Dedication

This book is dedicated to all of the carvers I have had the opportunity to train throughout the years. It has been a tremendous privilege for me to be able to teach many of these individuals, while being entrusted by numerous culinary instructors to come into their classrooms and work with their students.

Contents

CHAPTER 5 Template Design Technique 63

CHAPTER 6 Preparing the Carving Area 77

SAFETY WARNING: This book is a guideline to learn the art and science of ice carving. Many of the tools used in this text are dangerous and can easily cause serious injury to yourself or others. Should you choose to use the tools described, you do so at your own risk. The authors and Pearson/Prentice Hall Publishing Company cannot be held responsible for injuries or damages associated with the use of the tools and the techniques described in this book.

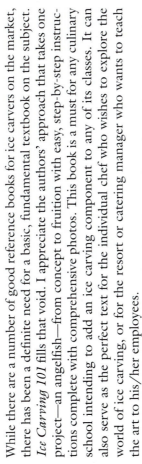

Foreword

While there are a number of good reference books for ice carvers on the market, there has been a definite need for a basic, fundamental textbook on the subject. *Ice Carving 101* fills that void. I appreciate the authors' approach that takes one project—an angelfish—from concept to fruition with easy, step-by-step instructions complete with comprehensive photos. This book is a must for any culinary school intending to add an ice carving component to any of its classes. It can also serve as the perfect text for the individual chef who wishes to explore the world of ice carving, or for the resort or catering manager who wants to teach the art to his/her employees.

I am happy to see that the book explores a few advanced steps and gives step-by-step instructions for another handful of projects. As one who understands the need to capture a record of carvings via photography, I am impressed with the chapter that discusses the art of photographing ice. You simply cannot grab a camera and take a picture. Carvers must understand the problems associated with photographing ice.

The unique and transient nature of ice as art is that it melts! Therefore, it is important to capture its finished beauty "for the record" in addition to having the image available for the carver's portfolio, Web site, and promotional advertising. A photograph meets those needs. This book gives basic, simple procedures that will allow for a visual record of completed works.

As a chef, professional ice carver, and mentor to many young culinarians, I appreciate the fact that there are safety tips sprinkled throughout the text as well as carver's notes. It is as if the authors are right there with you throughout the carving session.

Happy carving!

Michael Pizzuto, CCE, NICA Ambassador at Large

Preface

The beauty of sculpture lies in the art of creation and the science of practiced observation paired with skillful execution. *Ice Carving 101* shall groom beginning carvers toward a successful first experience with ice. If they have the professional desire, this book will propel them toward a lifetime career as an ice carver.

TO THE STUDENT

Ice carving is a grand spectacle in the culinary world. Most often, it is the focal point that brings life to an event. Public carving demonstrations always draw a crowd.

Some of the awe associated with the art of ice sculpture lies in wanting to know, "How do they do that?" The student who has never touched a sculpture block wonders the same thing and looks for guidance on how to begin.

Most professional ice sculptors have a story to tell about the first time they pressed a chisel into a block of ice. A student's first experience will undoubtedly be a memorable one. This instructional text demonstrates how to prepare the carver for all the steps required for creating a basic sculpture. Multiple pictures and diagrams are provided to showcase examples of each step in the process. With practice and perseverance, the beginner will develop a repertoire of display-quality sculptures and understand the techniques of how to pursue new designs.

The first-time carver needs inspiration to look at a block of ice and approach it with confidence. This is not a picture library of advanced type sculptures, though some additional designs are offered in Chapter 15. Such menageries of other publications may be entertaining to browse, but intimidating to the beginning student. Following the basic techniques outlined in this book will groom the the beginner to practice and achieve the more difficult designs with experience. The fundamentals of the tools, composition of ice, carving skills, and preparation are covered in detail. Each tool is introduced and reviewed as it relates to building a basic design. Transportation of ice from the full block to the finished sculpture is also outlined. Display technique and photography tips are offered to best exemplify the hard work involved.

TO THE INSTRUCTOR

The primary curriculum for the instructor is outlined in a one-, two-, or three-day session, depending on the needs of the program. All students will study the first day for a basic exposure to the art and science of ice sculpture with key words for review, discussion topics, and sample tests to quantify understanding of the student's comprehension. An instructor with ice carving experience may choose to end the first day with a carving demonstration to add to the program. Schools that lack the staff to demonstrate the actual carving process may opt to provide a lecture-only format or invite a guest chef to offer the technique exposure to this form of the culinary arts. Colleges with skilled instructors may use this text as a tool to deliver their own talents in a more structured format. The second day will encompass a practical carving experience with an emphasis on all students carving the same design for peer mentorship. The angelfish is chosen as the model design for simplicity and variables in tool usage. A third day may be incorporated for additional carving exercises. Instructors can choose additional designs from Chapter 15 or use compositions of their own or incorporate the students' design creativity. Schools with the budget for tools and sculpture ice will appreciate the support this text can offer such a curriculum.

TO THE PROFESSIONAL CULINARIAN

This book is also suitable for the private industry. Such training materials are often encouraged as a portion of the staff's continuing education. Should a hotel, cruise line, catering outfit, country club, or other similar concept have the desire to train on ice carving, suitable venues or instructors can be difficult to source. This text can serve as a self-study guide for the willing student. A mentoring chef could use this book as a preparatory tool for his or her apprentice.

Creating championship ice carvers is not the mission of this book. Instead, it lays the foundation for learning the art of ice carving. Once these steps are mastered and with continued practice, the student may pursue competitions at the professional level or even enter the Olympics of Ice Carving. "The world is your oyster."

About the Authors

Chef Michael Jasa, CEC

As a beginning ice carver attending the Culinary Institute of America, Chef Jasa became an active member of the Ice Carving Club. He served as the treasurer, and eventually he became the president for his second term. The club participated in many competitions and took the top three places in a nationally sanctioned competition of peers involving over forty competitors from more than a dozen schools. Chef Jasa was employed as an ice carver for the Breakers Hotel, Palm Beach, Fla.; the Grove Park Inn Resort, in Asheville, N.C.; and other corporate restaurant groups. These efforts have also led Chef Jasa to compete professionally in ice carving competitions. Such challenges have earned him gold and silver medals. Those achievements have led him to serve as a NICA-certified judge for international ice expositions. Chef Jasa has taught ice carving courses at Asheville Buncombe Community College, Asheville, N.C., two-hour continuing education courses for the American Culinary Federation, and the Florida Culinary Institute. Today, Chef Jasa is the proprietor of Culinary Artz.

Brenda R. Carlos

The inspiration to write this text has come with the support of Brenda Carlos, who has co-authored a number of Prentice Hall/Pearson Education culinary texts, including *The ACF's Baking Fundamentals; The ACF'S Cold Kitchen Fundamentals;* and *Knife Skills for Chefs.* She also served as publisher and managing editor for the Hospitality News Group, publishers of *Hospitality News for the Western US,* as well as the *International Education Guide.* Brenda is a regular contributor to the American Culinary Federation's *National Culinary Review* and has authored countless articles focusing on all aspects of the foodservice industry, event management, and running a business. She is the founder of BC Editorial Services and works with a number of hospitality clients. Brenda is an enthusiastic and dynamic speaker; she loves to speak to students and business owners about the culinary, hospitality, and event management industries. She is a former member of the International Foodservice Editorial Council and current member of Toastmasters, Int.

Chef Jasa was once tasked with the phone call to his parents to ask for the money to purchase his first set of ice carving tools. The only request was to make sure it was taken seriously and not to become a passing interest.

May this book be a testament to all students: If you have a dream and couple it with perseverance, your dream can become a reality.

In closing, we offer a few words of caution: Ice carving can be addictive!

Acknowledgments

This educational publication would not have been possible without the support of many generous contributors.

I would like to thank my mentors, who first took the time to show me the lessons found in *Ice Carving 101*. These mentors include:

1. From the 1990–1992 CIA Ice Carving Club, Chef Jaime Johnson, Instructor/Advisor, who stuck with me during the carving nights of my treasurer and presidential terms, and Chef Bill Williams, 1st Year Club President/Student/Alumnus, who coached me through my first carvings and helped with the composition of my early competition designs.

2. Fellow NICA competition judges Kevin McDonald, Hiroshi Noguchi, and the late Joseph Amendola with whom I've learned some of the finer points of sculpture evaluation.

3. Michael Pizzuto, for his lifelong guidance—from judging my competition entry to sharing his knowledge and wisdom as I wrote this book.

My appreciation is also extended to the publication team at Pearson/Prentice Hall for printing the first instructionally based ice carving book that reaches out to the ice carving community with the first-time carver in mind. William Lawrensen and Vernon Anthony are credited with making all the necessary allowances toward the investment of this mission.

The team at Jim Smith Photography was fundamental in transforming an ideal concept into a beautiful view of life through pictures.

There were many additional business ventures that also contributed to our photo shoot. The following are credited for their contributions:

Makita USA—For providing all the ice carving power tools necessary to create the ice pictured in this book.

Florida Culinary Institute—For offering the lab venue, utilities, and setting for a great photo shoot.

Ice Crafters—For lending the high quality tools necessary for illustrating those ice carving tools needed by professionals, students, or instructors alike.

Glo-Ice (aka Engineered Plastics Inc.)—For providing the display vehicles to showcase the illuminated, finished displays of ice sculpture.

Cheney Brothers, Inc.—For the generous gift of a freezer truck to hold all the extra ice and carved sculptures throughout an extended photo shoot.

I-Sculpt, Inc.—For providing insight on the mechanical production, and machined sculpture, of ice.

Cassidy Ice—For delivering premium quality ice for our photo shoot.

County Ice—For providing clear ice blocks for our use during any moment of the photographic productions, and many other times of need.

Unisource Marketing Group—For the understanding of the time, through my employment, to produce the fruits of this project.

Appreciation is also extended to my colleagues, Michael Pizzuto and Ami Novak, for participating in many of the efforts of this book and more.

The foundation of this work has been made possible through the inspiration and patience of my co-author Brenda Carlos. Brenda's experience and corroboration in writing educational textbooks has made this lesson to the ice carving community a well-written guideline to follow for the culinary enthusiast.

All who have been inspired by ice carving are the audience and supporters of this effort. May your interest in learning become the passion to know more about *Ice Carving 101*.

Michael A. Jasa CEC

It has been a pleasure to work with Chef Michael Jasa—through his skills and passion, the exciting world of ice carving truly came alive for me and I am now a huge fan of the art. I wish to acknowledge William Lawrensen and all the good people at Pearson Prentice Hall for their continual support of this book. I would also like to thank the Florida Culinary Institute for sharing their beautiful facilities with us during our photo shoot. This book certainly couldn't have been complete without the amazing talents of Jim Smith, our photographer, and his crew, who understood the challenges of photographing ice. Michael Pizzuto was an invaluable mentor throughout the photo shoot and also added his expertise to the manuscript. He was a true friend throughout the project. Finally, I wish to

thank my family, who continue to support me in my ventures and give me a reason to keep on going!

We would also like to thank the reviewers who shared their opinions and suggestions with us to strengthen the text. They are: David Bearl, First Coast Technical College; Drue Brandenburg, Johnson & Wales University, Miami, Florida; John Kowalski, The Culinary Institute of America; John Matwijkow, Unique Culinary Concepts; and David St. John-Grubb, Le Cordon Bleu College of Culinary Arts.

Brenda R. Carlos

The Professional Advantage

"A dazzling ice sculpture or carving as a centerpiece is an amazingly cost effective way to add glamour to any event. The spirit of a graceful ice sculpture may well fade away but the lasting memory of a sumptuous spread adorned with a dramatic ice sculpture will last forever."

Igloo Ice Bournemouth

Learning Objectives

After you have finished reading this unit, you should be able to:

- Discuss the value of ice carving in the foodservice industry
- Describe how ice carving lends itself to a spectator event
- Explain how an ability to carve ice makes you more marketable in foodservice
- Identify the business opportunities available for ice carving

Terms to Know

prism effect

sculpture charge formula

amortized value of your equipment investment

Once you have studied the content of this chapter, you should have a greater understanding of how developing the skills of ice carving can both enhance your professional qualifications as a culinarian and also lead to a thriving part-time or full-time business.

THE VALUE OF ICE CARVING TO THE PUBLIC EYE

Sculpting has been practiced as a major art form dating back to the Greek and Roman empires (Figure 1-1). Ancient Chinese art provides a glimpse into their culture (Figure 1-2). The study of ancient sculpture has given us clues about

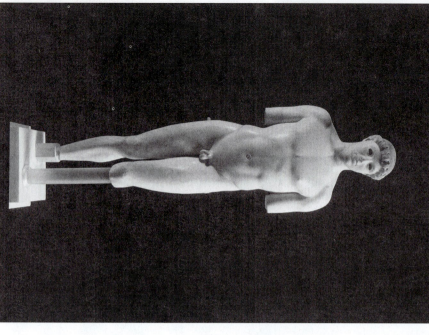

Figure 1-1

This sculpture of the Kritios Boy is from the Acropolis and was carved between 490 and 480 B.C. Today it is housed in the Acropolis Museum in Athens, Greece.

The Kritios Boy from the Acropolis. Greek (Archaic), c. 490-480 BCEH: 117 cm. Acropolis Museum, Athens, Greece. Nimatallah/ Art Resource, NY.

Figure 1-2

A sculpture of a female attendant carved during the Western Han period, second century B.C., gives us a glimpse into the dress and life of ancient woman.

Female Attendant. North China. Western Han Period (206 CE-99 CE), 2nd century BCE. Earthenware with slip and traces of pigment. H. 21 1/2 in. (54.6 cm). Asia Society, New York: Mr. and Mrs. John D. Rockefeller 3rd Collection. 1979.110. Photograph by Lynton Gardiner.

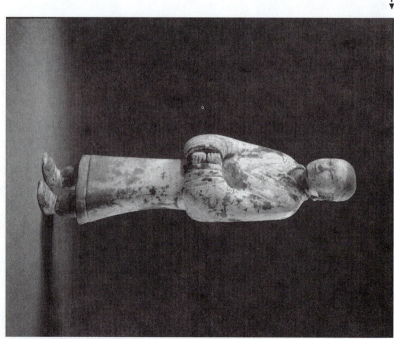

how early civilizations evolved. Ice carvings, unlike other sculptures of more durable materials, have not survived in their physical presence due to melting. Yet, the magical qualities of ice sculpture, as a form of artistic expression, have been a treat to society for as long as the medium has been available.

Most caterers, restaurateurs, and managers of hotels, resorts, and cruise ships are looking for a way to gain the competitive edge and elevate their events to a higher level (Figure 1-3). Ice sculptures create an exciting environment. They are sure to enhance any buffet table, serve as a centerpiece of the room to showcase a theme, or even be a structural component for serving food or beverages. Ice sculptures leave a lasting, positive image in the minds of most guests.

One of the unique features of ice carvings is that they come "alive" while on display. As they slowly melt, the image changes. Most ice sculptures displayed at room temperature and not exposed to wind or sunlight will last between four and six hours. Freezing temperatures of the core of the ice can help or hurt the qualities of ice. The sensitivities are described in this book. Fine

Sculptures of ice will leave a lasting memory to most any audience. A countless number of reviews have been made toward the quality of a Sunday brunch or a wedding. It is common to hear a remark similar to, "Everything was fabulous, and they even had an ice sculpture." The choice to include a great ice carving as a centerpiece will undoubtedly leave guests with the image of class and quality regarding the ambiance of the event.

DEMONSTRATIONS

Carving ice doesn't always have to take place in a commercial work area. There are some occasions when the actual carving process can become a live show for all to see and enjoy (Figure 1-4). When the chain saw starts buzzing, a crowd will soon follow. Public carving demonstrations are sure to draw an audience.

▲ **Figure 1-4** Tourists on the sun deck of cruise ship watch a chef carve an ice sculpture to be displayed on a buffet table.

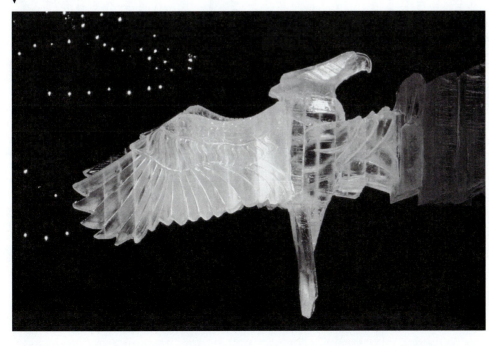

▶ **Figure 1-3**
A lighted eagle stretches its powerful pinions in an ice sculpture.

details such as facial features are the first to melt. This evolutionary process can intrigue guests.

A well-presented sculpture, enhanced by lighting, will create a multifaceted **prism effect**, which is a result of light refracting from its source and projecting into multiple angles and sometimes changing from white light to rainbow colors. The multiple images provided by refraction are limited only by the number of angles from which the carving can be viewed. These ever-changing qualities truly create audience appeal for ice sculptures.

Most cruise lines or vacation resorts include a carving demonstration as a well-staged show. Adults and kids alike will gather to witness this activity. Some localities of the United States, and even around the world, sponsor ice carving competitions as part of winter or culinary festivals. The colder areas often allow these carvings to remain outside on display for days or even weeks. Some resort areas, clubs, and other hospitality venues also feature this art as a public display for guest appeal.

MARKETABILITY

Chefs have gained the status of celebrities over recent decades. Open kitchens are growing in popularity among restaurant design layouts. This trend is fostered by the appeal of the guest wishing to witness "What is going on?" This movement toward the public display of culinary skills often requires the chef to be in the limelight. The demonstration of ice carving to the public is no exception to this concept.

A chef can either produce high-quality sculptures or, better yet, demonstrate them to the public while possessing a skill of marketable employment value. Many garde manger chef positions will require ice sculpture as a preferred qualification. Sometimes a pool of candidates for a culinary job opening will find the employer picking the chef with the ice carving ability over the rest. A career portfolio, which includes photographs and proof of ice carving experience, will tell the employer that the candidate is creative and possesses the ability to learn skills in addition to the mainstream expectations.

SCULPTING ICE AS A BUSINESS

A qualified ice sculptor does not have to be limited to performing this duty as a part of his/her full-time culinary position. There is always a market for those who can produce high-quality ice carvings.

The opportunity for additional income will stay with you throughout your career as long as you have the desire, the time, and the tools. In addition to the skills necessary to carve quality sculptures, one will also need the basic gear on hand so a sculpture can be created on a moment's notice. An entire list of carving gear is outlined in Chapter 4, Tools of the Trade. The basic necessities of gear include proper clothing, safety devices, hand tools, often a chain saw, and access to transportation and display equipment. Cold freezer storage is also needed. More commonly, the freezer is available at the display site. If not, the ice will be carved and stored elsewhere, and the ability to transport a finished sculpture at the appropriate time before the event will be required.

Carver's Note

A sculpture carved on site and displayed immediately will be a show-case for the carving portion, though the detail will melt rapidly unless the ambient conditions are very cold.

The most fundamental requirement is a source of sculpture-quality ice blocks. Without the ice, you have no ice sculpture. Depending on the location of the nearest ice block supplier, this can often be the greatest challenge to creating a sculpture business. As in most other business ventures, if there's a demand there is usually a supply. Here are a few options to consider:

- In some cases, the property hiring you may have the ability to order ice blocks and will store them on its premises.
- Employ your own supplier to deliver your ice to the required destination. You have more control over the quality of ice if you select the supplier.
- Partner with a purveyor. Many of the larger foodservice suppliers keep ice carving blocks on hand and will deliver them directly to your site.
- The final alternative would be to purchase an ice block maker of your own and also have the storage facility to hold your ice. This later option is usually only taken by the carvers who choose to make ice sculpture a full-time profession.

If the phone book or Internet searches do not leave you ample options for ice suppliers, try calling the purchasing department of neighboring properties (hotels or resorts) where you suspect they include ice carvings as an amenity. They will likely offer a referral. Networking in the professional community and simply asking around will usually provide you with options that will suit your needs.

Charging for Your Work

Carving ice can be a profitable business, as either a part-time or a full-time venture. The amount to charge a customer for an ice sculpture will vary based on the time invested in the project, as well as the expenses. The **sculpture charge formula** is an addition of the costs of your work added to the value of your time. A sculpture charge formula should be used to determine how much to charge for each carving. This formula is based on the expenses involved with producing an ice sculpture coupled with the value of your time and the quality of your work. Carvers with a reputation for excellence can command a higher price.

The sculpture charge formula considers the following expenses:

1. Cost of the ice.
2. Delivery of the ice, either as the raw block and/or as the delivered sculpture.
3. Set-up services, either by yourself or by others.
4. Rental or ownership costs of display vessels.
5. Storage of ice either at the display site or elsewhere.
6. Value of your time. This is the primary variable!
7. An advanced concept of costs would be related to the **amortized value of your equipment investment**, which is the expense to your business equally related to the amount you would need to charge for the payoff value of your investment in tools and supplies. (This value is paid off over a period of time as an internal expense of business costs as they relate to taxation and real property.)
8. Taxes and insurance.

The dollar valuation of the above list will often fall within the ranges listed below. Ultimately it is the demographic area as well as the law of supply and demand that will determine the value. Inflation over time will also raise the bar of expenses. The following estimate relates to the economy at the time of writing. Other currency or economics may reflect adjustments to this model.

1. The cost of the raw ice block = $40–$80.
2. Delivery of a single block sculpture, raw or carved = $20–$100. A solid block is heavier to transport, though damage to a finished sculpture is not a factor. Moving a sculpted block of ice can require additional skills, equipment, and preparation. This variable of cost depends on who is delivering the block and the distance traveled. If you put the finished sculpture in your own vehicle, the cost is little more than the gas. If you have a professional crew of two individuals drive the block 60 miles and deliver it on a Sunday or holiday, you could expect to pay a premium for the help.
3. Display services = from $0 to whatever your time and travel is worth. Many properties will have a chef or crew that is experienced in setting up ice sculptures. This means the carving can be delivered at any time prior to the event and stored in the freezer, a time/value savings. Other clients may need you to be there at the time of the event. This may add additional expense and time to the project.
4. Display materials = $0–$150. These display items may be rented and recovered, or purchased and left behind.
5. Storage of ice = $0–$20, depending on your amortization table to write off either your own freezer, your client's facility, or an ice house. Should you sculpt the ice at the block plant and have its workers deliver it, storage should be no problem. The ownership of a freezer is another option. A client with its own freezer is the best-case scenario.
6. The value of your time to produce an ice sculpture = ? This amount depends on your ability to market yourself, the quality of your work, and the value of your time. There may even be times when you will donate your time at a charity event.
7. Amortized value of your equipment investment = ? If you have purchased a large volume of ice carving equipment in a short period, you may write this off on taxes as a lump sum or as an expense that you spread over years of time. (Always consult a tax expert to see which method will work best for your circumstances.) Taking ownership of a carving studio with a block-making plant would most likely benefit from amortization. This dollar figure may not exist if you have not formed a business for tax purposes. Again, a financial adviser is recommended for evaluating your expenses. Business formation principles are rarely a concern for the beginning carver, though any professional in business will need to know the return on investment with capital equipment.
8. When starting a business it is always important to meet with a lawyer, business adviser and accountant to determine what licenses, insurance, and taxes are required. The cost of the fees (licenses and insurance) should be spread out throughout the year and reflected in the price of your work. Taxes should be collected when required.

Let's take a look at a hypothetical example for a single block sculpture:

1. Ice block cost $60
2. Delivery cost $30
3. Set-up services   1 hour of carver's time @ $15/hr = $15
4. Rental of display equipment $70
5. Storage of ice $0
6. Your time for carving
   and display   4 hours @ $15/hr = $60
7. Amortization of equipment $10 will serve as an example
8. Licenses, insurance, and taxes $10 (Depends on local jurisdiction)
Total cost to the client $255+

A carver who places a value of $25 an hour for his/her time would have a total cost to the client of $305. The most valuable lesson here is that your costs should be considered along with your time when quoting the cost of an ice sculpture.

Total Cost to the Client

The amount a carver charges depends on a number of factors. Beginners may be willing to sell a carving for a small fee or not charge for their time in order to have additional opportunities to practice. The fees go up depending on the expertise of the carver.

For those who pursue a business full time, hiring a business and tax adviser is recommended.

After following all the steps in this book, paired with practice and perseverance, you will soon gain the confidence to know when a project is within your ability and how to price it. Practice makes perfect, and the world is your oyster!

Pricing Tip

If a client requests an ice sculpture, most commonly the first question will be about the cost. A clear understanding of the job at hand is needed before the cost can be calculated. Use the above criteria to give you an approximate price range. Because the actual time involved will depend on a number of factors, give your customer a window of a price rather than a set figure. For example, a basic piece would run from $150 to $300 or more, where a multiblock display on New Year's Eve may run from $1,000 to $2,000. If you have experience, this is a good time to talk about the testimonials you have to offer. Now your credibility is established.

Summary

An ice-carving business can become the project of a hobby, a portion of your job description, or a part-time or full-time opportunity. The choice is up to the carver's ability and the local demand. A profitable business is dependent on the operational skills and marketability of the proprietor. The market of ice sculpture is open to all those who wish a grand display for their occasion.

REVIEW QUESTIONS

True or False

____ 1. Ice carvings come alive as they melt through gradual changes in their visual image.

____ 2. Most ice sculptures displayed at room temperature and not exposed to wind or sunlight will last between 5 to 10 hours.

____ 3. The amortized value of investment relates to the value of your time.

____ 4. A sculpture charge formula should be used to determine how much to charge for each carving.

____ 5. A sculpture charge formula is based on the expenses involved with producing the ice sculpture coupled with the value of your time and the quality of your work.

Short Answer

6. Describe the prism effect.

7. What are some of the safety considerations that should be addressed when carving for a public audience?

8. Explain what is meant by "amortized value of your equipment investment."

9. What are some of the factors that determine the delivery charges for the ice block, raw or carved?

10. Why do most carvers give clients an approximate price range for the projected job rather than a solid price upon the first meeting?

INSTRUCTOR'S NOTES

1. This is a good time to discuss the successes you have had in the ice-carving business or to invite a guest carver.

2. This portion of book study will be the first presentation you offer to your class.

3. Discuss the business importance to the content of this book.

4. Consider developing an extra-credit outline for students to aspire to higher grades. This may take place in the classroom or the carving arena.

5. This is the time to describe how the medium of ice sculpture delivers a living display. Refer to the first section of this chapter on the value of ice carving. This is the time to mention how ice takes on a new image as it melts.

6. The prism effect is something you could deliver to the class in the form of a properly lit ice sculpture or a small prism device.

7. Discuss how public speaking and taking the stage will exist at times in the culinary world.

8. Discuss this lesson with the entrepreneurial opportunities of developing an ice-carving business or any other proprietorship you wish to share.

9. If you have been one to negotiate price for an ice sculpture, discuss how you worked out the deal. This is the beginning of your lecture. Discuss how ice carving can be a business. This might be the perfect time to invite a successful ice carver to visit the class and share his or her experiences with your students.

Composition of Ice

2

"I am obsessed with ice cubes. Obsessed."

Drew Barrymore

Learning Objectives

After you have finished reading this unit, you should be able to:

- Discuss the differences of ice compared to other sculpture media
- Explain how ice is formed from water
- Describe the various levels of water quality for sculpture ice
- Differentiate between the methods of harvesting and manufacturing ice
- Identify how the clarity of ice affects the display quality and the design
- Describe how ice is frozen from the outside toward the inside
- Illustrate the process of making commercial-sculpture-quality ice
- Differentiate a clear-ice molding can from a still-freezing mold
- Explain the difference between clear-centered and feathered ice
- Describe the thermal qualities of ice and the tempering techniques of ice carving

Terms to Know

liquid state of water
solid state of water
crystallization
water filtration
reverse osmosis
sculpture-quality ice

oscillated freezing
lake ice
manufactured sculpture
   block
molded ice display
submerged-can method

feather
Clinebell method
impact damage
thermal shock
tempering
Arthur's Law

Most ice carvers would agree with Drew Barrymore in the opening quote. They are obsessed with ice cubes, though not the kind you find in a drink, but the giant blocks that can be carved.

Once you have completed the instructions in Chapter 2, you should understand how water turns to ice, the components of high-quality sculpture ice, and how ice is manufactured, harvested, tempered, and stored. This knowledge will prepare the ice sculptor for the ideal carving conditions, along with time management and purchasing insight to conduct a profitable sculpture business.

ICE AS A SCULPTURE MEDIUM

Sculptures are composed of various raw materials. Stone is one of the most durable sculpture media. Museums around the world contain sculptures made of ancient stone. Wood has been sculpted into the masterpieces of furniture and figurines, as its grain creates a unique pattern of nature. Ice is yet another medium of sculpture. Though its durability is not that of stone or wood, it can be carved in a small fraction of the time and possesses unique qualities.

Modern casting techniques have moved our world to know sculpture in a whole new way. Since the days of pouring liquids that could turn into a solid, we have known cast sculpture in both the artistic and simply functional means. Numerous metals, plastics, waxes, and other substances have been brought to their liquid state and molded into some type of sculpture. A common construction nail would be a metal example of a functional cast sculpture. A bronze or golden cherub may often be a composition of cast sculpture art. The medium of sculpture water must first be cast into a clear block of ice, which is an art unto itself. Casting a finished design of ice is rarely practiced over the production of raw rectangular sculpture blocks. The three-dimensional sculpture craft of ice carving will usually involve an ice block larger than the carving design, and it is reduced through relief sculpture methods. See Chapter 3 for the finer details pertaining to the differences between casting and relief sculpture.

FROM WATER TO ICE

For water to turn into ice, it must be exposed to freezing temperatures. This is an obvious factor. However, the process of which this water becomes frozen will depend on whether it becomes clear or cloudy. A common beverage ice cube would be the best example of this principle. An average household ice-maker will produce a cloudy cube as all the water is poured into a mold and then allowed to freeze without motion. Most commercial icemakers produce clear ice cubes as the water is slowly frozen while the liquid water flows over the freezing surface. This motion of the water is the discriminating factor between clear and cloudy ice. Commercial foodservice ice is also formed into the hazed nugget chewable variety often preferred for fountain beverages. The formation of ice cubes for beverage and the ice blocks for carving are entirely different processes.

By going back to basic chemistry class, we know that water expands when it freezes. If the entire exterior freezes, the liquid interior will have no choice but to expand within itself. This action produces microscopic air pockets, along with interior scratching, as the molecule walls of the ice become damaged from expansion, thus damaging the interior of the cube to a point where all these interior etchings are seen as cloudy ice.

A clear block, or cube, of ice is produced through a process in which air is never trapped inside the exterior of the water being frozen. If the freezing water is always in movement, as with a clear formation of ice. Mother Nature blesses us with a clear formation of ice. Lake ice is often clear, as the water is usually moving in some way or another underneath the cap. Manufactured clear ice will also possess some form of water movement during its production process.

This chapter will illustrate how clear ice for sculpture is handled.

THE SCIENCE

Water will turn from a liquid state to a solid state through freezing. The **liquid state of water** (H_2O) exists between 32° F (0° C) and the gaseous boiling point at 212° F (100° C). As water freezes or thaws, it will take on many types of microscopic formations. The freezing of water forms various crystalline compositions. The **solid state of water** exists below 32° F (0° C) and forms a crystalline composition based on its temperature.

A frozen block of ice can take on many forms of **crystallization**, a process in which multiple crystals form a variable solid mass based on its temperature. This matrix of crystals can interchange as the ice rises or lowers in temperature. These crystals can form the shapes of hexagonal plates, columns, star-like formations, and even long shards. The hexagonal column crystals form the best prism-like effects with light. This type of crystal is most often found at 20° F (−7° C) and at temperatures below −20° F (−30° C). The temperatures in this range will cause the crystalline composition to change many times. Higher temperatures will also alter these crystals and eventually lead to melting. This ever-changing reaction to ice resembles a "living" quality not found in other sculpture media such as wood or stone.

WATER QUALITY FOR ICE SCULPTURES

Ice is food. This concept applies to the beverages we drink and the sculptures we display next to food. The water used for ice sculpture blocks should be pure and sanitary. At a minimum, the water frozen for ice blocks should be cleaned of impurities through charcoal and micron sediment screens. Such water cleansing agents are types of **water filtration** systems used to purify water. Hardness of water may affect the color and taste of the block's runoff, so softened water is a desired quality. Water filtered through charcoal won't contain free chlorine, which could harm a food display or metal equipment.

Another form of water filtration is achieved through **reverse osmosis**, which is a process of pressurizing an impure liquid through a semi-permeable sheet of purifying membrane.

ICE HARVESTING—THROUGH HISTORY TO TODAY

Ice was harvested centuries ago for the use of its cold-storage qualities in keeping food or other goods fresh. In a more current fashion, we still use ice for the same purpose. Before the technology of modern refrigeration, naturally formed ice on a body of water was a precious resource. Ice blocks were harvested from lakes and brought to market as a valuable commodity. Their value prior to the 20th century was similar to that of the gasoline we use in our cars today. Many cultures needed ice for some reason or another. A display of grandeur may have even included a sacrifice of this precious resource to create a memorable component of a celebration in the form of a sculpture.

Any reputable sculptor will desire an excellent quality base structure for his/her chosen medium. It is essential to use **sculpture-quality ice**, which is defined as crystal clear blocks of clean potable frozen water. The clearest ice is created by pure potable water being circulated as it freezes into a block through a process called **oscillated freezing.** Naturally harvested **lake ice** can produce clear ice as the lake, or the elements above it, create the ideal movement of water. The nature of the outdoors and its water can be pristine or it can contain debris and other elements such as snow pockets. The microbial elements of unfiltered natural waters are rarely of a food-grade quality. Though some exceptions may apply, lake ice is best reserved for non-food-display purposes.

Manufactured ice is most commonly used for sculpture as it is properly composed of potable water with consistency in size and clarity. A **manufactured sculpture block** is man-made ice produced through refrigeration. This type of

ice is typically made of 37 to 40 gallons of pure water and molded into the shape of a rectangular cake weighing over 300 pounds and measuring 10 inches deep, 20 inches wide, and 40-plus inches tall in an upright position. Some regions will produce blocks as tall as 60 inches. Other block-making methods may yield a slight variance from the $10 \times 20 \times 40$ version, though this size is the industry standard (Figure 2-1).

A **molded ice display** is a finished block of ice for which the water was placed into a cast mold to form a complete display centerpiece. It is most often presented with a clouded center. This type of display does not contribute to the

Figure 2-1
This block was created in a commercial ice block plant and resembles the most common cubical dimension for ice carving.

art of ice sculpture, though its presence in the market deserves mention toward its value.

A molded block of ice can be cloudy or clear. The process of clarity depends on the method of freezing. A still-water freezing method within a solid mold will create a defined shape, but it will usually lack clarity. Some venues may allow this sacrifice in quality. This niche of an ice centerpiece represents casting sculpture over relief sculpture (Figure 2-2). More on this subject of casting versus relief sculpture will be expounded upon in Chapter 3, Art and Science of Sculpture.

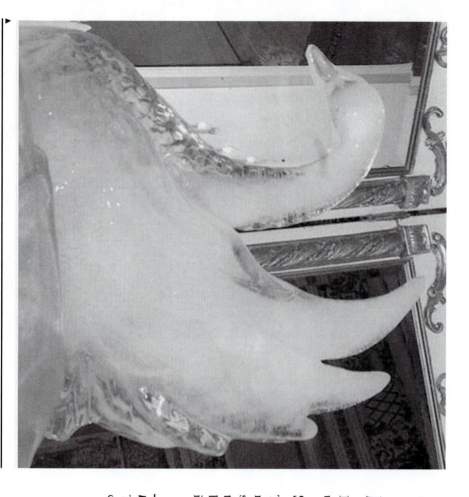

Figure 2-2   This is an example of an ice sculpture that was molded and not carved using traditional tools or the methods described in this book.

Figure 2-3
This commercial block plant will create nearly clear ice for sculpture purposes. The process takes approximately 48 hours.

MANUFACTURED ICE PRODUCTION

Besides the natural forms of ice, ice can be manufactured in various ways. Two popular methods are the submerged can and the Clinebell (Figures 2-3, 2-4, and 2-5).

Submerged Can Method

The **submerged can method** is a sculpture ice production method in which a metal can is submerged into a freezing bath and frozen from the bottom and sides toward the center. This method dates back to the early days of manufacturing ice for household refrigeration. Ironically, the standard-sized sculpture block was not created for the art of ice carving. Instead, the turn-of-the-century ice-carving plants were making ice in the 10 × 20 × 40 dimension at a time

Figure 2-4
The ice is harvested from cans.

Figure 2-6
This block demonstrates the interior elements of a feathered block of ice.

Figure 2-5
A Clinebell blockmaker. The Clinebell system produces ice with total clarity.

Pro's Corner

Professionals will often develop their design to work around the center of the ice. This may involve multiple segment carving along with ice re-assembly. See Chapter 14, Advanced Skills, for ice reassembly lessons.

Clinebell Method

The **Clinebell method** is a brand name associated with a horizontal method of ice-mold production in which the aeration is controlled from the bottom to

when the horse-drawn buggy delivered ice regularly for cold storage needs. This service was nearly as common as a postal delivery today. The home refrigerator was more commonly called an icebox. The smaller cubes for household use were most often cut or broken from larger production blocks. These larger blocks are the typical shape of modern blocks we use for ice carving today.

Large steel-alloy cans capable of holding 300 pounds or more of water are submerged into a bath capable of a holding its liquid state at a temperature below 32° F (0° C). A car's radiator is often filled with such an antifreeze solution. This solution is cooled through modern refrigeration methods. The water within the open-top can is frozen from the bottom and sides.

The key to this ice becoming clear is a combination of the water being oscillated by an air pump along with the ability for this air to escape from the surface. The oscillation is often produced through an aeration device placed into the block. This element will keep the water moving as it freezes. At some point this aeration device must be removed or it will be frozen within the block. The manufacturer will use various methods to remove the aerator. Any portions of liquid remaining within the block, after the aerator is removed, will become feathered and lack clarity as the water expands into the block and creates air pockets. This cloudy interior portion of sculpture ice is known as the **feather.** The larger the feather, the less clear the block will be throughout its cubical structure (Figure 2-6).

This form of feathered ice must be realized as an unclear element to the carving design. Advanced techniques of ice reassembly will result in professional carvers cutting around the feather and scrapping the cloudy center. A single, un-detached block will result in a cloudy center to the finished display

Figure 2-7
A Clinebell block of ice in its freshly harvested form, after production and ready for carving.

ICE STORAGE

Ice must be stored below freezing temperatures to stay solid. Although this is an obvious fact, there are many variables to freezer temperatures in the world of foodservice. The range of 32° F to −10° F (0° C to −12° C) is most often seen in the kitchen and ice carving areas. The colder temperatures are better for long-term storage, though the warmer freezing conditions are ideal for the actual cutting and carving of ice. This concept creates a dual application of the ideal storage conditions for ice carving.

A colder sculpture block will have a longer shelf life under long-term storage as well as on display. The drawbacks to a colder block will be the shock factor created when exposed to an alternate environment. Two primary categories of damage may occur: impact damage and thermal shock.

Impact Damage

Impact damage is the destruction of ice through vibration, agitation, or direct impact on the ice's surface. Ice is far more brittle in its colder states. Agitation or impact damage will be greater as the ice is colder. The vibration or bouncing of a moving vehicle may cause cracking and breakage. Direct impact on a solid surface will usually impose damage on any ice sculpture.

Thermal Shock

The destruction of ice through a shock in temperature exposure with damage often leading to cracking or sharding is known as **thermal shock**. An extremely frozen block, suddenly transported into the sunlight of a warm day, may decompose upon the exposure to the heat and rays of light. This type of thermal shock could cause internal shattering. For this reason, the block should be treated with ice tempering as it changes environments.

TEMPERING ICE

Ice tempering is a critical element to the preparation of carving ice. Tempering eases the thermal shock to a block of ice by gradually adjusting the frozen internal temperature of the ice to a softer and more adaptable state for cutting and the elements of warmer conditions. This prepares the block for the exposure to the elements of the working environment. A block of ice from a very cold storage area may shatter upon removal during exposure to thermal shock. Such shock will happen when the exposure exceeds 40° F to 80° F (14° C to 27° C) above the

the top as it freezes. The exterior walls act as the freezing agent, as opposed to the submerged can method. A plastic liner is used for each block to prevent fusion to the side walls. The liner is discarded from the harvested block after the freezing process is complete. These ice-sculpture blocks are known for total clarity within their center and the lack of any feather whatsoever. One of the large side dimensions may expand beyond the standard-sized measurements. This lack of smooth sidedness on a single-sided composition may be a negative factor for many template applications. However, the internal clarity will often outweigh the one uneven side when it comes to the best quality ice sculpture medium (Figure 2-7).

storage environment. Heat, rain, humidity, air movement, and natural sunlight will become factors in the destruction of sculpture ice. Ice tempering is a critical element to the preparation of carving ice. A properly tempered sculpture block of ice is softer for cutting, less abusive to the carving blades, and unlikely to shatter from thermal shock. The ideal carving block temperature for indoor carving is at the freezing point of 32° F (0° C). Carving outdoors in the sunlight may require temperatures below 20° F (−7° C) or lower if the sculpture is to endure the rays of the sun. A canopy from the sunlight is preferred for outdoor ice carving. Always temper your sculpture ice if moving to a rapidly changing environment.

Tempering for display may be needed for extreme conditions. An example could be a subzero storage segment of ice delivered to the sunlight in a hot area. The heat, light rays, humidity, and air movement may harm the ice. A shaded area is the first line of defense for an ideal outdoor carving condition. A cooler area is better for a longer carving time. Many carvers prefer to carve at room temperature. Cooler indoor areas are often best for ice carving, drainage requirements permitting. The allowance of time to ideally carve or display ice is directly proportional to the temperature conditions of the carving area. Tempering ice to its next environment is a required procedure of ice sculpture.

An internal ice temperature of 20° F (−7° C) or above will often yield a display-quality centerpiece or carving medium with fewer chances of thermal shock. Any ice stored below 20° F (−7° C) will require tempering to its alternate conditions. An ice temperature change exceeding more than 40° F (15° C) should incorporate tempering to ensure a high-quality sculpture. This principle applies to what this book calls **Arthur's Law** of thermal ice degradation, which states that a solid state of water (H_2O), as ice, will deteriorate from heated thermal shock in direct proportion to the change of its temperature environment. The slightest adjustment of a few degrees will begin microscopic changes to the crystalline structure of frozen water. Drastic temperature changes may incur the cracking, shattering, or sharding as the exposure variables become greater.

The most common practice for tempering ice is to move the block from the storage freezer to the higher temperatures of a refrigerated cooler. In most foodservice areas, this rarely creates a variable of more than 40° F (15° C). An alternative method can involve setting the ice in a room-temperature area while protecting the surface with a plastic bag or thermal blanket during the tempering process. The time required for tempering will depend on the variation to its final destination. A period of one to three hours is most common for ice tempering. Once the surface becomes clear and the block begins to melt, it has tempered and it is ready for carving. When ice is first removed from a freezer, it often becomes white and hazed on the surface. This is an initial sign of thermal shock, though it may not become destructive to the interior if proper tempering is applied. The surface should become clear before carving begins. A finished sculpture removed from the freezer can handle more of a temperature swing as the elements of vibration and cutting are reduced. However, a finished sculpture being exposed to a variable of more than 80° F (27° C) should be tempered to avoid potential damage.

SUMMARY

Before carving or displaying ice, a worker must anticipate the environment. A clear judgment of what will happen throughout the carving process will prepare sculptors for their work and price of services. The cost of a raw block of ice will depend on its clarity, delivery requirements, and water quality. The remaining value of sculpture-quality ice blocks will rest on supply and demand. Properly tempering a block of ice for carving or display will ensure a well-staged venue. The knowledge of the composition of ice will prepare a sculptor for the best provisions as they relate to purchasing, storage, and the handling requirements for ice carving.

REVIEW QUESTIONS

True or False

_____ 1. An average household icemaker will produce a cloudy cube because all the water is poured into the mold and allowed to freeze without motion.

_____ 2. Crystallization is a process in which multiple crystals form a variable solid mass based on its temperature.

_____ 3. Hard water makes stronger, clearer blocks of ice.

_____ 4. The white, cloudy interior portion of sculpture ice is known as a feather.

_____ 5. Arthur's Law states that a solid state of water will deteriorate from heated thermal shock in direct proportion to the change of its temperature environment.

Multiple Choice

6. The _____ of water is the discriminating factor between clear and cloudy ice.
   a. temperature
   b. motion
   c. hardness
   d. softness

7. Reverse osmosis is a type of
   a. crystallization process.
   b. water filtration system.
   c. freezing method.
   d. sculpture ice production method.

8. Sculptures made of lake ice are best reserved for
   a. outdoor events.
   b. banquet centerpieces.
   c. non-food-display purposes.
   d. any event.

9. A typical man-made ice block is made of _____ gallons of pure water.
   a. 20 to 30
   b. 37 to 40
   c. 45 to 52
   d. 50 to 60

10. Centerpieces made from water that is placed into a cast mold are called
    a. form displays.
    b. cast displays.
    c. processed pieces.
    d. molded ice display.

11. The submerged-can method was first used for
    a. household refrigeration units.
    b. ice carving.
    c. foodservice walk-in coolers.
    d. conjunction with medical surgeries.

12. The Clinebell method uses aeration that is controlled from the _____ as it freezes.
    a. bottom to the top
    b. top to the bottom
    c. from the outside edges to the center
    d. diagonal points

13. Ice is far more _____ in its colder states.
    a. brittle
    b. durable
    c. shatter-proof
    d. feathery

14. The destruction of ice through a shock in temperature exposure with damage often leading to cracking or sharding is known as _____.
    a. impact damage
    b. tempering
    c. thermal shock
    d. feathering

15. Tempering eases the block of ice by gradually _____ the ambient temperature variable.
    a. increasing
    b. adjusting
    c. lowering
    d. none of the above

INSTRUCTOR'S NOTES

1. Discuss how ice differs from other media of sculpture.
2. Expound on the sources of ice, both from natural resources and from manufacturers.
3. Explain the quality of ice as it relates to clarity.
4. Discuss how ice is made to outline the variables of this medium.
5. Prepare a role-play scenario of how to temper ice for an ice carving venue.
6. Outline the sculpture ice available in your local market.
7. Exemplify the importance of tempering ice.
8. Discuss Arthur's Law as it has been described in this unit.

3

The Art and Science of Sculpture

"I choose a block of marble and chop off whatever I don't need."

Alexander Pope
Second Book of Horace (ep. 1,1.146)

Learning Objectives

After you have finished reading this unit, you should be able to:

- Describe the difference between modeling, casting, and relief sculpture
- Explain the term *scale*
- Identify the steps needed to create an ice sculpture moving from a line drawing to a two-dimensional silhouette image to a completed three-dimensional image

Terms to Know

sculpture	relief sculpture
modeling sculpture	three-dimensional sculptures
casting sculpture	scale
	template
	silhouette image
	third dimension

The Cambridge Advanced Learner's dictionary defines sculpture as, "The art of forming solid objects that represent a thing, person, idea, etc. out of a material such as wood, clay, metal or stone, or an object made in this way" (Figure 3-1). In all, a **sculpture** is a three-dimensional image that conveys a thought or message.

Whether using marble, clay, wood, metal or ice, "sculptors record the full range of human experience in ways that are sometimes shocking, sometimes touching, but always exciting to see, to touch and to experience," says artist Palani Williams (Figure 3-2).

Sculpting ice requires a combination of artistic vision paired with the basic skills of cutting, shaping, and assembly (Figure 3-3). Ironically, the artistic portion is rarely the most important element. Many first-time carvers may become intimidated by any form of sculpture as they feel it requires a superior mind for creative beauty. However, carving ice is often not so difficult if a scientific approach is practiced in reproducing a proven design. As an example, upon completion of this course, a willful carver may encounter the opportunity to work in an environment

where another finished sculpture is stored in the freezer and viewable to the student seeking to learn. By using the basic techniques, one could apply the steps to reproduce a piece similar to what the original sculptor created (Figure 3-4).

It's all there in black and white, or perhaps in water and cold air, in ice carver's jargon. Re-creating an existing design is often the easiest way to advance and practice. The experienced carver will move quicker through a design once the steps have been run through at least one time. Chefs often relate this concept to following a recipe. Once the dish has been taken step by step from a list of instructions, it becomes simpler each time to reproduce the preparation (Figure 3-5). Eventually, the method no longer requires the step-by-step process, and cooking from the heart takes over. It's the understanding of the theory paired with practiced skills and memory that makes reproduction so simple. Original ice-carving designs will take longer because the steps will require more planning and preparation. The application of basic technique will always be the catalyst to the artistic vision of how a solid block of ice becomes a finished sculpture.

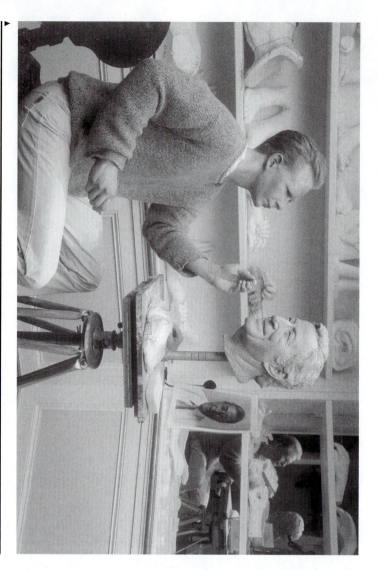

Figure 3-1   There are no limits as to what can be depicted in sculpture.
Demetrio Carrasco © Dorling Kindersley, Courtesy of Madame Tussauds, London.

Figure 3-2   A variety of media and tools are used in sculpture design.
Stephen Oliver © Dorling Kindersley.

Figure 3-3
The tools used by ice carvers are similar to those used by sculptors working with other mediums.

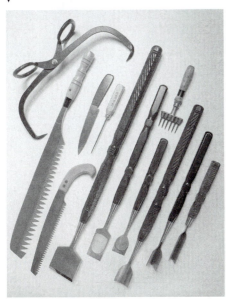

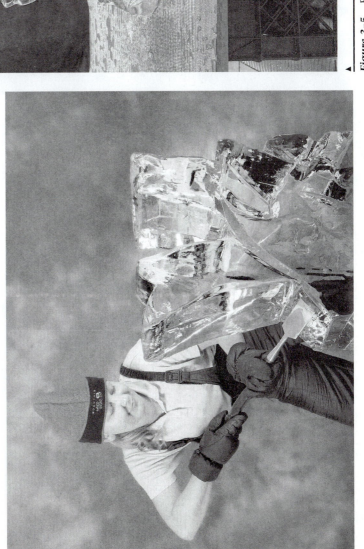

▲ ***Figure 3-4***   Ice carving combines art and science.

Before moving forward to the elements involved in ice carving, we should take a step backward to identify the types of sculpture. Sculpture is often broken down into four basic categories: modeling, casting, relief, and 3-D. All sculptures possess some or all of these techniques.

Modeling Sculpture

Modeling sculpture creates an image by assembling pieces over one another. When creating a modeling sculpture, the artist uses materials such as clay, wax, or plaster and gradually adds more and more of the material to build a three-dimensional form (Figure 3-6). Modeling is an additive process.

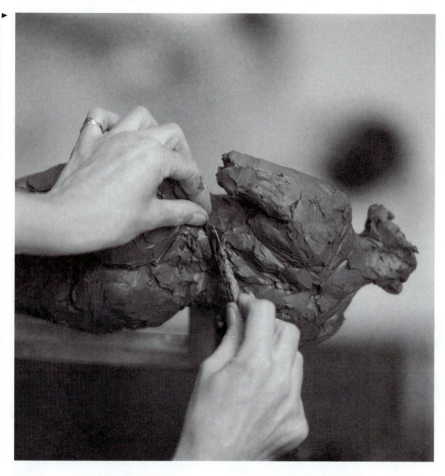

▶ *Figure 3-6*   A sculptor fashions a clay figure with her skillful hands.

▶ *Figure 3-7*   A chocolate marzipan rose and leaves. Ian O'Leary © Dorling Kindersley.

Modeling sculpture in the culinary world is often practiced in pastry art with piping bags extruding a formed shape of pastillage, gum paste, marzipan, cooked sugars, salt dough, tallow, or chocolate (Figure 3-7).

Small or large components are created and then assembled, edibly glued, or stacked to form an image of the designer's intentions. Vegetables can be cut and assembled, with each vegetable becoming a component in the overall sculpture. Modeling is rarely used in ice carving. Some exceptions may apply when snow or shavings are used to add to the design. Advanced ice work may require modeling pieces into a greater form through stacking and welding. However, the pieces are rarely molded from water and formed from the carver's fingers or other tools. Such segments are usually formed from a larger section of preformed frozen ice.

Casting Sculpture

Casting sculpture creates an image by pouring a liquid into a mold, which then cools and solidifies into the shape of a sculpture (Figure 3-8). The casting process enables the artist to duplicate the original piece of sculpture done in wax, clay, or plaster. Molten bronze or other substances are poured into the mold, replacing the area previously filled with the original medium. Once it hardens, the sculpture is cleaned and finished.

Casting sculpture in culinary arts is often done with cooked sugars, tempered chocolate, or gelatin. The medium is melted into a liquid and then poured in or on a preformed cast. The medium then becomes solid by cooling to form an image of sculpture (Figure 3-9). Sculpture ice is initially made by the casting of water into a standard-sized container and then frozen, as was discussed in Chapter 2.

Some operators feel that creating an ice sculpture from a mold filled with water and left to harden in the freezer will give them an ice sculpture. This form of casting does not possess the crystalline qualities of a true ice sculpture, though it may convey the shape and image of the cast.

Figure 3-9   A chocolate centerpiece is made by pouring hot white and dark chocolate into molds. Once the chocolate is firm, it is released from the mold and combined to create a beautiful showpiece.

Figure 3-8   *The Bronco Buster* by American painter and sculptor Frederic Remington (1861–1909). Remington modeled his bronze sculptures in wax first. Casts were made and the wax was melted away. Molten bronze was poured into the cast and left to harden. This process is known as the lost wax method of casting sculpture.

Frederic S. Remington, "The Rattlesnake," 1905. Bronze, 23–3/4 inches high. Amon Carter Museum, Forth Worth, Texas, Presented in Honor of Boone Blakeley for Service to Amon G. Carter, Sr. and the Carter Family, 1914–1995. Acc. no.: 1995.3.

Figure 3-10 An artist is fashioning this relief sculpture to show the front half of a person's head.

Relief Sculpture

Relief sculpture is the creation of an image by removing portions from a solid medium. The carved shape rises above the background but is not detached from it. There are various degrees of relief, depending on how far out the form stands from the background (Figure 3-10). Also note how this technique is applied to food (Figure 3-11).

Three-Dimensional Sculpture

"I say that the art of sculpture is eight times as great as any other art based on drawing, because a statue has eight views and they must all be equally well made."

Italian Baroque goldsmith and sculptor, in a letter
to Benedotto Varchi, January 28, 1547

Benvenuto Cellini (1500–1571)

Cellini is talking about three-dimensional (3-D) sculptures. **Three-dimensional sculptures** have height, width, and depth, compared with two-dimensional, which have height and width but no real depth. 3-D sculptures can and should be viewed from all angles. Modeling and casting sculptures often end as 3-D images, as do ice carvings. The carver can use an endless supply of designs that are carved, chiseled, drilled, and altered to create an artistic 3-D image that immerges from the block of ice (Figure 3-12).

GETTING STARTED

An ice carving starts with a basic idea of what the finished sculpture should look like. As discussed, an identical model (not necessarily to scale) is often the best guideline to follow when forming the basic and finished detail (Figure 3-13). For example, a toy doll could be used to re-create anatomical features when carving a human figure (Figure 3-14). Humans, by the way, are some of the most difficult images to carve. The same applies to animals, which make up another popular category of designs. In the area of logo design, a model or drawing is often referenced. In one way or another, a new design requires the artist to visualize what the finished sculpture should look like. To a novice, this often poses a great challenge. But you don't have to be a fine artist to produce attractive ice sculptures. Just follow the techniques in this book and learn the basics. Practice what you learn, and it won't be long before you're producing ice sculptures that will make you proud.

For ice carving, it is critical to remove the largest pieces around the entire sculpture first before starting with the smaller details (Figure 3-15). Most ice carvers don't have the luxury of carving in a freezing environment. Additionally,

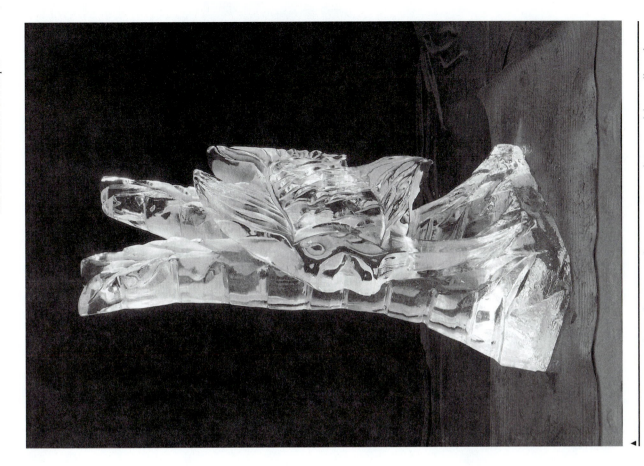

Figure 3-12 This three-dimensional ice carving can be viewed from all angles.

Figure 3-11 Elegantly carved fruits, using relief sculpture methods, are on display during a Thai festival in Los Angeles, California.

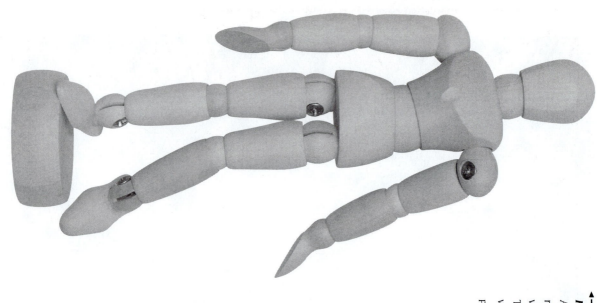

Figure 3-13
A photo, doll, or artist man-
nequin can serve as a model
when carving a human figure.
This type of model can help
with action shots.

Figure 3-14
Dolls can serve as
models to show mus-
cles and facial fea-
tures and basic
anatomy.

most folks aren't very comfortable working in such conditions. This leaves a natural progression of melting as the carving is produced. It would be foolish to carve the head of an animal with all its detail of eyes and snout before starting the rest of the body. By the time the piece is completely cut out of the block, the head and all its detail will have melted away. This approach could be tried with wood, but it is inherently impractical with ice. A step-by-step system should be followed to gradually remove portions from the entire piece simultaneously. All the big pieces are taken off first, leaving the shaping and detail work for last.

APPLY THE SECOND DIMENSION

Next, we must apply the flat image of the second dimension. This step is executed by composing a line drawing (sketched to scale) of the finished sculpture's silhouette image (Figure 3-16). **Scale** is an exact proportion of two sized images. For example: 1 inch on a paper drawing equals 5 inches in life-size dimension. This relationship would be referenced as a scale so that 1 inch on the template represents 5 inches on the sculpture.

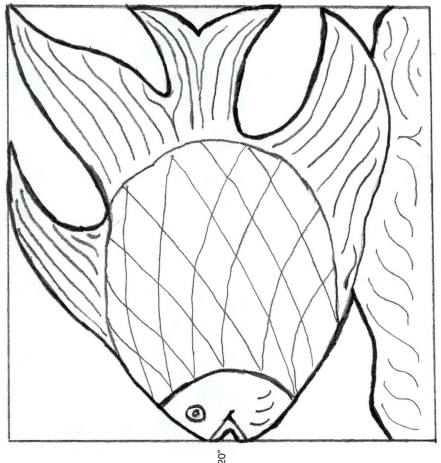

20"

20"

Figure 3-16   Compose a line drawing sketched to scale.

CREATE THE THIRD DIMENSION

Apply the template and remove the ice within the lines of the second dimension to create a **silhouette image**, which is the two-dimensional side view drawing (Figure 3-18). Once the template is applied and ice removed within the lines of the second dimension, the silhouette image of a sculpture will be carved into the **third dimension**, which gives the depth of a finished sculpture when viewed from all angles.

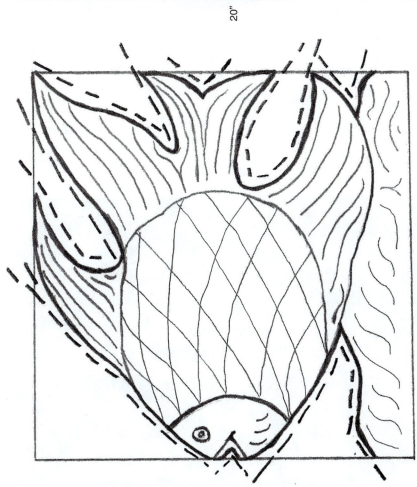

Figure 3-15   Always remove the largest pieces of ice before working on the small details.

The line drawing is most often drawn for the front (or most visually exposed) side of the sculpture. For example, if you were drawing a fish, it would be the outline of the side view where the thickness of the fins and mouth are not yet observed. The creation of this line drawing is a fundamental basic skill that must be learned in order to form most sculptures. This line drawing is often transformed into an actual-sized template, which will be applied to the ice (Figure 3-17). A **template** is a pattern, which can be used as a guide to transform the initial image to a life-sized marker on the ice. The template design instruction is outlined in Chapter 5.

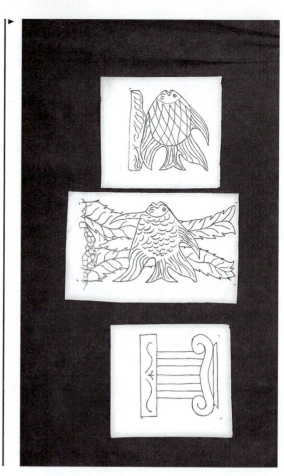

Figure 3-17   Templates are used directly on the ice to make the line drawing take shape.

Figure 3-19
Notice how the coral and the fish are cut away from the silhouette image.

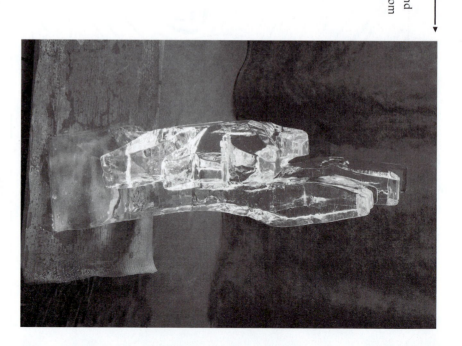

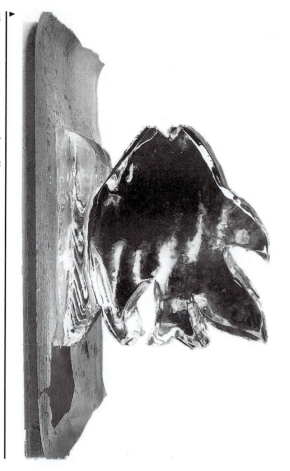

Figure 3-18   Creating the silhouette image.

The third dimension is often realized by turning the sculpture medium around 90° for a side view. The carver must now formulate where the sections will be removed to create a flat or curved image and how to shape it to form the third dimension of the design. More advanced designs may require only a portion of the second dimension to be removed. For example, in the design of the angelfish placed on a background of coral, the coral will be removed in the front where the fish is positioned and the fish segments will be removed in toward the back where the coral spans from top to bottom (Figure 3-19). The third dimension ice removal will be cut away from specific areas, yet seen from a side view (Figure 3-20). This concept is also referred to as compound depth segment, which is described in further detail in Chapter 9, The Large Cuts. This can often be the most challenging to visualize for a first-time carver. However, some designs are rather simple. One could imagine where a

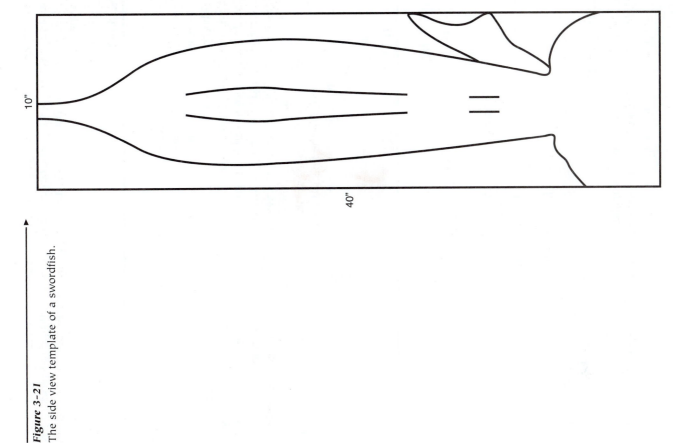

Figure 3-21
The side view template of a swordfish.

Figure 3-20
This side-view drawing of the coral and the fish illustrates where the third-dimension segments will be removed from the silhouette image.

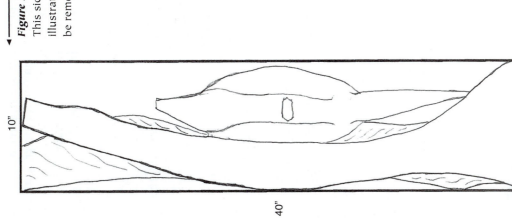

silhouette of a swordfish was created within 10 inches of ice. The carver then turns the ice sideways to make the dorsal fin more slender than the body, and then to create the tapering flow from head to tail and so on (Figure 3-21). Once again, the familiarity with the design, or models to copy, will be the guiding light to seeing this part of the project. As the cuts are made from this step, the carver should take regular moments to step away from the sculpture and view it from a variety of vantage points. (Step back at least 5 feet.) This allows the eyes to see the proportion in a larger subject, such as a 300-pound block of ice.

More details on carving the third dimension are discussed in Chapter 10.

SUMMARY

A number of basic sculpting techniques have been incorporated into the culinary world. This unit gave a brief outline of the basic types of sculpture and how they are used in culinary arts.

Creating a design from an idea starts with knowing what you would like the finished piece to look like. Sculpting ice is no different. You begin by composing a line drawing. It is applied as a template. Once the drawing is etched on the ice surface, the ice is removed within the lines to create a silhouette image. The third dimension is sculpted by imagining where the wide and skinny portions lie within the side view of the silhouette carving. This systematic approach will guide an ice carver to create sculpture in a simple step-by-step manner. Once the large pieces are removed, the sculpture really begins to take shape. From this point, the carver should see all the proportions of the finished piece in spite of its lacking any detail or finished surfaces. This is done by stepping back and looking at the sculpture from at least five feet away, which will allow the eyes to see the proportions correctly.

REVIEW QUESTIONS

Matching

Match the term with its description.

1. Silhouette image
2. Modeling sculpture
3. Scale
4. Sculpture
5. Template
6. Casting sculpture
7. Relief sculpture

a. artist adds materials to create the form
b. uses a mold
c. removes portions of a solid form
d. a two-dimensional side view
e. a pattern
f. a three-dimensional image
g. an exact proportion of two sized images

Short Answer

8. Which form of sculpture most applies to ice?
9. Why is it important to remove the large pieces of ice completely before beginning the detail work?

10. Discuss how a carver moves the sculpture from two to three dimensions.
11. Which design would likely be simpler for a beginning ice carver: a stationary fish or a fish on a coral background? Why?
12. Why is a model or scale drawing necessary for visualizing the finished sculpture?
13. Why should a carver stand back and view this sculpture while carving the three dimensional cuts?

Match the culinary application with the correct type of sculpture

14. Marzipan
Philip Dowell ©
Dorling Kindersley.

a. Casting sculpture

15. Squash
Andreas Von
Einsiedel © Dorling
Kindersley.

b. Relief sculpture

16. Chocolates

c. Modeling sculpture

INSTRUCTOR'S NOTES

1. Some students exhibit a natural fear of ice carving. This is the perfect time to share your own personal experiences and reminisce about your first ice-carving experience. If you haven't done much ice carving, call your local ACF chapter or NICA and invite one of its members to come to class and share their experiences.

2. After reviewing the preceding chapter, ask the class for comments on how they visualize a project coming together from an idea to a sculpture. Discuss the moving from preparatory drawings or models to two-dimension formulation followed by three-dimension shaping.

3. You may add to the program by bringing in the visual aid of models, toy dolls, animal figures, or any other props that support visual guidance.

4. Conduct an oral quiz of the material covered in the first three chapters. The discussion thus far has covered sculpture in general paired with the medium of ice. Specifics of ice carving will follow.

5. Consider offering a short break at this time. The class will reconvene with a display of tools discussed in the next chapter.

Tools of the Trade

4

"Man is a tool-using animal. Nowhere do you find him without tools; without tools he is nothing, with tools he is all."

Thomas Carlyle

Learning Objectives

After you have finished reading this unit, you should be able to:

- Identify the uniform and gear necessary for ice carving
- Explain the application of various ice carving hand tools
- Describe the qualities of various power tools used in ice carving
- Explain how to sharpen and store a chain saw
- Understand how to properly sharpen and store hand tools

Terms to Know

ice carving hand tools
flat carver power tools
ice carver power tools
chain
chain saw bar
die grinder
disk grinder
heat gun
power blower
iron
ice compass
small balancing level
large level

nail board
metal plates
freezing spray
hand broom
ice carving tool box
chisel caddies
hand truck dolly
flatbed dolly
extension cords
power strips
work tables
carving platform
padded blanket

elastic straps
extruded polystyrene
insulation sheets
display pan
display lights
crane lifts
whetstones
rotary whetstone machine
grinder
triangular V-notch stone
curved gouge stone
chain link file
chain saw assembly

When Thomas Carlyle penned his famous quote, he probably wasn't thinking of ice carving but his words certainly apply to this art. No ice carving can take place without some basic tools. In this chapter, readers will gain an understanding of the tools and equipment needed to get started in the rewarding world of ice carving.

Wearing the proper clothing and protective gear is basic. Before tools are discussed, we will introduce basic attire.

CLOTHING

Gloves

Gloves not only keep the hands dry and warm when working with ice, but they also protect the carver's hands from the sharp edges of both ice and equipment. Each type of glove offers unique advantages, depending on your work conditions (Figure 4-1). The most important thing to remember is to wear them.

- Latex foodservice gloves are sometimes preferred. They give the carver full dexterity, and they offer a slight barrier between the ice and sharp edges. Latex gloves are inexpensive and readily available. The main drawback of using this type of glove is that it offers little protection from the cold and not much protection from sharp edges.
- Insulated gloves have proven effective in ice carving. The lining offers warmth and protection from the cold. These gloves may be a little stiff, and it can be hard to feel the tools and the ice.
- Netted safety gloves are also another option, as they offer great agility when touching the ice and protect hands against sharp blades. Such gloves usually

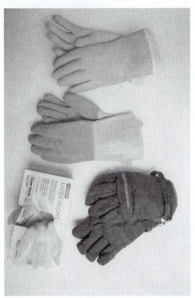

Figure 4-1
The type of environment in which you work will determine the type of glove to wear.

don't provide much thermal protection for those working in freezers or cold areas.

- Skier's gloves are another option for the cold carving areas. Always use the ones tailored with finger slots, instead of the mitten types. These will offer some of the best warmth as they were designed for that purpose.

Shoes

Because carvers stand as they work, it is important to wear comfortable shoes, but that is not all carvers need from their footwear. Shoes should be water resistant or waterproof to keep feet dry and warm (Figure 4-2). This type of shoe can also protect the carver from electrical shock. In many cases, carvers work in cold environments, and warm shoes or boots are appreciated. Rubber is often the best material, although textiles are often included in today's shoe designs. Shoes with slip-resistant soles are also very helpful. The proper choice is to stay safe and warm, but always remember that water repellence is a key factor in the choice of proper shoes.

While working with both electricity and melting ice (water). Wearing the proper shoes can prevent shock. In many cases, carvers work in cold environ- ... [the ice carver is often in a shock zone]

Socks

Keeping your feet warm and dry is important, and wearing the right type of socks is essential. When working in a cold environment, wear water-repellant and thermally lined socks, such as those designed for skiers or hunters

Figure 4-2
Footwear should be comfortable and water resistant.

(Figure 4-3). Thinner socks will work in warm areas, especially if you have adequate protective boots or shoes.

Pants

Leg wear should protect the carver from the weather, water, and sharp equipment. Professionals often wear ski shells or heavy-duty overalls (Figure 4-4). The standard chef-style pants will also work when a water repellant apron is worn and the weather is warmer. Absorbent cloth pants, such as jeans, are not recommended for ice carving.

Shirt or Jacket

Shirts or jackets are worn in layers based on necessity of staying warm and dry. A standard T-shirt for warmth with a good chef's jacket will often be suitable if an apron is worn and the weather is warmer. A ski shell or a warm-weather working jacket is often worn in colder areas. A long-sleeve shirt or jacket also acts as a barrier to sharp edges.

Long-sleeve cuffs can be a safety concern, especially with the use of power tools. Cuffs should not dangle into your work zone. Keep the cuffs rolled up, strapped to the wrist, or inserted into your gloves. Additional layers underneath the top layer may be needed, depending on the temperature. Layers can always be removed if the carver warms up.

Wear what you need. As long as you stay dry, you will be in good shape.

Eyewear

Eyewear is a safety precaution recommended for protection from shards or shavings of ice that may fly your way when ice is chipped off the block (Figure 4-5). This is particularly important when using a chain saw or other tools that throw debris in a scattered fashion. Protective eyewear will also protect a student from other carvers working in the vicinity. Colder weather may merit a set of skier's goggles.

Figure 4-5
Eyewear protects the eyes from flying fragments of ice.

Earplugs

When using power tools, it is recommended that carvers protect their hearing by using earplugs (Figure 4-6). There are many styles on the market, and the carver will want to select a pair that is comfortable to wear and that blocks out most of the loud noise.

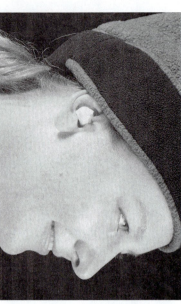

Figure 4-6
Earplugs should be worn whenever loud power tools, such as the chain saw, are used.

Apron

An ice-carving apron is the best protection from water (Figure 4-7). It should be waterproof and cover the top and bottom areas of your clothing. If water-repellant clothing is worn, an apron may not be needed.

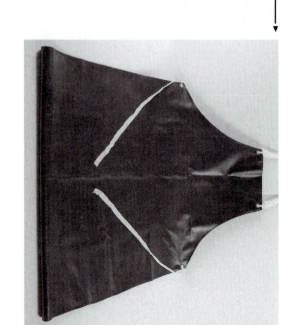

Figure 4-7
Ice carving aprons help keep the carver dry.

The average chef's gear is designed to breathe with the heat of the kitchen. Such aerating kitchen garments are perfect when working with food, but they may be less suitable for ice carving.

Head Gear

Head gear is a safety precaution as well as a thermal protection (Figure 4-8). A hard hat may be worn for the best safety when using power tools. A thermal cap is worn for the best warmth in a cold area. A standard baseball cap can be a

Figure 4-8
Proper head gear is an important element of an ice carver's dress code.

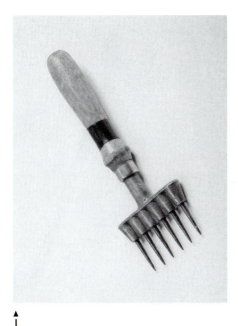

Figure 4-9
Carvers should consider wearing a back brace when lifting or moving heavy blocks of ice.

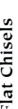

Flat Chisels

Flat chisels for ice carving are designed to be held by the hands and driven through ice and water; they are used for multiple purposes, including flattening surfaces, removing large and small segments of ice, and rounding corners (Figure 4-11). The balance of an ice chisel is drawn more toward the head for leverage purposes rather than the center, which is how most woodcarving chisels are made. Wood and stone chisels are driven with a hammer; thus the center fulcrum. Because ice is a softer medium, the head is the balance point of a good ice chisel. An ice chisel will always have a beveled side and a flat side. The beveled side should be at an angle close to 20°. The flat side of precision ice chisels will have a concave area on the underside to allow water to flow through it during use.

Figure 4-11
Flat chisels come in a variety of handle lengths and head widths.

moderate choice of both. Ice-carving head gear is an option that is best used for safety and comfort.

Back Brace

A supportive back brace is often worn by people with jobs that require heavy lifting; it reminds them of proper lifting technique (Figure 4-9). As ice carving can often result in lifting 50 pounds or more, this type of brace is recommended.

Ice Carving Hand Tools

The beginning carver will rely on a number of basic hand tools when creating a sculpture. The **ice carving hand tools** are the basic cutting implements used in ice carving to produce an ice sculpture. With experience, the carver will understand the importance of each tool. Prior to that, a student should try to become familiar with the basic tools and their uses.

Six-Prong Chipper

The six-prong chipper is the most basic hand tool for ice carving (Figure 4-10).

- This tool is used as a pencil for transferring a line drawing or a template.
- In addition, this tool can remove massive amounts of ice through careful strategic strokes.

The best way to store this tool is to insert it into a wine cork.

Figure 4-10
Six-prong chipper.

Basic hardware store chisels may be counterbeveled or balanced toward the center, and they are struck with a mallet or hammer. These are signs of stone or wood chisels, but they can work with ice in a more primitive way. They are also less costly than specialty ice chisels. A handyman's set of home-duty wood chisels is available for less than $100, but a single, top-quality ice chisel would often cost more for the single piece. The investment is proportionate to the carver's dedication to ice carving and its career opportunities.

Figure 4-12
Large flat chisel

Figure 4-13
Close shot of the chisel head.

Large Flat Chisel

The large flat chisel is the warrior's sword of ice carving (Figure 4-12). This heavy-duty chisel is valued at $200 to $500 or more, which is merited for regular use by a professional. The large flat chisel will leave a clean surface. The six-prong chipper, used for major segment removal, will leave a jagged surface. The large flat chisel usually has a long handle, which is heavy at the head to provide a driving force at its tip and is always gripped with two hands for stability.

Large flat chisels are used for the following carving jobs:

- The 3- to 5-inch blade will shear large segments of ice. (Professional carvers will also use a power tool to remove large areas of ice.)
- The blade will also aid in creating a flat surface in a traditional fashion.

Medium Flat Chisel

The medium-width flat chisel is handy in both the long- and short-handled varieties (Figure 4-13). The width is usually from 1 to 3 inches.

- A long-handled version will drive through the ice and help clean out a narrow area.
- The short-handled version is good for shaping and rounding corners.

Small Flat Chisel

A small flat chisel is usually 1 inch or narrower (Figure 4-14).

- This tool is used primarily for the fine detail shaping.
- It is also used to work out any small holes surrounded by the ice design.

Narrow Flat Chisel

A narrow chisel is needed when the carver works in a tight space (Figure 4-15).

- The narrow flat chisel works in confined spaces.
- It is also used for fine detail shaping.

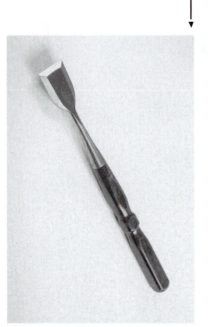

Figure 4-14
Small flat chisel.

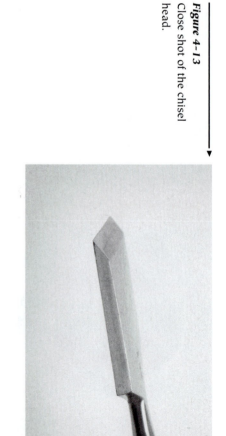

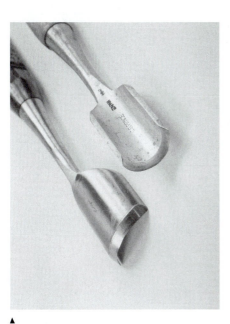

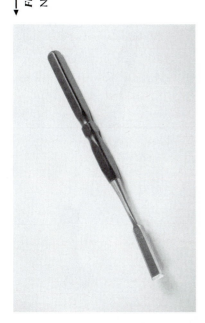

Figure 4-15
Narrow flat chisel.

Figure 4-17
The chisel on the left is the exterior beveled gouge chisel, and the one on the right is an interior beveled gouge chisel.

Figure 4-16
V-notch chisels come in a variety of sizes.

V-Notch Chisels

Large V-Notch Chisel
The span of the angle of V-notch chisels can vary from 30° to 45°.

- The large V-notch chisel is used for large decorative finishing lines and defining corners between segments of a sculpture.

Small V-Notch Chisel
The small V-notch chisel is a shorter hand tool than the larger variety and is used for more intricate work. It will usually measure less than 1 inch (Figure 4-16).

- This chisel is used for finer detail lines on the finishing work.
- It can also serve as a marking tool for the template transfer.

Interior Beveled Gouge Chisel
The interior gouge chisels are available with either short or long handles. They are used for a number of specialty carving techniques. The tip of this type of chisel has a curved rounded shape with the beveled side on the interior of the blade.

- The interior bevel of this chisel will round off narrow ball areas like grapes or the interior curves of a turn, such as the upper portion of a swan's neck.

Exterior Beveled Gouge Chisel
Similar to the interior beveled gouge, this chisel has a curved rounded tip with the beveled side on the exterior or outside of the blade (Figure 4-17).

- The exterior bevel on a gouge chisel is ideal for creating a curved impression within a flat surface, such as scooping out a bowl.
- This chisel is also handy for rounding off a 1-inch ball or other curved surface such as a small animal's kneecap.

Hand Saws

All ice saws have angled teeth designed for ripping only during a pulling motion. It is important to notice the difference between an ice saw and a tree trimming saw (Figure 4-18). A wood saw often has centered teeth, and they glide through the cut more than remove ice. Use of a wood saw may require additional pressure and may lead to breakage of the ice. Woodworking handsaws are not recommended for ice carving.

The teeth of an ice saw are slightly offset, which enables them to glide through the ice by removing the ice from the channel while cutting (Figure 4-19).

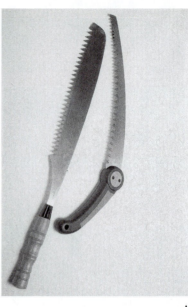

Figure 4-18
The tree-trimming saw is above and the ice saw is below; notice the difference in the teeth.

Pistol-Gripped Saw

The pistol-gripped saw has a curved handle and a blade between 10 and 16 inches long (Figure 4-20). This tool is used for various purposes:

- It can be used to make a relief cut in a small detail area and for the rounding of an interior curved area.

- Pistol-gripped saws are sometimes used to remove medium or smaller sized segments from the design portion of a sculpture.

Medium Hand Saw

The medium hand saw is usually 16 to 20 inches long.

- It is used for larger relief cuts or large segment removal. (However, a chain saw is often used for this purpose.)

Figure 4-19
Some of the teeth on an ice saw are slightly off center, helping the blade clean a path as it saws.

Figure 4-20
Pistol-gripped saw.

Large Hand Saw

The large hand saw is a monstrous cutting tool usually measuring from 20 to 36 inches in length or more (Figure 4-21). The large hand saw is rarely needed by a beginner. However, if one is available, it is a great sensation to feel the cutting power of this tool.

- These are used for splitting raw ice blocks when a chain saw is unavailable.

- They can also be handy for the advanced technique of stacking multiple blocks whereas the blade is driven through the seam to join the surfaces together. One who builds a castle wall would use this saw for such a purpose.

Awl

Also known as an ice pick, an awl is a single-pointed shaft of metal with a handle (Figure 4-22).

- This tool can be used for tracing along the ice within the lines of a solid template.

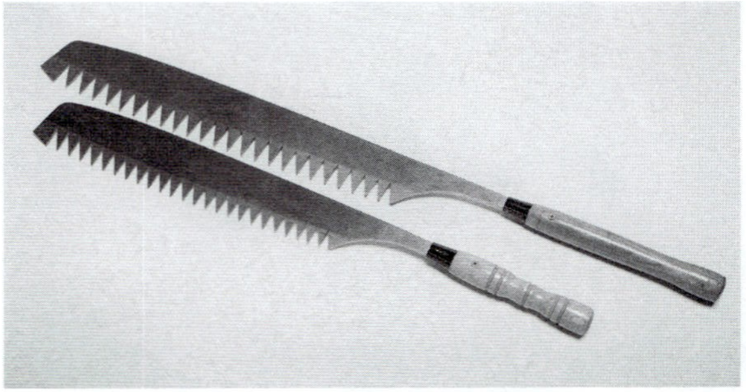

Figure 4-21
Comparison shot of medium and large hand saws.

water to leave a drop-like segment hanging from an area during the freezer storage phase of a finished sculpture. The ice knife will clean up such imperfections with ease.

Ice Carving Power Tools

Ice carving power tools are mechanically driven electric tools used for speed and specialty application. A beginner should learn all the functions of the hand tools before moving on to the utility of power tools. Power tools are often limited in the classroom for cost and safety reasons.

Safety precautions are of critical importance to prevent accidents and shock when using power tools. Never operate power tools without experience or supervision and training.

Chain Saw

The chain saw performs various tasks for an ice carver, including:

- Splitting raw blocks of ice.
- Removing of large unwanted segments from the ice design.
- Boring holes, or design-surrounded segments, that are larger than the width of the chain saw bar.
- Tracing over a well-adhered template as a replacement to the six-prong chipper and chisel method described in Chapter 8, Application of the Template.
- Shaping the design (though power saws rarely leave as clean of a surface as a flat ice chisel).
- Carving finishing lines by using the tip of the bar. (However, these types of decorative channels are usually considered a crude form of decoration compared to V-notch or gouge chisel strokes. Some carvers may consider this method faster and will leave an impression that may last longer on display. A straight die-grinder bit can also leave the same type of channel.)

The chain saw is the fundamental power tool for ice carvers (Figure 4-24). Although hand tools are best for beginners, professionals will often do 80 percent or more of their cutting with a chain saw. This power tool comes in various sizes and shapes, though the principle is the same for all of them. A chain with multiple shearing blades is driven around a cutting bar by a motorized sprocket. The electric version is preferred over the gas variety for ice carving. This preference is due to reliability, noise, exhaust fumes, and the weight of the gas variety. Gas saws are preferred only in an outdoor area where power is unavailable (a rare

Figure 4-22
Awl.

- Another purpose is rapid destruction of ice blocks during a breakdown period of display. A stabbing motion directly into the ice with an awl will split blocks in record time.

A wine cork is the best sheath for this tool, as with the six-prong chipper. Rounded and pointed tools such as the awl or six-prong chipper are inexpensive and often considered disposable when they become dull. Keeping their points protected during storage will greatly extend their life.

Ice Knife

The ice carving knife is similar in shape to a boning knife, though it has the single-sided beveled blade of a chisel and is heavier for greater leverage (Figure 4-23).

- This tool can be used for some of the rounding and shaping.
- Another common purpose is to clean up areas of frozen water drops once the carving is displayed. It is not uncommon for small accumulations of

Figure 4-23
Ice knife.

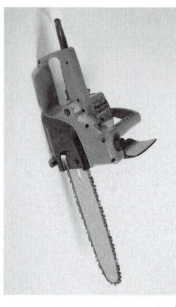

Figure 4-24
Chain saw.

instance for chefs and carvers). Electric saws are rated for power by amperage. A weaker saw may have only a 4- to 6-amp rating, and a heavy-duty commercial saw may have a 10- to 15-amp motor. The speed of a chain saw is measured in feet per minute (FPM), which measures how many feet of chain travel past a point on the bar in 60 seconds. The faster saws are recommended for ice carving. A weaker saw may have a rating of only 1,600 FPM, and the best saws can exceed 5,500 FPM.

The more powerful saws drive through the ice faster and last far longer. Cost and dedication level for usage will be a factor in choosing a chain saw for ice carving. Safety precautions are critical with chain saws. Safety notes are outlined throughout this book on the usage of this tool. Refer to this chapter's segment on chain saw care and maintenance for details on caring for your saw.

Gas-Powered Chain Saws

Gas-powered chain saws are typically not suggested for ice sculpture, as they vibrate much more than electric chain saws and are heavy. They are also outlawed in most competitions and are environmentally harmful. However, they occasionally become useful in some unique applications. Harvesting lake ice might be one example. Those who carve ice in cold weather may have the opportunity to carve lake ice. However, the average classroom will use manufactured sculpture ice instead. Sculpting ice where power is not available may be another reason to use gas-powered saws. Otherwise, the gas saw is very handy for tree trimming and other chores in the woods, though rarely a good option for ice carving.

Anatomy of a Chain Saw

The **chain** is the cutting blade for a chain saw (Figure 4-25). The length is measured in drive links, and many varieties are used based on the length of the

Figure 4-25
The chain.

cutting bar. If one were to simply count the links on the chain, this would determine the size. A 45 DL chain is often used for a 12-inch cutting bar.

Most chains have ripping blade links in between. The guide links are designed to keep the cutting bar straight and remove debris, especially for use with wood. Chains must be kept sharp or they may damage the sculpture more than carve it. Some thrifty carvers sharpen their own chains with a file. (See the techniques outlined in the back of this chapter for sharpening procedures.) Others may have their chains professionally sharpened a few times for a nominal fee. When expense becomes no object, new chains can be applied regularly. New chains are often priced between $15 and $50 or more. The lifespan of a chain depends on its care (prevention rust damage), the density of the medium being cut, the temperature of the ice, and misuses such as driving the blade into concrete or other dulling surfaces. (A colder, harder block of ice in 0° F [18° C] air will be far denser than a softer, tempered block of ice at 32° F [0° C]). A chain that is allowed to rust may become dull after the first use.

A primary safety precaution is keeping the proper tension of the chain along the bar. A chain that is too loose may fall off its track, breaking the chain and possibly causing bodily injury. See the instructions later in this chapter for tensioning techniques.

The **chain saw bar** is the guide to the cutting surface of the chain (Figure 4-26). Bars are available in various lengths and widths. The length varies from 12 inches to 24 inches or more. The shorter bars are easier to handle, and the longer ones can be useful for heavier utility work such as splitting blocks. A 12- to 16-inch bar is most commonly used for ice carving. The width is usually from two to four inches, and the narrower bars will maneuver more easily.

Figure 4-26
Chain saw bar.

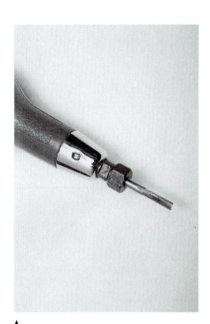

Figure 4-27
Die grinder.

Some chain saws will have a tip or kickback protector on the bar. This is designed as a safety measure for use of cutting wood and preventing kickback, which is a hazard that takes place when a moving chain touches a very dense area. It can cause the saw to suddenly swing upward. Kickback will never happen when applied to ice as the medium is always consistent and far softer than wood. This tip protector must be removed for use on ice carving as the tip of the bar is often used for sculpture technique. The method of removal for the protector will vary based on the brand of the saw. Another option is to purchase an aftermarket chain saw bar with the tip protector left off. Such aftermarket parts are sold by outside equipment manufacturers of chainsaw parts. Always store your chain saw in a dry area with adequate lubrication on the chain, bar, and sprocket components to preserve its quality for the next sculpture to come.

Die Grinder

The **die grinder** is a high-speed rotary tool similar to a router (Figure 4-27). The die grinder is long, narrow, and straight, as opposed to a hand drill or a router, and its speed is far faster than a drill for shearing ice. A drill will often turn at a speed of around 2000 revolutions per minute (RPM) or slower for boring straight holes. A die grinder can turn as fast as 25,000 RPM or higher and do the job much faster. The shape of this tool lends itself to be held like a large pencil for channeling scroll work where a pistol-gripped hand drill would not provide the same balance and precision.

- Die grinders can scroll a straight or angled channel within the ice's surface or mill an exterior portion of the sculpture for shaping.
- Some professionals will use this tool with a milling bit, as an alternative to chisels, for shaping. This method is a faster way to shape ice once you become accustomed to the feel of this power tool. This practice is not recommended

for beginners, as learning hand chisel technique is a fundamental lesson. We draw attention to the die grinder as it is becoming a more popular application for professionals.

Die Grinder Straight Bit

The straight bit comes in various widths, depending on the size of the channel desired (Figure 4-28). Most widths are available, from $\frac{1}{8}$ inch to $\frac{3}{4}$ inch and larger. A straight bit is also available with a single flute or a double flute. The flutes are the cutting blades built onto the bit. The double-flute variety is preferred as this provides twice the cutting surface.

- A straight bit will drive a narrow channel into the surface of the ice. This is commonly done for decorative lines or scrollwork where sand or snow is

Figure 4-28
Die grinder straight bit.

used to fill the channel as an advanced technique. More details on scroll-work are explained in Chapter 14.

Die Grinder Angled Bit

The advantage of using an angled bit with a die grinder is speed. When used in tandem with a hand chisel, a deeper grove can be created compared with using a V-notch chisel alone (Figure 4-29).

- An angled bit replicates the shape of the V-notch chisel due to its conical design. Various angles and widths to form the groove are available.

Die Grinder Milling Bit

A milling bit is either straight or angled (Figure 4-30). These bits are often de-signed with two to four flutes down the shaft for maximum shearing ability.

Figure 4-29
Die grinder angled bit.

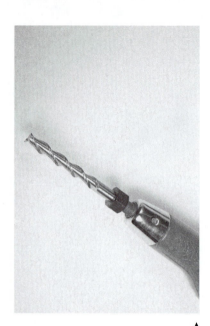

Figure 4-30
Die grinder milling bit.

- Die grinder milling bits are designed for shaping the exterior portions of the work, or for rapid insertion into the surface.

Disk Grinder

A **disk grinder** is a power tool with a sanding or grinding disk, which turns in a rotary fashion (Figure 4-31). The disks come in various grades of texture, though the course sanding types are usually preferred.

- Disk grinders are used to grind away flat or curved surfaces.
- This tool would be used to replace the surface shaping that a flat chisel pro-vides. Once again, with the safety factors involved, this alternative to hand tools is not advised for beginners.

Figure 4-31
Disk grinder.

Heat Gun

A **heat gun** is much like a hair dryer although it often uses far less air flow, runs hotter, and is often insulated better to prevent electrical shock (Figure 4-32).

- Heat guns enable the carver working in a freezing area to induce controlled melting. Controlled melting smooths out rough edges and adds clarity to the surface.

Power Blower

A **power blower** is much like a hair dryer without the use of heat and usually of-fers a much higher air velocity (Figure 4-33). These commercial tools are usually insulated better than hair dryers for the purpose of safety from shock.

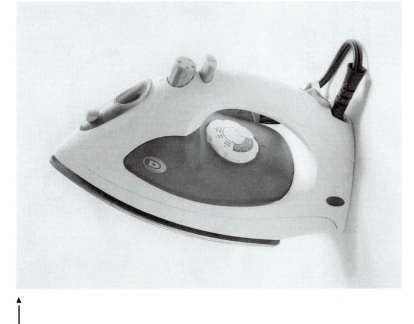

Figure 4-34
A household iron can be useful for ice carving.

• This tool efficiently blows ice shavings and pieces off the carving during the cleaning process.

Iron

A household laundry **iron** is commonly used for heating metal plates or other surfaces so they will be warm enough to melt the ice on contact (Figure 4-34). The placement of this tool is usually in a dry area away from the water and carving zone. Application of the iron directly to the ice has been seen though not advised. This is due to the critical safety precautions of GFCI protection, which is mandatory for use with this tool. Irons were not originally designed nor insulated for use in heavy water environments. Never use an iron in an ice carving area without the full GFCI protection from electrical shock.

• Creating a perfectly flat surface is usually the goal of this application.

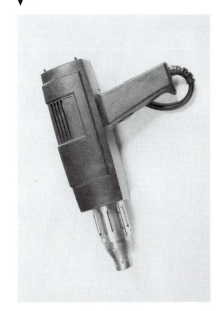

Figure 4-32
Heat gun.

AUXILIARY TOOLS

Ice Tongs (Double-Handle or Boston Tongs)

Ice tongs are a hinged set of metal spikes used to lift and carry ice (Figure 4-35). The Boston variety is built with two separate handles and made for holding with two hands.

Ice Tongs (Single-Handle, Cincinnati or Kansas City Tongs)

The Cincinnati or Kansas City–style tongs are built with a single handle linked to the back of the hinged area. Some ice carvers prefer single-handled tongs, but they are not recommended for beginners when moving large blocks of ice. They are good for transporting smaller blocks up to 50 pounds.

• This type of tongs is gripped with a single hand or both hands on the same handle.

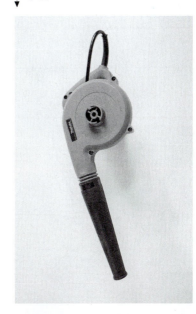

Figure 4-33
Power blower.

Figure 4-35
Double-handled Boston
tongs shown above;
single-handled Kansas City
tongs shown below.

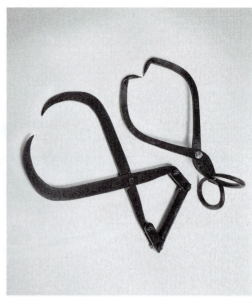

Figure 4-37
Levels.

Levels

Levels are used to test the surface or sides of an ice block (Figure 4-37). A **small balancing level** is a handheld tool, approximately 8 to 12 inches long.

- It is used primarily for stacking segments of ice on display so they are kept centered and balanced.

A **large level** is typically 48 inches long and includes lines of measurement.

- Large levels are used for measuring areas of raw ice blocks or leveling larger platforms of multiblock sculptures.
- They can also be used for ensuring that the carving platform is level.

Nail Board

A **nail board** is a plank with two handles on top (Figure 4-38) and multiple nails or screws inserted through the top to the bottom (Figure 4-39). They are

Figure 4-38
Nail board with handles
on top.

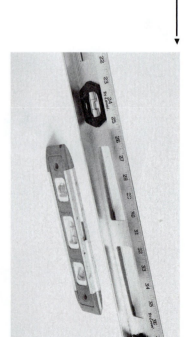

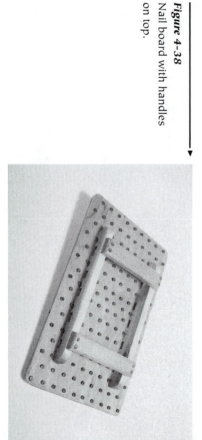

Figure 4-36
Ice compass.

Ice Compass

An **ice compass** is a metal hand tool (Figure 4-36) with two sharpened points that are expandable from a hinge. One point rests in the center of the circle to be marked while the other scratches the marking line of the circle pattern.

Figure 4-39
Screws protrude from the bottom of the board.

available in various shapes, though rectangular is most common, and are from 1 to 3 feet wide. Nails or screws are usually set from ½ to 1 inch apart. In spite of its name, screws are more commonly used for durability.

- A nail board is used to scratch a flat surface on the ice.

Metal Plates

Metal plates are commonly made of rigid sheets of aluminum (Figure 4-40). They can be built in various shapes and sizes for either small or large surface applications.

- Metal plates are used to form a clean flat surface on the ice. Creating a flat surface is handy for multiple reasons, including the preparation for an ice sheet to be decorated or scroll filled, stacking segments of ice with a clean seam, or ice welding. These techniques are too advanced for a beginning carver, though they are widely used in the industry.

Figure 4-40
Metal plates.

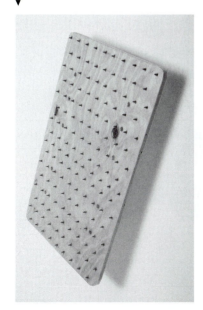

Figure 4-41
Freezing spray.

Freezing Spray

Freezing spray, popularly sold as gum remover, is a can of gas that emits a freezing spray upon application (Figure 4-41).

- This can be used as a temporary application to chill down the surface of the ice.
- Freezing spray is needed for quick repairs of ice on the display table and sometimes used for ice welding and template adhesion.

Caution should be taken with the use of freezing sprays for two reasons: excessive freezing and the potential as a fire hazard. Excessive freezing may occur if too much spray is applied, which can crack the surface of the ice. Keep in mind that thermal shock is sensitivity for the crystalline structure of sculpture ice. Holding the can too close or spraying for too long may damage the ice. The compounds inside the can are stable under pressure in the liquid state, but once released into the atmosphere, they boil into a gas that becomes very cold. Depending on the compounds, they will reach temperatures of −10° to −40° F (−23° to −40° C).

A greater hazard is the safety involved with the flammability of this gaseous substance. Such sprays often contain butane or propane gases. As these gases are essentially fuels, extra care must be taken to avoid using them near open flames; power tools, which create internal sparks; and other sources of extreme heat. Freezing sprays are commonly used in the industry though are rarely needed by the beginner. Exercise extreme caution when using freezing sprays.

Hand Broom

A **hand broom** is a small handheld broom made of straw or nylon (Figure 4-42).

- Hand brooms are used to sweep excess shavings or ice particles from the sculpture during the cleaning process.

Figure 4-42
Hand broom.

Ice

There is no correct size or shape to an **ice carving tool box**, as some carvers may use a mechanic's stacking drawer system and some may use a single-chambered box (Figure 4-43). A good feature to notice would be an extended overall length so that longer tools can be stored.

- A tool box is commonly used for housing all the smallwares in a single dry caddy that can be carried to a job site.

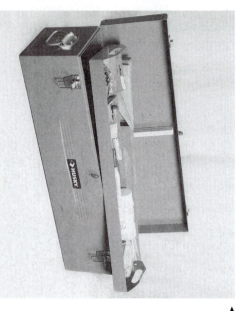

Figure 4-43
Ice carving tool box.

Figure 4-44
Chisel caddy.

Chisel Caddies

There are many shapes and sizes of **chisel caddies** (Figure 4-44). They range from a small golf club–style bag to an elongated suitcase, a durable vinyl bag, or a padded wooden box. All these choices store long-handled tools in a protective case.

- A chisel caddy is a protective holster for the storage of ice chisels.

Dollies

A **hand truck dolly** is a wheeled hand vehicle (Figure 4-45). The wheels of this type of dolly can vary. The versions with inflated rubber tires are the most preferred as they handle bumps very well. Ice does not respond favorably to impact

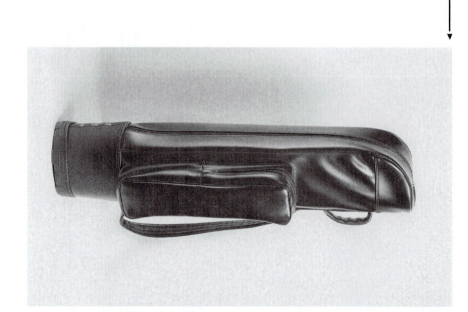

Figure 4-46
Flatbed dolly.

- A flatbed dolly is a low-profile hand vehicle used to transport items. Most hospitality establishments use this tool in the receiving department to transport cases of food or other goods. Sculpted ice is often moved on the flatbed between the freezer to the display area. This can be the case because more surface area becomes an advantage or because the stewarding staff will find only this resource on display day.

Extension Cords

Extension cords used for ice carving are a safety concern (Figure 4-47). Many carving venues may be 20 to 50 feet away from a reliable power source.

- Extension cords are a vital requirement for the use of power tools. Because water and electricity are joined, it is recommended to use high-quality

Figure 4-47
Extension cords.

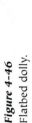

Figure 4-45
Hand truck dolly.

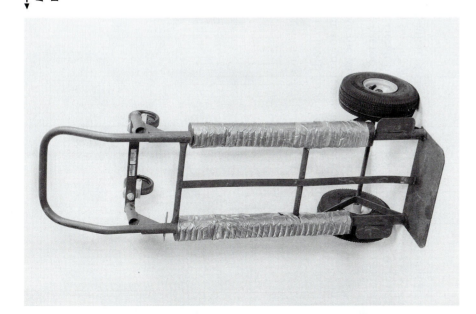

during transportation. A smooth ride is always the key to success in the transportation of ice.

- This tool is capable of hauling payload in an upright position.

The rigid-wheeled varieties are not recommended. The addition of padding along the upright supports protects the ice from breakage during transport. Insulated padding will also prevent the embossment of ridgelines into the ice as it melts.

A metal **flatbed dolly** should have protective padding on its surface (Figure 4-46). Cardboard would become a minimum shock protection, and blankets, cardboard, or other padded barriers will prevent the ice from sliding or taking damage during transport.

extension cords. An outdoor-rated power cord is always the right choice, as the indoor variety will not handle the electrical load with its wiring nor be insulated for a water-laden environment. A 16- to 14-gauge wire rating is best for the heavy electrical load. For extended lengths beyond 75 feet, a 12-gauge cord may be needed for tools that draw over 10 amps. Refer to the manufacturer's recommendations on sizing extension cords for electrical tools. This information is usually listed in the owner's manual or can be acquired from the factory directly.

Ground fault circuit interrupter (GFCI) receptacles are electrical outlets used for safety against electrical shock (Figure 4-48). They include test/reset buttons to ensure their function ability.

- The receptacles are designed to stop the current of electricity if a short occurs, such as through the operator of a power tool. This safety precaution is always recommended for use with power tools in wet work areas. A portable version can be built with a receptacle, outdoor receptacle box, 8 feet of heavy duty cord, and an insulated plug.

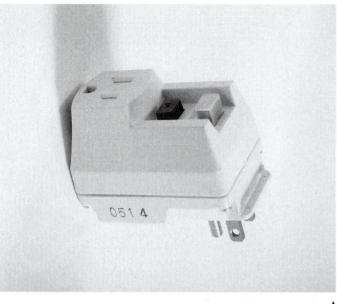

Figure 4-48
Ground fault circuit interrupter.

Figure 4-49
Power strip.

Power Strips

Power strips are electrical receptacle splitters (Figure 4-49).

- Power strips are handy for work areas that use multiple power tools. By using power strips you cut down the number of extension cords in the work area or having to trade out the plugs when you change tools.

It is important to remember that too many tools working at once from a single power strip can overload the circuit breaker. Because most professional carvers will be working alone, only a single tool will be used at a time, which is never a problem. See a further explanation of electrical requirements for a carving area in Chapter 6.

Work Tables

Basic **work tables** are recommended for the storage of hand tools and small power tools in the ice-carving area (Figure 4-50).

- Work tables protect hand tools from foot-traffic accidents and keep them away from puddles of water.

A standard 6- to 8-foot banquet table will be fine. Line the table with terry cloth towels or Styrofoam to protect both the tools and the table surface.

Carving Platform

A **carving platform** is a pedestal used to raise a block of ice to an appropriate working height, and it keeps the ice clean of dirt on the ground (Figure 4-51).

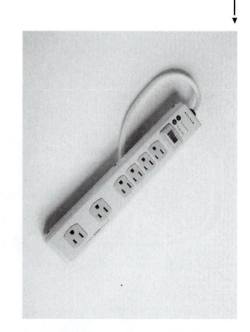

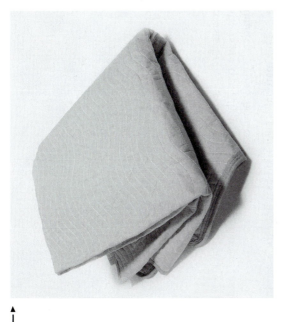

Figure 4-52
Padded blanket.

Figure 4-50
Work table.

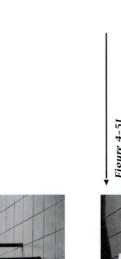

Figure 4-51
Carving platform.

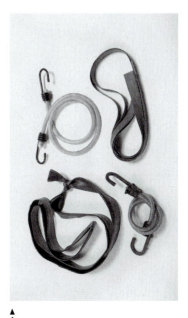

Elastic Straps

Elastic straps, such as bungee cords, are flexible securing bands of rubber (Figure 4-53). Specialty rubber straps are also available. An economical option would also consist of splitting an old bicycle tube in half and tying the ends together.

• Straps are used to secure blankets or templates on the ice.

Insulation Sheets

Extruded polystyrene insulation sheets are a high-density style of foam and capable of handling the full weight of ice blocks (Figure 4-54). This material

Figure 4-53
Elastic straps.

• When a carving platform is used, a carver can gain a better leverage angle when working on the lower portions of the ice sculpture. Various heights and materials can be used for carving platforms. See Chapter 6 for further details on platform varieties.

Padded Blanket

A **padded blanket** is used for the protection of the ice during transport as well as for protection from defrost degradation during long-term freezer storage (Figure 4-52).

• Straps or bungee cords are usually used to keep the blanket secured to the ice. Quilted moving blankets are usually the most functional and economical.

resists breakage and flaking, which can create a mess during cleanup. Such sheets are typically used as a building material, and they can be purchased from builders' supply houses.

- This material is best used as a liner for a carving platform or even a protective surface for tools and carving gear.

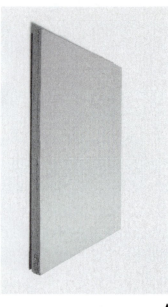

Figure 4-54
Extruded polystyrene insulation sheets.

Display Pan

A **display pan** is the vessel used for presenting an ice sculpture (Figure 4-55). Many options are available, from elaborately decorated stands, rotating carousels, and lighted glow pans to economical roasting pans or watertight boxes, which may be wrapped with a tablecloth for presentation.

- A proper display pan will have a tube built in for the drainage of water. Otherwise, the pan should be extra deep or water will have to be removed during the display period in a room-temperature environment.

Figure 4-55
Display pan.

Display Lights

Display lights enhance the appearance of an ice sculpture (Figure 4-56).

- In some cases, the room used for display may have track or ceiling lights suitable for illuminating the sculpture. However, this is often not the case. Small battery-operated insertion lights or AC-powered clip-on table lights are often used when track or ceiling lights are not available.

Figure 4-56
Display lights.

Crane Lifts

Crane lifts operate with either a motorized or hand-crank winch to raise the platform (Figure 4-57).

- A crane lift is used for lifting ice from the ground to display height. This tool replaces the basic manpower of lifting a heavy block onto a table. Although these cranes can be a substantial investment and they occupy considerable space, they are very handy when the display staff may not be capable of lifting heavy objects.

Whetstones

Whetstones are sharpening stones used for honing ice chisels (Figure 4-58).

- Whetstones are available in various grit ratings, which measure the number of grains per cubic inch. Chisel sharpening whetstones range from the courser 800 grit to the finest 6,000 grit styles. See the notes on chisel sharpening for further details on whetstones.

Figure 4-59
Rotary whetstone machine grinder.

Rotary Whetstone Machine Grinder

Rotary whetstone machine grinder is a flat wheel that turns mechanically while a water source constantly moistens the stone to prevent burning out the temper of the chisel's metal (Figure 4-59).

* A rotary whetstone machine grinder is a specialty power tool designed specifically for honing chisels (Figure 4-60).

Triangular V-Notch Stone

The **triangular V-notch stone** is a specialty sharpening stone designed for honing the interior portion of a V-notch chisel (Figure 4-61).

* The V-notch chisel's interior must be flattened after honing the beveled side. The triangular stone is very handy for this purpose.

Figure 4-60
A flat chisel is being sharpened on a rotary whetstone machine grinder.

Figure 4-57
Crane lift.

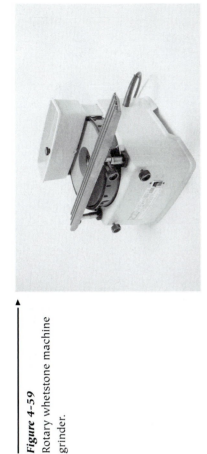

Figure 4-58
Whetstone.

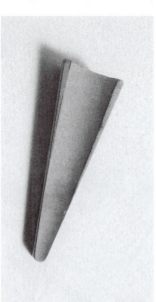

Curved Gouge Stone

The **curved gouge stone** is a half-moon-shaped tool (Figure 4-62).

• This tool is a specialty sharpening stone designed for honing the curves of a gouge-shaped chisel.

Chain Link File

A **chain link file** is an abrasive metal rod (Figure 4-63).

• It is designed specifically for sharpening the links of a chain saw chain.

CHAIN SAW CARE AND MAINTENANCE

Like most tools, chain saws require specialized care and maintenance in order for them to run at their optimum ability. Properly maintaining the chain is the key to a high-performance carving experience. The motor assembly and drive bar also require attention. This section illustrates how to keep the chain saw in top form.

Figure 4-62
Curved gouge stone.

Figure 4-61
Triangular V-notch stone.

Figure 4-63
Chain link file.

Chain Saw Assembly

The manufacturer's **chain saw assembly** instructions should be followed as each brand varies slightly. Some basic elements are common among all saws (Figure 4-64 and Figure 4-65). Because it is possible to put the chain on backward, take notice to keep the cutting blades facing forward from the top of the bar.

Chains

Tensioning the Chain

The tension of the chain should be tight enough to keep the guides on track with the bar. The chain should have enough slack to glide smoothly around the bar. Here are a few tips to remember when tensioning the chain:

• A chain set too tight will bind up during operation and prematurely wear out.
• A chain too loose may run off the guide track of the bar and possibly derail, break, and injure someone nearby.
• Chain tension can be checked in the idle state by pulling the chain toward the middle of the bar.
• A rule of thumb for proper tension is to have a gap, from chain to bar, equal to the thickness of one pencil or 3 to 5 millimeters.

To adjust the tension:

1. Always unplug the equipment when making adjustments or cleaning any power tool.
2. Begin by loosening the guard plate screw by one full revolution. This will keep the bar secured in position while allowing it to slide back and forth along the bar guide.

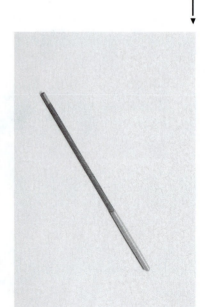

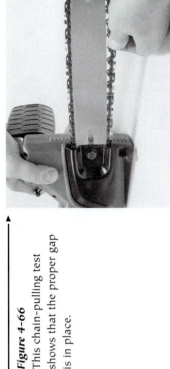

Figure 4-66
This chain-pulling test shows that the proper gap is in place.

3. Next, adjust the tensioning screw to the desired setting with a screwdriver. Keep in mind that a proper test will not be possible until the guard plate screw is retightened and the chain pull test is reapplied (Figure 4-66).

    Note: Chains will loosen during extended use, and the tension should be checked regularly.

"A Clean Chain Is a Happy Chain"

Saw chains, made of high-carbon steel, are capable of achieving very sharp edges through miles of cutting while remaining chip resistant. A downfall to this compound of steel is the tendency to rust. Once rust sets in on any metal, the blade will never be the same. This also applies to chisels made of similar steel.

Steps to Chain Maintenance:

1. The best way to maintain a sharp chain is to keep it dry and oiled.
2. Remove the chain after each carving session and dry it with a towel. Take the time to dry off the remaining components of the saw so the chain does not rest in water during storage.
3. Once the chain is reassembled, use the chain oil pump to apply oil and rotate the chain along the bar a few times by gripping the chain with the towel and pulling.

Chain Oil

Clear food-grade machine oils are suitable for the oil pump, chain, and bar sprocket. Never use cooking oil of any kind for lubrication

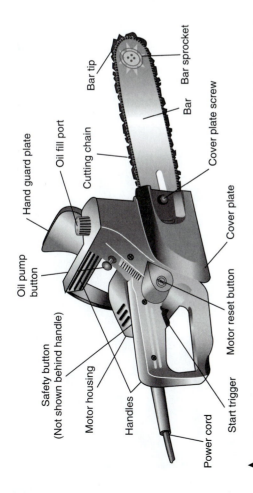

Figure 4-64   This diagram illustrates the image of a fully assembled chain saw with a label and line to the following areas: motor housing, cutting chain, bar, bar tip, bar sprocket, cover plate, cover plate screw, start trigger, safety button, oil pump button, oil fill port, power cord, handles, hand guard plate, and motor reset button.

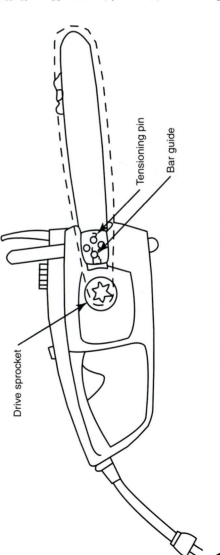

Figure 4-65   This diagram shows the saw with the cover plate removed to illustrate the following components: drive sprocket, bar guide, and tensioning pin.

as it will gum up and damage the equipment. "Bar and chain oil" is a commonly sold product. New saws sometimes come packed with a sample bottle of bar and chain oil. This type of oil is fine for the average user who cuts wood and trees. The standard bar and chain oil looks like a thin motor oil; it is great for machinery but is too dirty for carving ice. It also is not food-grade quality. Seek recommended resources of this book for sources of food-grade machine oils.

Lubricating the Chain

Always keep the chain lubricated for a smoother carving experience and extended life of your equipment.

1. To load the oil pump, remove the cap, apply a funnel, and fill the reservoir as needed (Figure 4-67). Filling to the top is not necessary, although a full tank keeps you from repeating this drill as often.

2. Press the oil pump button as needed throughout the carving session to keep the chain and bar lubricated (Figure 4-68). There is no defined rule for how much oil is needed, although an average would be two pumps for every five minutes of running time. You will hear the difference in the sound of chain as it runs with and without oil.

Figure 4-67
Filling the oil pump with oil.

Figure 4-68
The oil pump button should be pushed to release oil to the chain and bar throughout the carving process.

chain link file in its correct position during sharpening. The file is best applied with a pushing motion and not allowed to touch the blade during retraction. All chains have blades on opposite sides to move evenly through the medium. The filing motion is best done on all of one side first.

2. Next move to all the remaining links of the opposite side for the efficiency in the steps of self-sharpening (Figure 4-69).

Guide Bar

Always use a guide bar with a sprocket built into the tip. Some bars are available without this feature, but they are not recommended. Most sprocket bar tips have a small port for application of oil.

1. Use a dropper to apply a few drops of food-grade clear machine oil to this hole. In lack of a dropper, pour a small puddle over the hole area while laying the bar flat.

2. After the oil is applied, rotate the sprocket a few turns to work the oil into the inner housing (Figure 4-70).

Motor Housing

The motor portion of the saw should be a durable low-maintenance portion. The best health plan for any machinery is to keep tools clean and dry after carving and during storage. Heavy-duty versions of electric chain saws have replaceable motor brushes. These brushes are spring-tensioned blocks of carbon located near the side of the motor and are easily removed with a screwdriver. They should be checked now and then for wear. If they become completely worn, this condition will damage the saw and render it useless. Replacements are always available from the chain saw factory or its distributors.

Chain Sharpening

The ripping blades of a chain saw can be kept sharp through regular maintenance. A professional sharpening service will have the equipment to perform this quickly at a nominal charge.

1. An economical option would be to sharpen your own chains with a chain link file. The top blade should be filed to a 30° angle and the side blade should be filed to an 85° angle. This is achieved by properly holding the

HAND CHISEL CARE AND MAINTENANCE

Notes of expertise on chisel sharpening and maintenance are provided by Michael Pizzuto of Samurai Chisel Sharpening Service, Golden, Colorado.

Even though electric power tools, lathes, Computer Numerical Control (CNC) machines, and computer controlled instruments are being used in ice carving, hand tools remain the bedrock of ice sculpture technique. Knowing how to properly maintain hand tools is imperative. Chisels made especially for ice carving range in cost from $100 to $500 each, so it is important to keep them in shape. With proper handling, storage and sharpening, chisels should last for many years.

It is not hard for chefs to relate to the value of sharp tools. Just as a sharp chef's knife performs the job easier with safety and efficiency, so does a sharp chisel. A properly beveled chef's knife is sharpened at a 20° to 22° angle. Ice chisels that measure less than 3 inches are typically sharpened at a 19° angle and those measuring 3 inches across or more are sharpened at a 20° or 21° angle.

Sharpening Stones

It is preferable to have three whetstones with varying degrees of grit (Figure 4-71). Expect to pay $20 to $40 per stone. They last a long time and are easily transported to job sites. While water or oil can be used on whetstones, water is preferred. Water is often readily available. Water also allows the stone to dry without leaving an oily residue or glazing of the stone's surface. If using oil, it must be machine-grade oil, not cooking oil. Cooking oils will gum up. Sharpening stones have grit, which ranges from coarse (800 grit) to medium fine (1,000 grit) and to finishing

Figure 4-71
A variety of whetstones with different degrees of grit is needed.

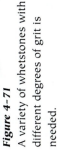

File

30°

Saw chain

Figure 4-69   Notice the correct file placement for chain sharpening.

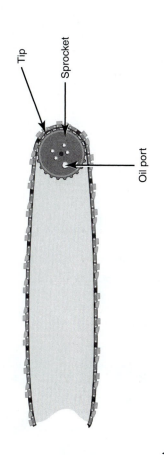

Tip

Sprocket

Oil port

Figure 4-70   Find the tip, sprocket, and oil port of the guide bar.

(6,000 grit). As you sharpen, you will move from the coarser to the finer. Nicked and damaged chisels will need additional sharpening with the coarser grades first. As the chisel becomes sharper, it should be moved and sharpened with the finer grade stones.

Several types of materials are used to manufacture sharpening stones; natural and man-made are two primary categories. It is recommended to use the natural Arkansas hard stones or man-made stones from Japan. You can purchase these stones at a well-supplied hardware store or at a woodworking supply store, or you can refer to the ice carving specialty suppliers listed in the appendices of this book.

Carver's Note

Do not use traditional three-way sharpening stones used to sharpen kitchen knives as the stones are too coarse and will become difficult to form the ideal edge. Mechanical grinders are another option as they can sharpen a number of tools quickly. However, they are expensive and heavy, and those designed for chisels (as shown earlier in the chapter) may only include one grade of stone. These types of grinders must have water or oil continuously applied to the stone during the sharpening process or the chisel will become damaged from excessive heat. A severely chipped or damaged chisel can be ground to restoration quicker with a machine grinder than by hand with a sharpening stone. The sharpening surface of a mechanical grinder for chisels must be flat. *A standard circular bench grinder (commonly used for knives) can never be used for chisels as it will not maintain the proper angle.* For this reason, it is usually not advised to send your ice chisels to be sharpened by a knife sharpening service unless the workers specifically understand the principles of chisel sharpening and have the proper equipment to do the job. The appendix of this book provides resources for chisels to be sharpened by ice carving professionals.

Follow These Steps to Sharpen a Flat Chisel

(Gouge or half round and V-shaped chisels will need special consideration.)

• **Determine the Angle of the Chisel Blade**

Use a protractor to determine the correct angle. You can obtain a protractor from a drafting supply or office supply store. The protractor will help you check the angle during the sharpening process. Hold the protractor up against the chisel and check for the proper angle, depending on the size of the chisel (Figure 4-72). Check the angle of the blade periodically throughout the sharpening process to ensure that the correct angle is being maintained. Damage can

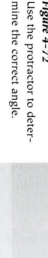

Figure 4-72
Use the protractor to determine the correct angle.

occur to the blade if a proper angle is not preserved, and carving effort will be significantly increased.

To maintain the angle during the sharpening process slowly lift the chisel on the wet stone until the surface tension of the water creates a "line" against the cutting edge. As long as that "line" of water is there on the wet stone, the proper angle is being maintained (Figure 4-73).

• **Chisel Sharpening Technique**

Expect to spend 20 to 30 minutes on each tool.

1. Soak the stone in water or oil for 15 minutes or until it is saturated. This will allow the metal particles to wash off the surface of the stone and avoid glazing of the stone's surface. Again, water is the preferred medium.

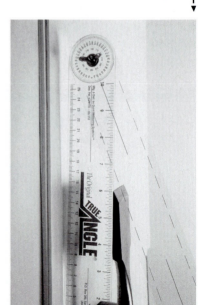

Figure 4-73
Hold the back of the chisel with one hand. Place the guiding hand with the thumb on top of the chisel and the rest of hand creating a wedge underneath the chisel.

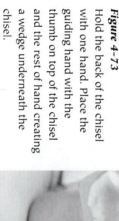

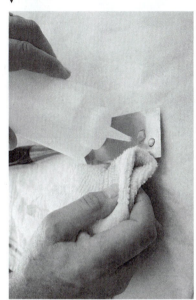

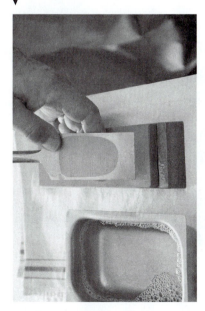

Figure 4-74
The chisel's cutting surface should have a flat contact with the stone. Imagine cutting a paper-thin sliver of the stone off with each stroke. It is as if you are finely shaving the stone.

2. Select a suitable work surface. Find a level surface that is waist high, such as a 36-inch kitchen worktable.

3. Secure the wet stone on a damp towel. The towel will prevent the stone from moving once pressure is applied.

4. Never hurry when sharpening. Be relaxed; concentrate on holding the chisel's cutting surface in flat contact with the stone (Figure 4-74). Place your hand gently and firmly with the thumb on top of the chisel's blade. Slide the rest of the fingers around behind the blade against the back of the chisel to create a wedge. (Your other hand can be holding the chisel's handle.) Those who hurry have a tendency to lift the chisel's handle and go past the correct 19° or 21° angle. Use the method above to find the "line" on the wet stone, which will keep the blade at the proper angle. Sharpening the chisel at a larger angle will ruin its cutting edge. The angled side needs to be sharpened at least twice as much as the flat side.

5. Use methodical, even strokes as you push the blade from the front of the stone to the back. Remember to use the same amount of pressure throughout the stroke from one end of the chisel's blade to the opposite end. This avoids pushing harder in the middle of the stroke, which will create a depression in the stone. Always push evenly on the forward stroke but ease up entirely on the backstroke. Apply additional water or oil as needed to keep the stone from getting dry and watch to maintain the "line" of water for proper angle.

6. The normal process generally takes 100 forward strokes on each side of the blade per stone. Progressively moving from coarse to fine stones and finally to a polishing grit stone will complete the process.

7. Always use the protractor between each stone to monitor the degree of the angle. Keep the stone wet and maintain the angle by watching for the surface tension line of water.

8. Immerse the sharpened chisel in moderately hot water (120° F). Dry completely, removing all water droplets, which can cause rust and pitting. Dry the wood handle, especially where the metal joins the wood.

9. Oil coating of the blade or handle may be necessary for chisels that are stored in a humid environment (Figure 4-75). Machine-grade food-safe oil is again recommended.

V-Notch Chisel Sharpening

1. The angle of the cutting surface, from the top of the wings to the base of the angle, must be maintained at a proper 90° angle. Use the protractor to determine the angle.

2. The blade should be parallel to the stone (Figure 4-76). Using an incorrect angle can damage the blade (Figure 4-77).

3. Begin by following the sharpening stroke procedure described in the flat chisel section.

4. Repeat the same motion for each of the two sides of the V.

5. The interior section of the V may need to be straightened with a triangular V-notch sharpening stone. There may also be small metal shavings or burrs to remove. Keep the stone flat inside the chisel (Figure 4-78). During this maneuver, wear gloves for safety.

Gouge Chisel Sharpening

Gouge chisels are among the most difficult to sharpen, as they will require a rolling motion on a flat stone in combination with the forward strokes applied on the flat and V-notch chisels.

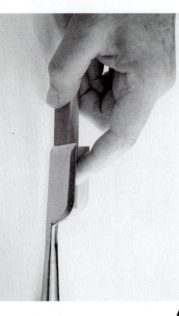

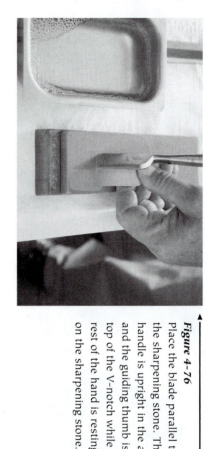

Figure 4-76

Place the blade parallel to the sharpening stone. The handle is upright in the air and the guiding thumb is on top of the V-notch while the rest of the hand is resting on the sharpening stone.

Figure 4-77

This photo illustrates the incorrect way to hold the chisel against the sharpening stone. It must be parallel to the stone.

Figure 4-78

The final step in the sharpening process is to lightly work the stone along the inside of the V-notch chisel. Place your index finger firmly on the top of the stop to keep it pressed against the chisel.

Figure 4-79

Begin by placing the blade at the top of the stone.

Exterior Angled Chisel

1. Begin by holding the stone in place on the workbench with either a clamp or placed on a towel.

2. Using the protractor, determine the 19° angle of the blade. As the blade is pushed along the stone, apply a pivoting half-circle motion to hone the entire surface of the blade. Start at one end of the stone and rotate the blade as it is pushed to the other end of the stone (Figures 4-79, 4-80, and 4-81). This will require practice. Repeat as needed.

Figure 4-80

Twist the chisel as it moves from one end of the sharpening stone to the other.

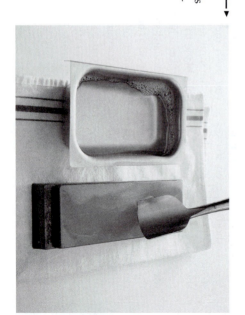

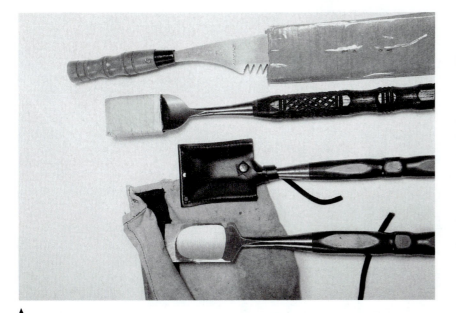

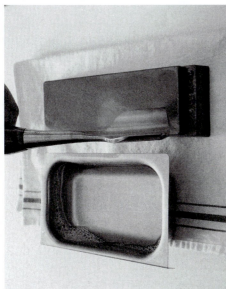

Figure 4-81
The process continues until the blade has been rotated to the opposite side and moved to the other end of the stone.

Interior Beveled Gouge Chisel

Interior beveled gouge chisels require a separate type of sharpening stone, which is cylindrical or completely round as shown in Figure 4-62.

1. Secure the chisel handle on a table or, preferably, in a vise.
2. Take a water-saturated stone and push and curl the stone along the inside curvature of the U-shaped gouge. Again, the angle is important to monitor.
3. Interior beveled chisels may take additional time for proper sharpening, so be careful and patient.

Carver's Note

Extra safety precautions must be followed during this particular technique, because the round stone is pushed toward the chisel's cutting edge. Two safety methods can help prevent a cutting injury to the hand while holding the stone: Use a cut-proof safety glove similar to those worn when cutting foods on a power circular slicing machine. Or, wrap the end of the stone with a small towel, thus protecting your fingers you push the stone against the inside chisel curvature.

ICE CHISEL STORAGE

Never store chisels without protective blade covers. The goal of a protective case is to preserve the costly investment from damage by water or impact. Store each chisel individually in its own protective cover. The razor's edge of the high car-

bon steel blade is brittle and can chip if it hits the metal of other tools. There are a number of ways to protect chisels, and it seems that each carver has his or her favorite method (Figure 4-82). Here are a few options:

1. Some professionals will simply wrap each chisel in a dry terry cloth towel or piece of canvas and secure it with an elastic band (Figure 4-83). As long as the towels are dry, this will prevent moisture from damaging the metal and provide protection from damage.
2. Another option would be to create a protective sheath with cardboard and tape. This type of sheath is made by cutting a strip of corrugated cardboard to the length of the chisel's head and long enough to wrap around the entire body with a slight overlap. This should be done in a fashion that a slight outward angle will be set on the insertion side of the sheath. This angle will allow the chisel to enter easily and also create a catch zone toward the back,

which secures the sheath during storage. Once the cardboard cover is formed, secure its structure by wrapping with heavy-duty tape.

3. A leather sheath with an anchoring strap can also be used for protection either on its own or in tandem with a cardboard cover.
4. Canvas makes a durable sheath that will last for many years.

Keeping chisels dry is the most critical element to proper storage. As with the chain of the power saw, the metal will rust if it is in contact with water. A towel is easy to replace, while specialized cardboard or leather becomes a fixture. The cardboard or leather sheath options require extra care to prevent them from holding water. A perfectly dry chisel can rust if placed in a wet sheath. The best way to avoid a wet sheath is never to place a wet chisel inside. Once a sheath becomes wet, it must be dried or replaced. A clothes dryer will often suffice for the drying process.

Ice carving chisels should be transported in a protective case or caddy. Many versions are available.

Drying of Chisels

Once the carving process is complete and the ice has been properly stored or displayed, it is time to care for the equipment. The chisels must be thoroughly dried with absorbent paper or cloth.

Figure 4-83
One way to protect the blade is to wrap the chisel in a terry cloth towel or piece of heave canvas and secure it with an elastic band.

Condensation will also occur on cold metal as it warms up. Frozen ice crystals buried within the microscopic grooves of the metal, or even moisture in the air, can create hidden collections of water after a proper drying process on cold steel. Those who work in colder weather will need to take an additional step of warming up the metal before the drying process begins. This warming procedure is easily done by insertion of the chisels into a hot bath for 30 seconds. The fresh hot water will also benefit your chisels if a high salt-water or chlorinated water condition exits at the job site. Always dry chisels thoroughly after each session of ice carving. A valuable chisel can become heavily damaged from only a single act of carelessness. Properly dried and protectively stored chisels will last for years and require less sharpening maintenance.

SUMMARY

Like most crafts, it is important to use the right tools for the job at hand. The most basic gear begins with the proper clothing for safety and comfort. Hand tools range from the simple six-prong chipper to chisels and on to an array of specialty tools. Power tools are also commonly used for ice carving. The use of power equipment will usually rise in proportion to the carver's experience level. The beginning carver should not focus on power tools without first learning how to carve with hand tools. As with other tools, it is important to treat them with care, keeping them clean, dry, and as sharp as necessary.

REVIEW QUESTIONS

Short Answer

1. List the pros and cons of using latex gloves when carving ice.
2. Explain the safety concerns associated with long sleeve cuffs while carving.
3. Describe the major carving jobs that can be done with a large flat chisel.
4. Explain the difference between an ice hand saw and a tree-trimming hand saw.
5. Describe the uses of freezing spray.
6. List the steps to chain maintenance.
7. What type of oil can be used to lubricate a chain saw?
8. List three types of sheaths commonly used to protect ice chisels.

Multiple Choice

9. Ice carving _____ is the best protector against water.
   a. head gear
   b. apron
   c. gloves
   d. jacket

10. The most basic hand tool for carving is a
    a. chisel.
    b. awl.
    c. handsaw.
    d. six-prong chipper.

11. Flat ice chisels always have a beveled side and a _____
    a. flat side.
    b. pointed tip.
    c. notch at the end.
    d. interior beveled gouge.

12. Which of the following carving tasks is *not* done with a chain saw?
    a. splitting raw blocks of ice
    b. boring holes that are smaller than the width of the chain saw bar
    c. tracing over a well-adhered template
    d. trace along the ice within the lines of a solid template

13. The die grinder is similar to a
    a. router.
    b. nail board.
    c. rotary whetstone grinder.
    d. chisel.

14. The purpose of an ice compass is to
    a. lift and carry ice blocks.
    b. draw a circle on the ice.
    c. determine the strongest end of the ice.
    d. scratch a straight line on the surface of the ice.

Matching

Match the chain saw part with its description

_____ 15. Kickback protector
_____ 16. Guide links
_____ 17. Chain

a. the cutting blade
b. guide to the cutting surface
c. must be removed for use on ice

_____ 18. Chain saw bar
_____ 19. Oil pump button
_____ 20. Tensioning screw

d. removes debris
e. controls slack in chain
f. keeps chain and bar lubricated

INSTRUCTOR'S NOTES

1. The review of this chapter during lecture is best outlined with a show-and-tell table full of equipment. It isn't necessary to obtain every item on the list in this chapter. Primarily focus on the tools that the students may be using if they are to be carving any ice during class, or simply cover the basic tools needed to carve the angelfish design in this book or any other basic sculpture.

2. The advanced tools listed are for exposure to the industry of ice carving and not necessarily meant to be used by the students. For example, a first-time carver should not be concerned with complex ice welding. However, you could demonstrate how to use the metal plates if class time allows and you are inclined to showcase this.

3. It is a good idea to highlight the tools listed in this chapter that you would like to demonstrate or make a part of the class discussion.

4. This list of equipment is also a great reference for testing material. A written test could include "fill in the blanks" or "matching" from this list. An oral class participation quiz could take place with "name that tool." Bonus points or extra credit could be applied to tools not specifically covered in class demonstration though mentioned in this book. This application will demonstrate who read the material and who did not.

5. Demonstrate the process of breaking down the chain saw for drying and oiling, then follow with reassembly.

6. Demonstrate the process of properly drying and storing a hand chisel.

7. Demonstrate the process of properly sharpening chisels. Show the motion and angle preservation during the sharpening process in an imaginary way while holding the chisel in the air.

Template Design Technique

5

"Every journey begins with but a small step."

Mattie J. T. Stepanek

Learning Objectives

After you have finished reading this unit, you should be able to:

- Explain the purpose of a template
- Identify the types of templates used for ice sculpture
- Describe the carving design and show where it will fit within the ice
- Discuss the principle on utilization of ice
- Create a line drawing sketch for a template
- Expand a line drawing sketch into the full-sized template
- Describe the purpose of a side or top view drawing
- Demonstrate how to properly store a template

Terms to Know

template

preparatory line drawing

paper template

solid template

freehand drawing

tracing

template expansion method

This chapter focuses on some of the small steps that must be taken before beginning a carving project. Once you have learned these steps, you should be able to produce a template suitable for use for ice carving. This exercise begins with selecting a design, preparing a line drawing sketch, and then transferring the image to a life-sized template to be applied during the carving process. Upon completion of this chapter, you will be prepared to begin an ice carving through the steps outlined in the coming chapters. Chapter 8 will discuss how your prepared template will be applied and used on the ice.

USING A TEMPLATE

A **template** is a life-sized version of a carving design made of a disposable or permanent medium to transfer a line drawing image to the face of an ice block. A freestyle approach to carving can be very difficult when visualizing how the end result will come about. A minimum preparation is to have a **preparatory line drawing**, which is a scaled-sized sketch of a sculpture design on paper. It resembles what the finished piece should look like. This line drawing is typically a two-dimensional silhouette front view of the largest face of the ice. The preparation of a template will provide a life-sized version of this line drawing. Such a tool is ideal for transferring the guide lines onto the face of the ice before the actual cutting begins.

TYPES OF TEMPLATES

Templates are generally divided into two major types: paper templates and solid templates.

Paper Template

A **paper template** is a life-sized version of the preparatory line drawing sketched on paper (Figure 5-1). Paper templates are most commonly used as they are relatively simple to make, and they adhere well to the ice. They also allow a carver to tap markings through the paper or cut directly through to the ice as described in the scrollwork section of Chapter 14. We will primarily focus on the use of paper templates during the lessons of this book.

Solid Template

A **solid template** is a life-sized version of the preparatory line drawing, which is cut into a durable sheet of cardboard or wood (Figure 5-2). Solid templates are

Figure 5-1   The picture shows an example of a paper template for a half-block angelfish.

used for carvers who wish to repeat a design over and over again and use the same template. A solid template is made through the same process of drawing the paper template; however, the additional step of cutting the lines with a razor or even a jigsaw will apply. Such solid templates can be used directly on the ice for the template transfer, as described in Chapter 8, or can be used to quickly trace out additional paper templates.

FITTING THE DESIGNS WITHIN THE ICE

This concept begins with reviewing the size dimensions of the ice block being used. As discussed in Chapter 2, a common full-sized ice block is roughly 40 inches tall and 20 inches wide. Consequently, a square-cut half block will have a face measuring 20 inches high and 20 inches wide. The depth is not important at this stage of

PREPARING A SCALE DRAWING

The first step is to determine how the chosen design fits into the confines of the ice block. Some carvers prefer using a scale drawing. They start with a sheet of paper and create a scale dimension of the life-size block of ice. For example, start with a letter-sized sheet of paper measuring 8½ inches × 11 inches. The block can be marked as a 4-inch × 8-inch rectangle for a full block of ice, or draw a line through the middle of the rectangle for a half block. The scale would be 1 inch of the drawing equals 5 inches on the life-size template or face of the ice. A side-view rectangle can be handy as well (Figure 5-3). It is best to use a pencil and have a good eraser ready, as you may find yourself making changes as you go.

Use this model to begin finding how your design will fit into the ice you are about to carve. If the carving is a logo, it should fit within the square or the rectangle. If it is an animal, it should also fit inside this spectrum to become a simple relief sculpture. Most basic designs will fit within the confines of a single block. Furthermore, the designs will have to be within the block's dimensions unless you are qualified to begin the advanced steps of ice reassembly. As a beginner, you should stick with the simple designs.

Some designs may require modification to become structurally sound for ice sculpture. An example might be how a flamingo with thin legs will need support to keep the carving viable throughout the display period (Figures 5-4 and 5-5).

The angelfish design is primarily used in this book as a model for the beginner to practice an exercise of a half-block design. The same fish can be carved within a scene of coral to enhance the image to a full-block sculpture (Figures 5-6 and 5-7).

The concept of incorporating a simple design into a greater display is a common idea among sculptors. Being able to make the idea fit within an ice block will come with time and experience.

USE OF ICE

An ice carving design should incorporate as much of the ice as possible while still maintaining an appealing and proportionate image. Just as any chef would never want to throw good food in the garbage, why waste ice if it isn't necessary? This concept begins with the planning and drawing stages of developing your design and corresponding template. If the ice is there, try to use it. Look at

Figure 5-2   This picture shows the same design of the angelfish cut out of cardboard to form a solid template.

the template design. The third dimension may be visualized later with the help of top- or side-view drawings.

Note: Ice blocks that have been stored in freezers for an extensive period may shrink slightly. Always plan your template drawing to fit inside these dimensions rather than stretch beyond them.

Pro's Corner

Some advanced designs may involve cutting a single ice block into multiple pieces. When these segments are stacked or reattached, they may produce a finished sculpture outside of the dimensions listed above. As this course of Ice Carving 101 is focused on beginning techniques, this concept will be left as an auxiliary subject discussed in Chapter 14, Advanced Skills.

TEMPLATE DESIGN WORKSHEET

20"

40"

10"

Figure 5-3   This diagram shows what a blank preparatory line drawing page should look like for a full block. The side view box is shown as an option. A line could be placed through the middle of the page to prepare for a half-block drawing. A full-page depiction of these diagrams is available in the appendices at the end of this book.

Figure 5-4

This diagram shows a sketch drawing of a flamingo and how it would fit within the dimensions of the ice. Take particular note that the realistic looking legs are nice on paper although they won't support the sculpture throughout the display period.

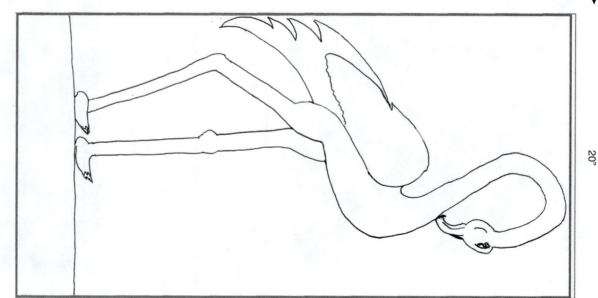

20"

40"

20"

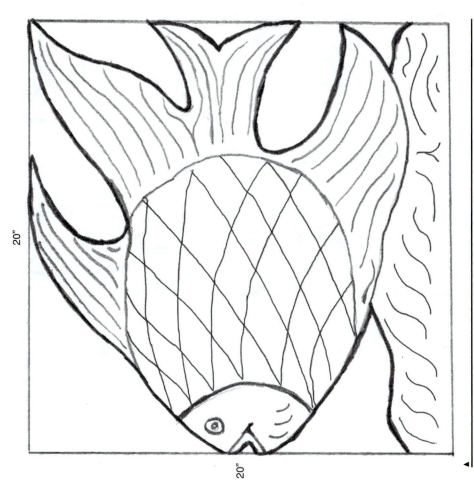

20"

Figure 5-6 The half-block angelfish is drawn within a square to depict how the design will fit within the face of the half block you intend to carve.

Figure 5-8, which demonstrates how a swordfish can be accurately designed as a smaller sculpture and still look good. However, the second diagram illustrates how a similar design stretches to the edge of the block area, thus using more ice (Figure 5-9). In general, it is commonly easier to carve larger sculptures as your tools will have more room to maneuver around the ice.

Figure 5-5
The same flamingo has now been modified with slightly thicker legs and a scene of tall grass to offer primary structural support.

40˝

20˝

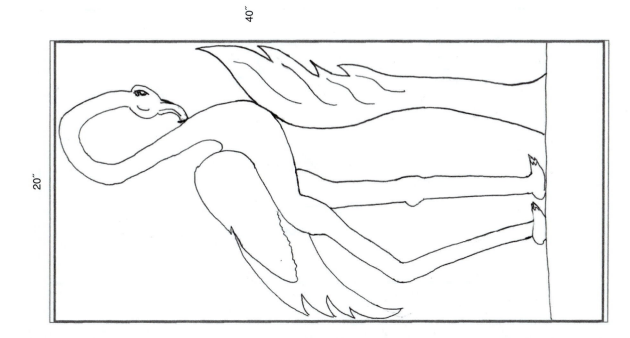

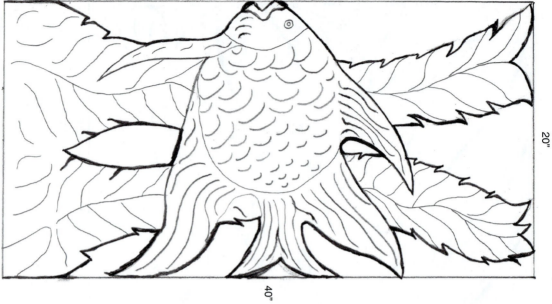

20"

40"

Figure 5-7
The same angelfish is now incorporated into a full-block design with the addition of a coral scene in the background. Notice how the coral will structurally support the entire fish.

Figure 5-8
This swordfish design does not use the ice to its fullest potential.

20"

40"

lines are all you need for making the life-sized template. However, filling in the details will help in visualizing how the whole design will come together. Such interior line details will also come in handy toward the end of the carving process when you're looking to apply detail. For example, the scales of the angelfish, shown in Figure 5-6, will be useful when you're referencing the preparatory line drawing during the finishing details, though these lines are not needed for the expanded template you will apply to the actual ice.

If you attempt a freehand design, don't get frustrated if you end up scrapping five or so initial drafts. It is also important to stress that this should be a clean line drawing with simple lines. There is no need to apply shading as one would do for an artistic portrait. A clean line drawing will be beneficial for the expansion process described in the next section of this chapter.

Sketching a template line drawing can be created with freehand drawing or tracing. **Freehand drawing** is the practice of sketching a design on a blank sheet of paper, and **tracing** is a method of drawing in which an existing image is placed either over or under a comparable image of the intended design and copied to a blank sheet of paper. The easiest way to sketch a preparatory line drawing is to use something as a point of reference. The best tool would be to copy a proven ice design. This provision is available through references offered at the end of this book.

An original design can also be assisted with a picture of a similar image. Depending on your ability to copy what you see, you could try transferring the design freehand or by tracing. Tracing is generally done in one of two ways.

1. Use a thin writing medium known as tracing paper over the picture or drawing you are duplicating. Draw the picture you see as a line drawing for the ice carving you plan to present.
2. Position the blank drawing paper on the bottom and the model drawing or picture on top. Use a sheet of carbon copy paper between the two sheets of paper. Use a ballpoint pen to trace the perimeter of the model image, thus transferring the lines you'll need for the template.

In either case of tracing, it is advised to tape all sheets of paper to a flat surface so they do not shift during the tracing process.

Sometimes your model picture or drawing may not exactly fit in your perimeter square or rectangle of proportion to the ice. If this is the case, mark over your first draft lines again with your pen or a fine-tipped marker to make the lines bolder. Use a second set of tracing paper with your scaled square or rectangle already-drawn on the paper. Now work to make any areas breeching the lines fit within your block template. You may need to bring in an arm, a leg, or some other appendage of the design. Sometimes, you will need to eliminate a feature to make this fit into a single block.

THE LINE DRAWING SKETCH

While applying the principles described in the preceding section, sketch your preparatory line drawing design on paper with the appropriate square or rectangle drawn out to resemble the area of the ice you plan to carve. The perimeter

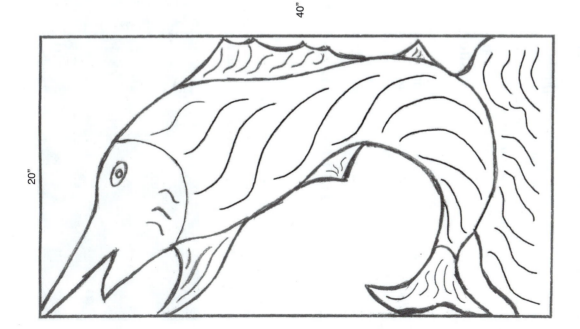

Figure 5-9
This design is similar to the one in Figure 5-8, yet the appendages span to the perimeter of the block and therefore use more ice.

20"

40"

The image you are copying may not provide the structural support needed for the finished ice sculpture. If this is the case, modify the sketch to follow the principles described earlier in this chapter. The flamingo, illustrated in Figures 5-4 and 5-5, is a prime example.

Pro's Corner

Appendages that stretch beyond the lines of a single block are often carved separately from a spare section of ice. These are reattached through various methods. A sculpture stacked on a base structure would be a primary example (Figure 5-10). A vertical seam that defies the center of gravity is far more difficult and requires advanced skills. These skills are not the focus of this book, though an introduction is covered in Chapter 14, Advanced Skills.

CREATING A FULL-SIZED TEMPLATE

At this point, you should have finished a preparatory line drawing. Now it is time to expand this image to the size of the actual template. The process known as the **template expansion method** is used to create a full-sized template from a small preparatory drawing. It can be done in several ways. Some of these methods include the use of professional printing, overhead projectors, and the gridline copy method. Each method has its features and benefits.

Template Paper Options

The paper used for templates should be absorbent to provide better adhesion when it is applied to the ice. This rules out the use of parchment. Parchment, known for its lack of absorbency, is a staple in commercial kitchens, though not ideal for ice carving template usage. A wax-lined butcher's paper is also a poor choice of medium for the same nonstick reasons.

Some examples of ideal template paper may come from a classroom-sized easel pad, a large roll of plain paper at least 20 inches wide, or even newspaper

Figure 5-10 This image portrays a finished sculpture reassembled to a second carving of a base structure. Gravity will fuse the ice together. This is a simple form of ice reassembly.

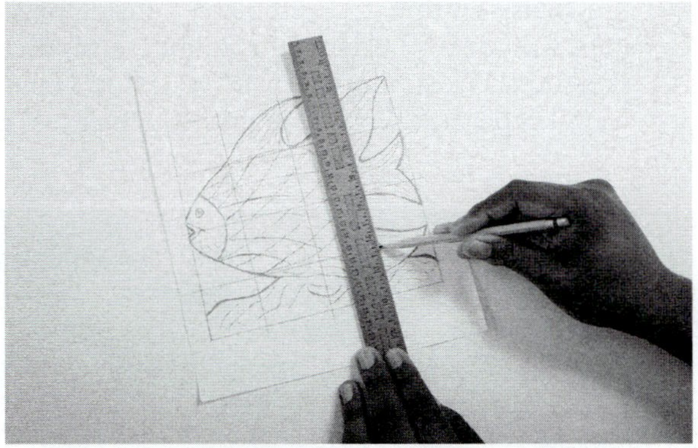

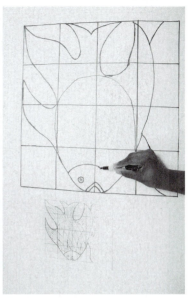

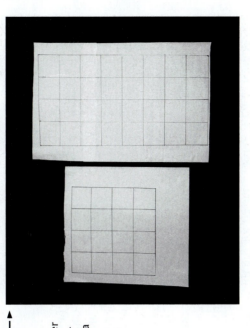

Figure 5-11
This image illustrates how the grid lines are placed on your line drawing.

Figure 5-12
A full-block grid is drawn on a full-size sheet of paper within a 40 × 20-inch rectangle. Draw the same for a half block on the smaller sheet in a 20 × 20 square.

Figure 5-13
Draw the angelfish within the grid lines and follow a block-by-block copy until the entire image comes together.

with the use of a red marker. If you don't have access to paper large enough to form a single sheet to cover the block, it's okay to tape two pieces together. The paper should be slightly larger than the block, so you can fit the entire image on your template paper. For example, if your block is 40 inches high and 20 inches wide, select a piece of template paper that is at least 44 inches long and 24 inches wide. You can always trim the paper after you have transferred the image.

Template Expansion Methods

1. Professional Printing—One may take a simple line drawing to a professional printing outfit and ask it to be enlarged onto the paper and size dimension of your choice. A digital image of this drawing may be an advantage for the printer, so additional fees may apply if they need to do this for you. This option can be rather costly, but it is available in many areas. You may be charged for the cost of producing a poster-sized image of your work. Again, this option comes at a price; and most professionals would make it a "do it yourself" project to conserve on the extra expense.

2. Overhead Projectors—If you have access to an overhead projector, this can be the most accurate way to expand your line drawing in a quick and simple way. Hang your life-sized template paper against the wall. Masking tape or painter's trim tape is good as it often won't strip the surface or leave too much glue residue. A professional might attach a long expeditor's ticket rail to the wall for a more functional alternative of hanging the template paper. Use a tape measure to outline the dimensions of the ice you plan to work on as a template perimeter. For use of an overhead projector, you will first need to copy your line drawing onto a transparency. This is easily done with a good copy machine. Be careful as some copiers produce too much heat for transparency passing and require a paper backing for proper flow through the machine. A few trial and errors or advice from a printing professional will aid in this effort. Once your transparency is formed, place it on the overhead projector. Adjust the projector so that your line drawing fits within the lines of the template. Use a marker to draw your lines to form the template. A bold color or black is often preferred by carvers. Be aware that some paper may bleed through to the wall. A second piece of paper or another backing medium may be needed to prevent markings behind your template.

3. Gridline Method—A set of thin lines will be drawn on both your line drawing and your expanded template paper. Work on a large flat table for this procedure (Figures 5-11, 5-12, and 5-13). Use each box to examine how these segments come together. Draw each box one frame at a time with a marker. Eventually, the expanded template will come together. This exercise is the most time consuming, and it is the most economical of all

methods. During the template transfer process described in Chapter 8, you will disregard these gridlines and use only the design you have sketched. Use a photocopy of your line drawing for the gridline work. Always keep a fresh image of your sketch as an original.

Pro's Corner

Freehand drawing skills will take over once you are comfortable with the lines of any particular design. The template process is the best way to plan a new design. A practiced design may eventually have you sketching freehand on the ice with the six-prong chipper as a pencil

Side- and Top-View Drawings

A side- or top-view drawing may also help along the way. The templates outlined in this chapter are focused on the front view, where a template is applied. Once the primary cuts of the second dimension are carved, as outlined in Chapter 9, you will not have the opportunity to apply paper in the form of a template. The surface to approach will be curved from the cutting work you've already done. A vision or line drawing of the side or top view will help in the actual carving process if you are unsure of what to do next. The lines of the third dimension must be sketched onto the ice with the six-prong chipper or the tip of the chain saw. Otherwise, you would simply start cutting away at the third dimension without a pattern to follow. The beginner will mark such lines with a chipper and hand tools. This is a required skill. See the third dimension preparatory drawing section of Chapter 10 for more details.

A great way to prepare yourself for the third dimension of ice sculpture is to plan your work by marking the lines of the side views and also the top view of what you picture the sculpture to look like. Professionals do not always prepare such drawings, which consume more time but are useful for the novice carver. The work involved in preparation for the carving process is directly proportional to the experience of the carver sculpting the design. A beginner will want to spend more time in the preparation phase. A top view is often a first step in seeing the third dimension. Most cuts start from the top, so knowing where to start is necessary. A preparatory line drawing will aid in knowing where to cut. These lines don't always have to be drawn on the ice. However, any guiding line is better than no preparation at all. Use a top- or side-view line drawing to follow as you make the first cuts on the third dimension work (Figures 5-14, 5-15, and 5-16).

Figure 5-14
This drawing shows the top view of the angelfish as an example of what a top view line drawing would look like.

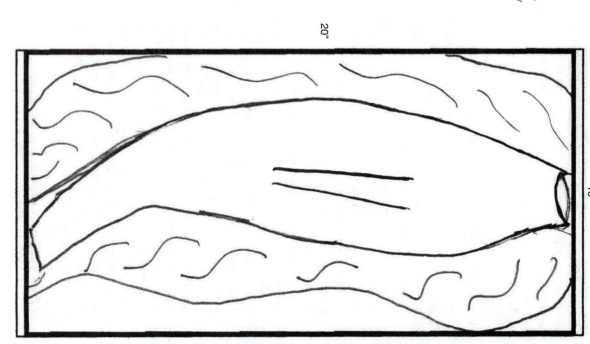

20"

10"

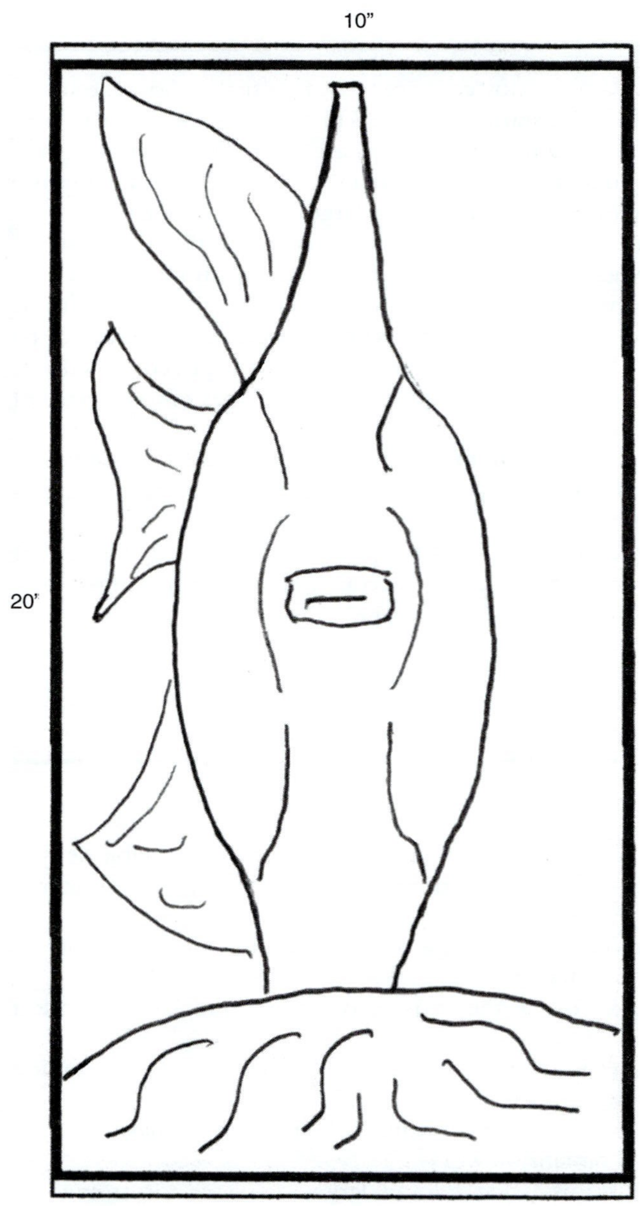

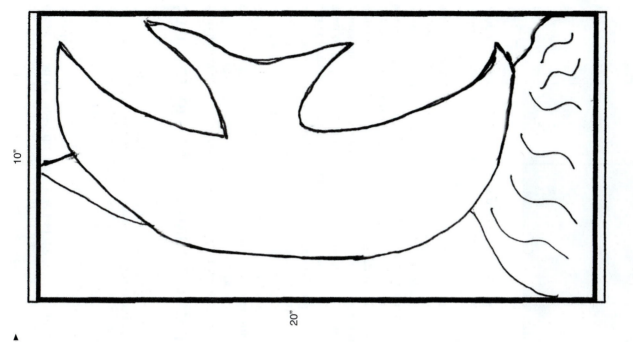

10"

20"

Figure 5-16
This diagram shows the preparatory line drawing of the tail backside view of the angelfish design illustrated in this book.

Figure 5-15
This diagram shows a preparatory line drawing of the frontal mouth view of the angelfish design illustrated in this book.

10"

20"

A side-view line drawing will assist a carver when approaching either side of the template face. It is most common for these two faces to have a separate image. As an example, the front side and the back side of the angelfish will have a separate image.

A side- or top-view line drawing is a preparatory step for approaching the third dimension of sculpture. This practice is recommended for first-time carvers. Once you have practiced a similar sculpture, you may have the intuition to work out the third dimension with only the second dimension template as a guideline. A side- or top-view line drawing will aid in visualizing the third dimension.

STORAGE OF LINE DRAWINGS AND TEMPLATES

A well-drawn preparatory line drawing is best stored in a sheet protector. This will preserve the image during use of the carving process, which tends to be a wet environment. The only good reason to remove this drawing from its sheath is to make a copy for reproduction and template expansion methods. Otherwise, leave your hard work stored in a binder along with any other designs you have stored in sheet protectors. This binder will grow thicker as you carve additional pieces.

The life-sized template should be stored dry until use. As the templates are rather large, you may wrap them into a roll or fold them. These vital tools will need to be laid out flat during use, so keep the template as flat as possible. The best option is to keep the template as flat as possible. Folding will create seams, which may resist fusion with the ice. The best option is to keep the template as flat as possible. Folding will create seams, which may resist fusion with the ice.

A thin paper medium will adhere to the ice well no matter what form the template has been reduced to for transportation. Thinner absorbent paper is the ideal medium for a one-time usage of template paper. Thinner paper will be easier to apply to the ice. A first-time carver should choose the thinner absorbent medium as an ideal choice.

Thicker paper will last longer in your repertoire files. Repetitive carvers may keep such documents as a record of their work. Some professionals will use a thick paper template as a tracing tool to quickly reproduce a disposable design on thinner paper.

Pro's Corner

Multiple template rolls are best stored upright in a tall bin suitable for holding several rolls of paper. A horizontal file will also work if the compartments are deep and hold only a few rolls of templates per file to avoid crushing. Folding and creasing is rarely practiced for long-term storage of paper templates.

SUMMARY

It is very difficult, particularly for novice ice carvers, to visualize how the sculpture should look when they are staring at a fresh block of ice. In order to plan out the steps needed to carve, a number of tools are used. The most basic step is to create a preparatory line drawing, which is a scaled sketch of the sculpture on paper. It usually shows the front view of the largest face of the ice.

Next comes the template, which is a life-sized version of the line drawing. There are a number of types of templates, each with its own advantages and disadvantages. The task of expanding the line drawing to an actual template can be done through a professional printer, with the use of an overhead projector, or by using the gridline method. Once the template is made, it is placed directly on the ice block and enables the carver to transfer the guide lines onto the face of the ice before cutting begins.

Because templates only show the front view, many carvers also create side- and top-view drawings, which will help in visualizing the steps needed to carve a three-dimensional figure.

Most carvers store their drawings and templates for future use. Those that can fit in a plastic sheet protector can be stored in a large binder. Larger templates may have to be rolled or folded for storage.

REVIEW QUESTIONS

True or False

_____ 1. A preparatory line drawing is a life-sized version of a carving design.

_____ 2. Solid templates are most commonly used as they adhere well to the ice.

_____ 3. Template expansion is the process used to create a full-sized template from a preparatory drawing.

_____ 4. The gridline method is the most economical template expansion method.

_____ 5. For use of an overhead projector, you will first need to copy your line drawing onto a transparency.

_____ 6. Use a top- or side-view line drawing to follow as you make the first cuts on the third dimension work.

_____ 7. Avoid creating seams when folding large templates for storage as seams may resist fusion with the ice.

_____ 8. Thinner template paper will adhere better to the ice.

Short Answers

9. List the advantages and disadvantages of using a paper template.
10. List the advantages and disadvantages of using a solid template.
11. Why should an ice carver use as much of the ice as possible?
12. What is the advantage of having a professional printer expand a template?

INSTRUCTOR'S NOTES

1. Explain what a template is used for and what materials can be used to create a template. If available, show a variety of templates to your students.
2. Describe how an image will become a line drawing used for preparation in the carving process.
3. Discuss designs that work well for ice and those that do not.
4. Outline the difference between a basic design that fits within a single block and carvings that stretch beyond the perimeter of a single full or half block.

5. Explain how freehand drawing and the tracing technique take place in producing templates.
6. Demonstrate how transferring a design into a life-like image is carried out through the various methods of template expansion.
7. Show how tracing can be applied by all methods described in this chapter: printing, overhead projection, and the gridline procedure.
8. Describe how professionals use templates and sometimes trace their sketch on the ice itself once they know the lines of their sculpture. How to use a preparatory line drawing is best shown at this point. Explain how a line drawing is referenced as a template.
9. Explain how the side- and top-view drawings precede the preparation of carving in the third dimension.
10. Display a visual image of how to use a sheet protector for preserving a line drawing along with commentary on storing life-sized templates.

Preparing the Carving Area

"Mise en place means far more than simply assembling all the ingredients, pots and pans, plates, and serving pieces needed for a particular period. Mise en place is also a state of mind. Someone who has truly grasped the concept is able to keep many tasks in mind simultaneously, weighing and assigning each its proper value and priority. This assures that the chef has anticipated and prepared for every situation that could logically occur during a service period."

The New Professional Chef, Culinary Institute of America, 7th edition

Learning Objectives

After you have finished reading this unit, you should be able to:

- Describe a typical layout of the carving area
- Discuss various carving platform options
- Review uniform safety
- Explain electrical preparations and safety
- Demonstrate proper tool storage
- Discuss water supply and drainage
- Describe ambient air management

Terms to Know

carving platform
protective liner or shield
GFCI

Ohm's Law
ambient air environment

wind velocity
sharding

Chefs understand the philosophy of *mise en place* and will find it helpful when preparing the carving area. When sautéing, a cook must have all the ingredients in place before assembling a dish in a hot pan; the ice carver too must be set for success before initiating the first cuts. This chapter will outline the various steps for creating a successful ice carving environment, which includes the preparation and organization of carving platforms, tool storage, power requirements, water supply and drainage, management of weather conditions, and safety tips. Seasoned ice carvers have developed the ability to anticipate and prepare for any number of logical occurrences. Having the state of mind mentioned in the chapter-opening quote will take some time to develop but starts with the organization of the tools and the preparation of the carving area.

Before the chisel ever touches the ice, the carver has important work to do. Without proper preparation, accidents can happen, ice blocks can be shattered, and potentially beautiful ice carvings will never be realized. Although the information in this chapter is not as glamorous as the sculpture portions, it is an important facet of successful ice carving.

THE CARVING AREA

An ideal carving area should be a space of at least 10 feet by 10 feet. More room is always nice, but less than this can be crowded and possibly unsafe to other carvers or yourself. The carving area should consist of a carving platform, a tool storage zone and the needed space to work around all sides of the sculpture without bumping into walls or other carvers.

The tool storage zone usually consists of a table or bench where all the carving tools are placed. It should have easy access to the carving platform. Whenever possible, each carver should have his or her own tool storage table. In classrooms, it is often necessary for students to share tools; and a common table is placed with easy access to the multiple carving platforms.

CARVING PLATFORM

A **carving platform** is the surface that supports the ice as it is being carved. For safety purposes, carving directly on the ground is not recommended. Tool damage can occur when sharp edges are driven into a solid surface such as concrete, pavement or tile. Carving on grass can be dirty and unstable.

The carving platform can be composed of materials such as wood, plastic, masonry, or concrete blocks (Figure 6-1). Sometimes milk crates, dish machines, or dunnage racks are used (Figures 6-2 and 6-3). It is best to place crates

Figure 6-1
Four concrete blocks are used to form a sturdy base.

Figure 6-2
Two milk crates set as a base platform.

Figure 6-3
A metal platform with polystyrene insulation sheet and rubber mat liner.

and should be smooth enough to slide the ice when intended, yet sturdy enough to endure the carving process.

UNIFORM SAFETY

Wearing the proper protective gear is important to the safety and comfort of working in the ice carving environment. Chapter 4 covers the clothing, tools, and accessories you would need for carving safely. Specifics of such safety and ice sculpture gear are reviewed here.

Clothing

You should wear pants, shoes, and top gear, which keep you warm, dry, and comfortable during the exercise of ice carving. The layers of warmth will depend on the ambient air in which you will be working. The water-repellent qualities of your clothing will keep you comfortable no matter where you work.

In the simplest form, the typical chef's attire of a long-sleeved jacket and rubber-soled shoes will suffice for a student learning for the first time. Extra layers should be worn under the uniform, especially in colder conditions. For those who have the opportunity and work in a colder area, a bib-style ski shell works very well along with a water-repellent jacket. For warmer conditions, keep to the lighter gear with water-repellent qualities (Figure 6-6).

Shoes

A student who is doing this as a required class project will get by with the standard leather antiskid kitchen shoes (clogs not included), but one who intends to advance in ice carving should invest in the proper shoes or boots. Shoes with a higher leg rise will prevent water infiltration. Boots should have contoured rubber soles to provide traction. Water-repellent boots with steel toe liners are the safest. Some have waterproof and selfinsulating liners—perfect for cold-weather carving. The boots worn by firefighters are ideal for this condition, along with cold weather socks if the conditions should require the warmth.

Gloves

Some sort of rubber glove should be worn while working with ice. Garden gloves of leather or cotton will seem protective, but they fail after becoming wet. The simplest form would be the food handler's latex gloves worn by culinarians everywhere; these will wear out during most carving sessions and require multiple replacements. Heavy rubber gloves are safe too, but they don't offer the agility that most carvers desire. Gloves worn by skiers are often used for

and racks on a nonskid mat to prevent the platform from skidding over a slippery floor. Be creative. Look around your school or workspace to see what might work for you.

The optimum platform height is typically 5 to 20 inches above ground level, which reduces the amount of bending required by the carver. An elevated work area also keeps the ice carving closer to eye level. All angles of the ice should be accessible to the carver. The surface area of the platform is usually between 22 and 48 inches long with a square or rectangular shape. Smaller pedestals allow the carver to get closer to the ice while larger platforms will support blocks in their lengthwise position. The larger variety will require the carver to bring the ice close to the edge when the base and lower area need attention.

The carving platform should be covered with a **protective liner or shield.** Liners are placed on top of the carving platform and are usually made of cardboard, high-density Styrofoam (polystyrene insulation works well), plywood, or even rubber mats (Figures 6-4 and 6-5). They should be at least ½-inch thick

Figure 6-5
Polystyrene insulation set on top of milk crates as a liner to the carving platform.

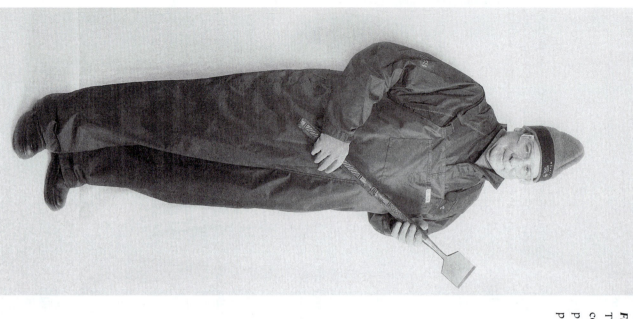

Figure 6-6
This carver is set for success with all the necessary protective gear including protective clothing.

colder areas as the fingers must stay warm to be comfortable with the exercise. Thin rubber gloves work well for those who wear them in warmer weather. In any case, hand guards of some sort are critical to prevent cuts from tool usage or even the hairline lesions caused by sharp edges of the ice. Handling ice with bare hands is never recommended.

Eyewear

Protection for the eyes is important when flying debris becomes a part of the carving process. This happens especially during the use of power tools. Glasses or goggles are recommended for this purpose.

Apron

A water-repellent apron made of rubber or plastic is handy if the carver is wearing clothing that may absorb water.

ELECTRICAL REQUIREMENTS AND SAFETY

The electrical service needed for power tools will depend on the types of tools being used and the quantity of tools at the carving site.

GFCI

A critical component of safety for working with water and electricity is to work with receptacles that have GFCI protection. **GFCI** stands for *ground fault circuit interruption*. A GFCI is designed to protect people from severe or fatal shocks. In essence it is a specialized circuit breaker like the ones found in your bathroom. When water and electricity intermingle while the flow of electricity is disturbed, the GFCI senses the problem and trips the circuit. Portable GFCIs can be plugged directly into a receptacle, and the power tool is plugged into the GFCI or those that are specialized extension cords. Just remember that using a GFCI receptacle is essential (Figure 6-7).

Amperage

It is important to determine the overall amperage load during your preparation process. Ideally each power tool will have its own receptacle and GFCI. A carving area with multiple carvers may not provide such a provision. Therefore, a basic understanding of electrical requirements is necessary.

Most 120-volt circuits in commercial work areas will have the horizontal slide on the left inlet of the power receptacle. This is an indicator of a 20 amp

Water Supply and Drainage

One of the easiest ways to keep the carving area clean is to hose it down periodically. This is easy when there's a water supply nearby with a hose and spray nozzle attached. For the finishing touches of the sculpture, it is handy to have a light spray of water to smooth out the rough edges and wash off the shavings stuck on the ice. If a hose is not available, use a water jug or spray bottle for this finishing work.

Water drainage and removal is always an important consideration when selecting the site for any ice carving event. When a carver shaves away particles of ice, they drop to the ground and create slush, which is slippery and cumbersome. Puddles sometimes form. Large chunks of ice can also be a hazard to foot traffic. Drainage and water removal is an important factor for safety and comfort in the ice carving arena. The indoor carving areas must have a drain nearby. The frozen areas of a walk-in freezer may be an exception, though they are rarely used for a class venue. The debris and water will be discarded and melted off in one way or another.

Outdoor carving areas will often provide water runoff, though the carving area must be maintained as a nonhazardous environment. For safety purposes, it is best to remove all loose ice at all times. Take regular breaks to clear and/or squeegee traffic areas.

Ambient Air Management

The air in which you carve has a lot to do with the success of the carving, not to mention the comfort of the carver. Some of the factors are out of our control, but others can be managed. The **ambient air environment** primarily depends on the temperature, wind velocity, and lighting of the carving area. Many variables can apply to these conditions depending on outdoor weather or indoor working areas. What can the carver do to manage these variables? Let's find out.

Air Temperature

Air temperature is the simplest factor to manage. It is easy to understand as ice is frozen water, and we tend to be most comfortable at the room temperature of 72° F (27° C). The colder the air, the less the ice will melt, and vice versa for warm air. Some carving venues can be created in refrigerated warehouses or similar outdoor venues where conditions are optimal. Extreme conditions or warmer air may require steps to be taken to lessen the effect of ice melting. These steps might include working under a tent, in a shaded area or working early morning or evening when the sun is not as intense.

Figure 6-7
Always use a GFCI plug when using power tools. Portable models are available.

circuit breaker and wiring to support such load. Many household outlets do not have this type of service and the electrical panel must be verified to know how many appliances can be connected to a single circuit. The amp draw of each appliance will also be a factor to gauge what tools can be connected to each circuit. Most power tools will list their amp draw on the serial plate. If this is not listed, then the total wattage of the appliance should be available and verified before using power tools.

To determine the number of amps required, we'll use **Ohm's Law**, which is a mathematical equation used to calculate the number of amps.

Ohm's Law: Watts/Volts = Amps

If the total amp draw is less than 80 percent of the circuit breaker rating, you can apply multiple appliances to the same circuit. An overload of appliances on one circuit may cause the breaker to trip, which creates a hazard and an undesirable delay in the activities of the day by requiring the breaker to be reset.

Note: When in doubt about your electrical needs, consult a professional electrician before staging your class or event.

Tool Storage

The hand tools needed for the carving session should be organized on a table with easy access for the carver. Use a cloth to keep the table and tools dry. Never set your hand tools on the floor or ground, where they can become an obstacle for those working in the area. Larger electrical tools and their cords should be kept out of puddles and away from walking areas. Always keep tools out of harm's way!

WIND VELOCITY

Wind velocity is the speed in which air is traveling. Air movement enhances the air temperature in an environment. This is similar to how a convection oven distributes heat more effectively and a freezer moves air to chill its contents. Be aware that a warmer condition paired with strong winds can hinder the experience of ice carving. It is best to pick a carving zone that is protected from such elements.

LIGHTING

It is easy to figure that ample lighting of your work is important for ice sculpture. However, because it is common to carve outdoors, the sunlight can be the worst enemy to a crystal clear block of ice. The sun not only imparts heat to cause melting, but the rays of direct sunlight exposure also can prematurely alter the crystalline structure of the water molecules and cause sharding within the block.

Sharding is a condition in which the internal crystals of the ice break apart to a degradation level and separate from the structure of the carving block. With pressure the shards can actually break off into sharp fragments. Sunlight can be endured if the ambient air temperature is below 20° F (−7° C), though this is rarely the case in a classroom environment. Therefore, a covered area should be set up for the ice carving zones. If a shed is not available, it may be necessary to erect a tent or canopy to provide such protection.

SUMMARY

Safety is the first and foremost goal for a successful work area. Proper gear must be worn to protect the carver from slippage and electrical hazards and to offer comfort during the exercise. Electrical safety and supply is critical to the success of ice sculpture. Create the ideal work environment to the best possible standards with the ambient air conditions and an organized work area with proper tool storage.

REVIEW QUESTIONS

Matching

Match the correct definition with the correct key word.

1. Sharding
2. GFCI

a. used to determine the amps required
b. condition in which internal crystals of ice break down

3. Ambient air environment
4. Ohm's law
5. Carving platform

6. Wind velocity

c. specialized circuit breaker
d. the speed in which air travels
e. determined by temperature, wind, velocity, and lighting
f. can be made of wood, plastic, crates, racks, or concrete

Short Answer

7. Why shouldn't an ice carver place the ice directly on the ground or floor to carve?
8. What special clothing should an ice carver wear?
9. Why is it important to wear protective eyewear?
10. You are in charge of an ice carving demonstration for your school. Three well-known ice carvers will come to the school to participate in the event. Carvers each will be using two 115-volt chain saws (1,000 watts each) and die grinders (230 watts each). You have decided to set up the carving area outside one of the kitchens on a covered patio that is 30 feet by 40 feet. List what you will need to set up in advance, including the electrical requirements.
11. Describe one way to keep the floor safe during an ice carving event.
12. What's the best way to prevent sharding?

True or False

_____ 13. The main purpose of a GFCI is to protect individuals from electrical shock.
_____ 14. The ambient air environment depends on temperature, wind velocity, and lighting of the carving area.

Multiple Choice

15. An ideal carving area should provide at least _____ of space for each carver.
   a. 8 feet by 8 feet
   b. 12 feet by 12 feet
   c. 10 feet by 10 feet
   d. 20 feet by 20 feet

16. A protective liner or shield should be used
   a. to cover the floor of the carving area.
   b. to cover the tool storage table.
   c. to cover the ice block before the session begins.
   d. to cover the carving platform.

17. Only one of the following types of footwear is *not* advisable for ice carving:
    a. clogs
    b. leather antiskid kitchen shoes
    c. water-repellent boots with a steel toe liner
    d. firemen boots
18. What causes thermal sharding?
    a. the hot sun
    b. improper amperage
    c. wind
    d. using the wrong tool for the job

INSTRUCTOR'S NOTES

1. A 22 × 30-inch platform is recommended for upright single-block pieces. A 48 × 48-inch platform is recommended for horizontal designs. Carving directly on the ground may seem simpler, though it may damage the tools and will inevitably be harder on the backs of those who spend the day stooping as they contact the ice. Raised platforms are highly recommended.

2. Choice of uniform is subject to company policy. However, the unique practice of ice sculpture may merit the allowance of students to show for class with either their standard chef's uniform or the recommended carving gear outlined in this chapter. Clothing would be a personal choice, though aprons, eyewear, and hand gear is best provided by the instructing institution.

3. This course can be offered without the use of power tools, though the use of chain saws in particular will reduce the class time necessary to complete a carving day. Power tools are often used by experienced carvers; supervised exposure is a benefit to each student. Yet, learning not to depend on power tools is an even greater lesson. Teach respect for hand tools and power tools as a fundamental part of ice carving.

4. Electricity is often the most difficult item to provide for multiple carvers using power tools. The supply of such tools is also an account of budget availability. It is advisable to check with a professional electrician to verify that the amount of power needed is available. A test should be conducted before the session by starting all tools that may be needed for the event at the same time. If successful, this test will ensure that circuit breakers will not trip during class.

5. It is best to prepare your class with at least two chain saws and two die grinders. A backup of each tool will ensure a smooth experience in case of a tool failure. A second die grinder will allow two tips to be handy instead of one for those who care to use them for finishing work. A disk sander may also be demonstrated, though it is not recommended for beginning carver instruction.

6. A student should always be supervised by an instructor during the use of power tools. Should tools not be available at each work station, it is advised to set up a power tool area where this use will take place. Students should have the opportunity to get the feel of all tools, though they don't necessarily need to use them throughout the entire process.

7. Tables for tools are recommended. A table provided for each work station would be a bonus, though sometimes it is not available. Tables to be shared among multiple stations will suffice as well.

8. Providing a single water hose to the carving area is ideal. Having a nozzle with a misting spray capability is also recommended.

9. Drainage is a factor of the facility you work with. A floor squeegee will always be necessary for the clean-up. A large trash receptacle is a good idea for clean up. A floor squeegee will always be necessary for the clean-up phase and the carving portions of class. Larger chunks of ice should be discarded immediately from work stations as they can become foot traffic hazards.

10. The carving area is optimum if held within a 40° to 60° F (4° to 16° C) environment. This condition prevents excessive melting. As this luxury is not always available, it is most critical to provide overhead protection from direct sunlight. A tent or shaded area is recommended for most outdoor carving areas.

Ice Transportation, Block Preparation, and Chain Saw Basics

7

"Before everything else, getting ready is the secret to success."

Henry Ford

Learning Objectives

After you have finished reading this unit, you should be able to:

- Describe how to lift and move a full block of ice
- Explain how to square the block
- Demonstrate chain saw usage
- Identify the steps of chain saw tip cutting
- Discuss chain saw line cutting
- Describe half block splitting

Terms to Know

hand truck dolly
corner balanced position
squaring the block

half block splitting
square half block
L-cut half block

chain saw line cutting
chain saw tip cutting

In Chapter 6 we discussed the need to prepare the carving area. Now it's time to discuss the preparation of the ice block itself. The first step is moving the tempered ice to the carving site. Before an upright block is placed on the carving platform, it must be squared. Because that process is done with a chain saw, we will also discuss some chain saw basics in this chapter.

MOVING ICE INTO POSITION

The only way to move a 300-pound block of ice that measures 40 × 20 × 10 inches is to use your body weight to manipulate it into its desired position. If the block is upright in the freezer, it's not too difficult to transport it with a **hand truck dolly**, which is a two-wheeled cart used for moving heavy objects by hand. This type of dolly consists of a vertical frame with handles at the top and a metal blade at the bottom that is inserted beneath a load. Once the load is placed on the frame, it can be tilted backward until balanced for easy pushing or pulling. Use a dolly that is rated for at least a 400-pound load. The dolly can be modified with padding to prevent the block from rubbing against the metal framework (Figure 7-1).

Another method of transporting ice is to use ice tongs. Before attempting this, students need to understand the principles of weight distribution, which will be discussed in this chapter.

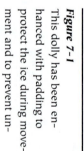

SAFETY NOTE

Always wear gloves and steel-toed boots. Many carvers use back support harnesses, similar to those worn in industrial workplaces, when moving ice.

Moving Ice with a Dolly

- With the block in the upright position and the dolly in front of the 20-inch face, use one hand on the back corner of the ice to lean the block backward slightly.

- Use the other hand on the dolly along with one foot on the axle to push the lower platform of the dolly underneath the ice (Figure 7-2). From this point, it is often easier to slide the ice fully onto the dolly rather than to push the dolly flush to the block.

- To pull the ice back onto the wheels, you'll need to use your weight. It is safest to learn this skill as a solo maneuver, though a helper should be

nearby in case assistance is needed and to open doorways. With one foot on the axle and one foot sturdily extended back, use one hand on the back of the ice to pull the block onto the dolly's wheels (Figure 7-3).

- Once the weight begins to move backward, move the ice-gripping hand back to the dolly for extra support (Figure 7-4).

- Move the block around as you roll the block to its destination. Work to maintain balance on the wheels as you roll the block to its destination. This is no time to be in any hurry. The weight should be slightly backward toward your body to allow control. However, holding the ice too far backward can make it heavy and unwieldy.

Figure 7-1
This dolly has been enhanced with padding to protect the ice during movement and to prevent unwanted melting from the heat of the metal.

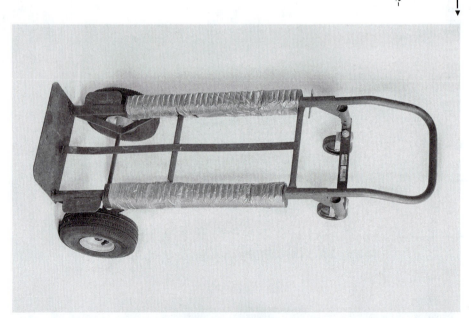

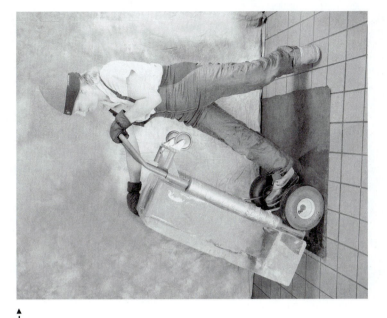

Figure 7-2
The block is held back slightly to allow the plate of the dolly to slide under the ice.

Figure 7-3
Note the hand and foot position as this carver moves the block back onto the wheels of the dolly.

Removing Ice from the Dolly

To set the block back into its upright position, reverse the technique used for pulling the block onto the dolly.

- Start with the feet in position and one hand on the back of the ice; slowly pull the block into the upright position.
- Once dolly is flat on the ground, tilt the block slightly backward just enough to slide the lower dolly plate out from underneath the block.

Moving Ice with Tongs

Lifting ice blocks with tongs can be dangerous if not handled properly. Use only tongs that have sharp points, which can grip the ice block without slipping. There are two basic types of tongs on the market: single handled and double handled. See Chapter 4 for a description. Preference is based on personal choice. For this exercise, we will use the double-handled style. Be aware that piercing the block too close to the edge may cause a portion to break off. An interior placement more than 3 inches from the edge is usually sufficient to prevent this damage.

To move an ice block with ice tongs, you should have the body strength necessary to lift approximately 100 pounds. An assistant may be required to get the first portion of the lifting under way. However, this assistance should only lighten the load and provide stability. The majority of control needs to stay in the hands of the primary lifter.

In addition to using a dolly for transporting ice, a carver may need to drag a block only a few feet or more using ice tongs. This can be done easily if the floor is relatively smooth and flat, and it is not recommended on ramps or bumpy, unstable surfaces. This practice is done in either the upright or the horizontal position. Learning weight distribution and tong placement will aid in this function.

Next we will explore a number of situations and show how to use tongs to properly maneuver an ice block.

Figure 7-4
To bring the block back into the upright position, one hand is placed on the back of the ice and the foot is extended as a counterweight.

Figure 7-5
Proper position for upright block movement. Note how the back is straight, the knees are slightly bent, and the arms are fully extended.

#1 Moving an Upright Block over a Flat Surface

There will be times when you need to move or slide the block of ice over the ground or floor. Follow these directions:

- Approach the 10-inch side of the block with the tongs in both hands and tines extended.
- Grip the ice while bending the knees slightly and lowering the arms to full extension.
- Once the tongs are secure, you should be able to stand up straight and flex your arms and shoulders so that the end of the block closest to you will lift slightly (Figure 7-5). This tong position will allow full advantage of weight distribution and help the block slide easily.
- Take baby steps backward to move the ice to its intended destination.

#2 Moving an Ice Block in the Horizontal Position

There will be times when the block is lying on its side.

- Insert the tongs approximately 5 inches diagonally from the corner of the block, which should allow the interior loop of the tongs to toggle back and forth between the side and top of the block.
- Once the tongs are securely fixed, extend your arms and legs to lift the end of the block slightly.
- Take baby steps to move the ice to its intended destination (Figure 7-6).

#3 Lowering an Upright Block

An upright block may need to be lowered to its side for squaring, block splitting, or positioning a horizontal design.

- While standing against the 10-inch side of the block, nestle one foot up against the bottom of the block with the other foot back.

Figure 7-6
Proper position for horizontal movement. Note how the position of the back, knees, and arms.

Figure 7-7
Note how the tongs are positioned approximately 8 inches inward and 4 inches from the top.

Figure 7-8
Pull backward on the tongs and use your body weight to initiate the backward motion. Note the position of the foot against the block to prevent slippage.

• Grip the tongs with both hands and set the points approximately 8 inches away from you on the top of the ice. The tines should be at least 4 inches down from the top though not bottomed out (Figure 7-7). The tongs should also be able to swing back and forth in this position. At the same time, allowing a sturdy rest against the top face for a proper grip when the block is lowered.

• With tongs in position, use both hands to gently pull the block backward, using your back foot as a counterweight (Figure 7-8). Some carvers may need assistance with starting this maneuver.

• As the block begins to move back, approach the ice with your knee and body to prevent it from falling toward you. With experience you will anticipate how much pressure to apply. The goal is to balance the block on its lower corner while securing movement with the tongs and your torso (Figure 7-9). The block is now in the **corner balanced position**, which is the point at which the ice is standing on its lowest corner and secured by the grip of the tongs and the torso of your body.

• To continue lowering the block, shift the tongs with both hands to the forward position against the top face of the ice. During this motion, you should slightly support the weight toward the torso of your body.

• Once the tongs are forward, take the foot that was up against the ice and step into a side-by-side foot position (Figure 7-10). This is a very critical

Figure 7-9
The body supports the block as it stands balanced on its corner.

Figure 7-10
To prepare for lowering, the feet must be spread apart and the tongs nested in the upper position. Note how the hand position has changed and the elbows are extended.

Figure 7-11
Keep the back straight as the block is lowered so that its weight is distributed between arms and legs.

time to keep your back straight to support the weight of lowering the block. Your elbows should be extended outward, which will help control the fall through use of your shoulder muscles.

- You should now lower the block slowly while squeezing the tongs. A fast drop may cause you to lose control and injure your back. Some carvers may need assistance for the lowering maneuver by having a helper grip the opposite side of the ice. It is important for this helper to only lighten the load and not take control, or else the primary block holder may lose his or her secure grip. As the block is lowering, it is again important to keep your back straight and not stoop over to prevent back injury (Figure 7-11).

SAFETY NOTE

If the block moves toward you out of control, quickly step away, release the tongs, and possibly sacrifice the block for the sake of your personal safety. A falling 300-pound block of ice can damage your body.

#4 Lifting a Horizontal Block to the Upright Position

This maneuver requires the most strength of all the moves. Don't attempt it unless you are certain that you can lift 100 pounds with the tongs. As suggested

Figure 7-14
The tongs are securely gripped with a single hand, and the other hand is placed on the back corner of the block.

Figure 7-12
Note the tong placement and position of the back and knees.

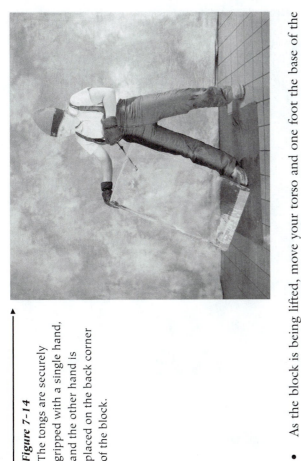

earlier, it is a good idea to have an assistant to get the first portion of the lift under way.

- Affix the tongs 8 inches from bottom of the ice block.
- With knees bent, back straight, and elbows flexed, swiftly lift the block into the corner balanced position (Figures 7-12 and 7-13).

- As the block is being lifted, move your torso and one foot the base of the ice, as done in the lowering process. Begin by
- Once the block is balanced on its corner, shift your hand position. Begin by securing the tongs by a pulling with one hand while gripping the top back corner of the block with the other (Figure 7-14).
- Using your back foot as a counterbalance, slowly allow the block to rest upright (Figure 7-15).

Figure 7-15
The back leg is used as a counterbalance for slowly lowering the block into the upright position.

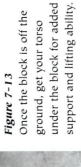

Figure 7-13
Once the block is off the ground, get your torso under the block for added support and lifting ability.

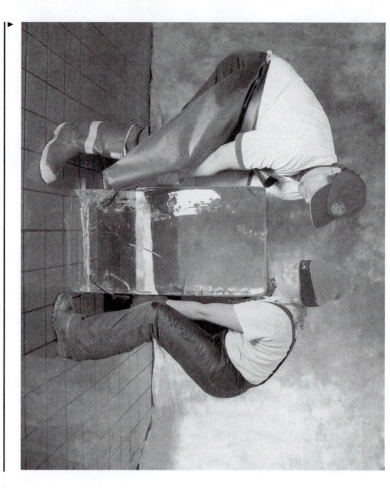

Figure 7-16   These two carvers are preparing to lift a block onto the platform. Note the position of the tongs on the ice so that the legs, not the back, do the work.

- Position the tongs in the lower third of the block. (The exact position will depend on the height of the lifter.) Most of the lifting will be done by the legs. Also consider securing a grip high enough to avoid being too top heavy, which may cause the block to lean sideways during lifting.
- Once the block is in the air, take baby steps sideways to position the ice or have a third participant move the platform underneath the elevated block.

SQUARING THE BLOCK

Before setting the block into its carving position on the platform, the bottom surface should be prepared through a procedure called squaring the block. **Squaring the block** is a process in which the bottom face is cut flat and perpendicular to

Figure 7-17
Marking your line for squaring the base.

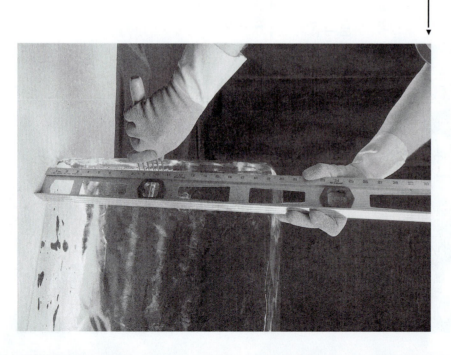

#5 Lifting a Block onto a Platform

The task of lifting the block onto the carving platform is best left to a dual team of stronger participants in the group who are capable of lifting 150 pounds each. However, it is possible to combine the lowering and raising technique with keeping the platform steady during the process. There are also lifting cranes designed for this procedure. See Chapter 4 for additional information on lifting cranes.

The most preferred method will vary depending on carving time and lifting ability. In general, having two strong carvers, each equipped with ice tongs, will be the quickest method.

- To lift the block onto a platform, begin by positioning the ice next to the platform (Figure 7-16).

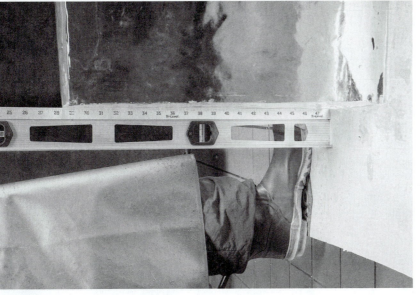

Figure 7-19
A properly squared block of ice.

the upright position of the block. Most sculpture blocks will have at least one uneven surface. This surface will often become the base because the clarity of the block is typically weakest on this end. Freezer exposure will also tend to round off any flat surfaces over time. Therefore, creating the flat squared surface under your base is necessary to provide stability during carving and display.

- Begin by setting the block on its side either on a platform on the ground with a liner.
- A 2- to 4-inch section is often removed for squaring. Place the block where this section will hang off the edge of your elevated surface.
- Apply a straight edge or level to the front face where the cut will be made and trace a line with the six-prong chipper to mark the cut (Figure 7-17).
- Use a T-square to transfer the line to the top face of the block (Figure 7-18).

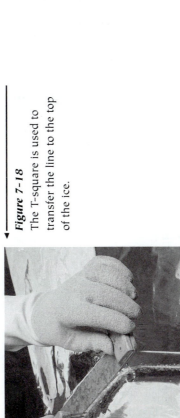

Figure 7-18
The T-square is used to transfer the line to the top of the ice.

- Use a chain saw to make this cut as described in the chain saw tip and line cutting sections later in this chapter.
- Once the block is squared, proceed with moving the ice to its carving position or make further cuts to form half blocks or other multiple pieces. The small plate left behind from squaring is often discarded (Figure 7-19).
- For specifics of chain saw usage, refer to the section featured later in this chapter.

HALF BLOCK SPLITTING

Half block splitting is the procedure of dividing a full block into two equal pieces. This is commonly done for smaller designs and to save on the cost of sculpture ice. The square half block and the L-cut half block are two primary

shapes formed when splitting blocks in half. The choice of the split will depend on the shape of the design.

The **square half block** is a 20 × 20 × 10-inch square formed by splitting the block down the center of the 40-inch face. To cut this shape, lay the full block into the horizontal position. Mark a line down the center over the top and side faces. This can be done with the level and chipper as described in squaring the block (Figure 7-20). Execute the cut as described in the section on chain saw line cutting (Figure 7-21).

The **L-cut half block** is a 20 × 35 × 5-inch upright block with a 20 × 5 × 10-inch base left attached for support (Figure 7-22). This form of a half block can be a very economical way to double your ice supply and still achieve an upright design. Based on the design, the thinner 5-inch profile can also be simpler to sculpt. The splitting process may require some practice, though.

Proceed with caution as your cuts approach the middle of the block. Although it is possible to make all cuts for the L-cut half block cleanly and perfectly, this rarely happens. A chain saw with a bar over 20 inches may

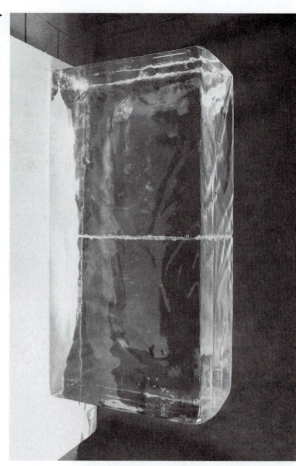

Figure 7-20   This block is marked for the square half block cut.

allow an exception to this exercise, though such tool usage is rarely seen with the exception of well-stocked professionals. Cutting beyond the line markings could damage the blocks. Therefore, perform regular inspections to see where the uncut portions remain. The uncut areas, requiring separation, are identified by looking for the clear (nonsnowy) sections within the ice.

- Begin the process by squaring both ends of the full block in the horizontal position. Remove as little ice as possible so the maximum height will be kept.

- Once both sides of the block are squared, use the tongs to lift the block into the upright position.

- Place marking lines on both of the 20-inch sides. One side will have the line 5 inches from the bottom, and the opposite side will have the line 5 inches from the top.

- Scratch a marking line down the center of each of the 10-inch sides. These lines should be drawn between the 5-inch base areas of the top and bottom

Figure 7-21   The completed square half block.

Figure 7-23
An ice block has been marked for the next step of cutting the L-cut half block.

Figure 7-22
The L-cut half block.

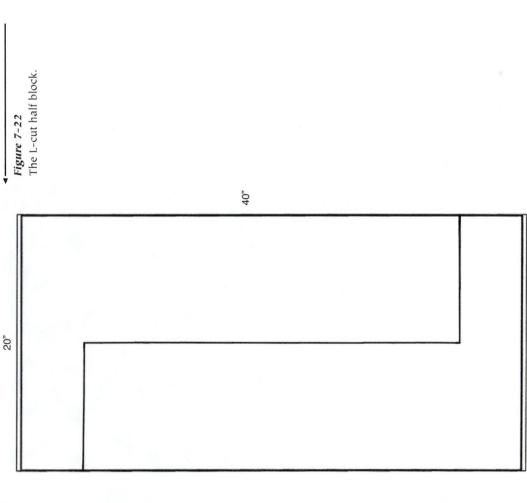

of the block. Lastly, scratch lines on the 10-inch sides to connect the center line to each of the respective base lines. This step will complete the markings for the L-cut block (Figure 7-23).

• Use a chain saw to cut the vertical line on one 10-inch side of the ice. Most saws do not have a blade long enough to cut through the entire

20 inches of the block, so this cut should go 12 to 15 inches into the block.

• The base cuts come next. Cut the bottom line first. Work the saw across the marking line a few inches at a time until the center is reached.

• The top portion base cut will now be done while following the same inch-by-inch cutting method.

• The block should now be lowered into the horizontal position for the final cut within the center. The uncut portion should be at the top of the lowered block. Insert the saw from the top to meet the opposite side cut made in the beginning.

• Ideally, all the major cuts have been made. However, there are often small areas where the ice was not completely separated (Figure 7-24). This area is best cut by hand tools, such as a hand saw. Once the ice is fully separated, the L-cut blocks are best divided by inserting a flat chisel into the upper portion of the side block cut (Figure 7-25). The two sections should break free at this point. If they don't, the block should be examined for remaining uncut areas.

• Use towels to securely grip the ice. This may be a good time to have a helper assist you.

• Once separation is evident, lift the sections onto their base (Figure 7-26). Any snow or unclean surfaces can be finished with a hand broom or flat chisel (Figure 7-27).

Figure 7-24
This last cut to divide the center should separate the two L-cut sections. Notice that the uncut section still remains clear.

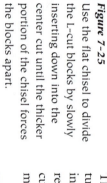

Figure 7-25
Use the flat chisel to divide the L-cut blocks by slowly inserting down into the center cut until the thicker portion of the chisel forces the blocks apart.

Figure 7-26
The carver lifts the separated block into an upright position on its base.

CHAIN SAW USAGE

The chain saw is the most utilized tool for ice carving. Although most any sculpture can be created with hand tools, this power tool gives the greatest time savings and utility to an experienced carver. A chain saw must be treated with respect, for its value as well as for its danger. All beginners should learn the art of cutting with and without chain saws; however, hand tool utilization is the primary focus for the first-time student. This course shall include exposure to both.

It is recommended that students use chain saws only under the close supervision of an instructor. Many cuts will happen faster with the chain saw, and its use will save the class time with tasks such as block splitting or major cut removal. An electric chain saw is typically preferred over a gas-powered version for reliability reasons paired with avoidance of noise and oil debris. Some venues may use gas-powered versions when electricity is not available.

Figure 7-28
The saw tip is inserted approximately one inch into the ice to form the tip cut.

Figure 7-27
The finished L-cut.

Chain Saw Tip Cutting

Inserting the first inch of the saw blade to mark a line is known as **chain saw tip cutting** (Figure 7-28). This is a common practice when cutting straight or even curved lines. Making cuts through a large section without this guiding step may cause inaccuracies. The saw is first turned on with both hands on the tool. The tip is then inserted to initiate the intended cut. This step will assist in guiding the saw through the deeper cuts to come.

Chain Saw Line Cutting

A cut that follows a straight line through the block is known as **chain saw line cutting**. Your eyes should remain positioned above the saw blade to assist in achieving straight cuts. The bar of the saw must remain perpendicular to the ice. The slightest variance in pitch can create an uneven cut by the time the bar

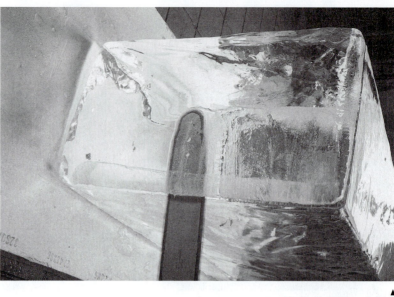

Figure 7-29
The saw is held perpendicular to the block to form a straight cut as the blade moves down the tip cut line and separates half of the intended cut.

reaches the opposite side of the ice. Most cuts will begin with a tip cut. Insert the bar halfway through the ice to continue cutting the line (Figure 7-29). This halfway cut will guide the bar as the final cut is taken. Complete the cut by inserting the bar completely through the ice (Figure 7-30).

Carver's Note

Let the saw do the work. Too much pressure may cause the chain to bind up and stall the motor. Having sharp chain blades and higher-powered saws reduces the likelihood that the chain will bind up.

Figure 7-30   The saw is driven through the entire block to make the complete cut while being held perpendicular to the cut.

SUMMARY

Lifting and transporting ice must be practiced safely and effectively. Moving the block to its desired position is a fundamental part of preparation. One should know how to lift and lower a 300-pound block safely and securely. Sharp tips are essential in the use of ice tongs. Forming half-block sections from the full block can be both economical and easier for the carver. A chain saw is to be handled with respect for its value and danger. Always keep both hands on the saw and your eyes above the blade while cutting.

REVIEW QUESTIONS

True or False

_____ 1. The typical ice block used for carving weighs 100 pounds.

_____ 2. The easiest way to move ice blocks long distances is to use ice tongs.

_____ 3. Sharp points on ice tongs can grip the ice block without slipping.

_____ 4. Lifting a horizontal block of ice to the upright position requires the most strength of all the moves.

_____ 5. The squaring process is almost always performed with a chain saw.

Multiple Choice

6. A standard ice carving block weighs
   a. 100 pounds.
   b. 150 pounds.
   c. 200 pounds.
   d. 300 pounds.

7. Ice tong tines should be placed more than 3 inches from the edge of the ice to
   a. prevent slippage when moving.
   b. prevent pieces of the ice from breaking off the block.
   c. drag a block of ice over a smooth floor.
   d. allow full advantage of block distribution.

8. The main purposes for squaring the ice block are
   a. to remove the ice with the least clarity.
   b. to ensure that there is a flat surface for carving.
   c. to provide stability during carving and display.
   d. All of the above.

9. The L-cut half block will measure
   a. 20 × 20 × 10 inches.
   b. 20 × 35 × 5 inches.
   c. 20 × 10 × 5 inches.
   d. 40 × 20 × 10 inches.

10. What tool is used most for ice carving?
    a. chisel
    b. chain saw
    c. ice tongs
    d. hand saw

11. Electric chain saws are preferred because
    a. they produce less noise.
    b. they don't leave oil debris.
    c. they are more reliable.
    d. All of the above.

12. Before setting the block into its carving position, the bottom surface should be prepared through a process called
    a. an L-cut.
    b. half block splitting.
    c. marking a line.
    d. squaring the block.

13. A cut that follows a straight line through the block of ice is known as
    a. chain saw line cutting.
    b. the tag line.
    c. the base line.
    d. None of the above.

14. Applying too much pressure to the chain saw may cause it to bind up and
    a. crack the ice.
    b. cause the bar to come off its track.
    c. skip off the ice's surface.
    d. stall.

INSTRUCTOR'S NOTES

1. Some students may not be qualified to lift heavy objects. This should be identified before anyone lifts anything. Lifting and transporting ice is a critical lesson and should be reviewed with all present. Allow as many qualified students as possible to practice transport and movement techniques.

2. Providing at least one set of steel-toed rubber boots is recommended for practicing ice transport. A few varied sizes will ensure that all will be comfortable. Many students may have this support built into their chef gear. If so, it is advised they keep those shoes on until all the blocks are in position.

3. You may wish to designate which of the stronger students will assist in the lifting of ice onto platforms.

4. Squaring blocks, with a small group of students, is a practice you may wish to perform before, or during, the practical class begins. The choice will depend on class time and qualified participants.

5. The use of power tools such as chain saws will be a factor of safety and utility provisions. The free use of power tools is not recommended for the first-time carving student. A designated power tool area may be set up for the major cuts. An instructor or adviser should be watching during all power tool usage.

Application of the Template

"Why should a craftsman not make use of all his tools if they will promote a greater communication and expressiveness?"

Don Ellis
American musician

Learning Objectives

After you have finished reading this unit, you should be able to:

- Apply and secure a prepared template to the ice
- Transfer the template design to the ice by dotting and scratching
- Create V-notch lines over the surface scratches to leave a life-size image of the original design drawing

Terms to Know

template adhesion
paper template
solid template
surface scratch
V-notch lines

Ice sculptors use templates to transfer their initial image to a life-size marker on the ice. This chapter will discuss how to attach a template to the flat surface of an ice block and leave behind the line drawing as a re-creation of the original scale drawing.

The template first must be secured to the ice in a process called **template adhesion.** It is important that the template stays in place during the transfer process, which is the step that creates the guideline impressions on the surface. As you can imagine, it would be almost impossible to accomplish a proper transfer if the template shifts.

As discussed in Chapter 5, a template can be formed out of various mediums. We will begin by discussing paper templates, which have many advantages for beginners.

PAPER TEMPLATE APPLICATION

Paper templates, which are created for single or limited use, apply much easier to the ice compared to other templates as they're usually more flexible, form fitting, and capable of freezing directly onto the ice. Paper is also easier to cut through.

Position the Template

Follow these steps when applying a paper template:

1. Begin by establishing your base. It should generally be about 5 inches high for a single-piece design. Measure up from the bottom of the ice block. Five inches is usually enough to support any carving. A supporting base must be substantial enough to withstand the transportation process; otherwise, cracking may occur when moved. Shorter bases or the absence of a base altogether may apply for some designs.

2. Determine where the template should go. Your template should fit within the block of ice (Figures 8-1, 8-2, and 8-3).

Template Adhesion

Template adhesion is a critical step. There are two ways to stick the template in place: freezing it or securing it with straps.

Figure 8-1
A properly positioned paper template.

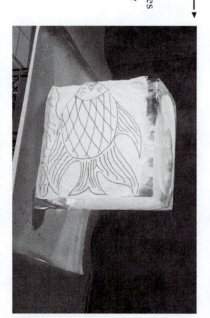

Figure 8-2
This template has been positioned too low and does not leave enough structure for the base.

Figure 8-3
This image was improperly placed with the lines outside the block, thus distorting an accurate transfer of the intended design.

Figure 8-5 The hand broom can be used to press out air bubbles between the template and the block of ice and to smooth the surface of the template.

Freezing Method

Freezing can be the simplest method. As was discussed in Chapter 2, the block must be tempered before carving in warmer conditions. Tempered ice with a 32° F (0° C) surface temperature will have a wet surface. When the ice is wet, position the paper template on the ice. The moisture will allow the paper to adhere to the ice. In a few minutes it will freeze directly onto the ice block if temperatures are favorable, that is, if the ambient air and elements do not interfere. Be aware that working in higher temperatures may require additional freezer exposure as the surface may become wet again during the transfer process. Simply set the block, with the template in place, back in the freezer for 10 minutes or so. Another alternative would be to use a freezing spray, although the adhesion may only be temporary, depending on the weather (Figure 8-4).

Figure 8-4
The easiest way to secure the template is to freeze it directly to the ice block. Some conditions may require the use of freezing spray.

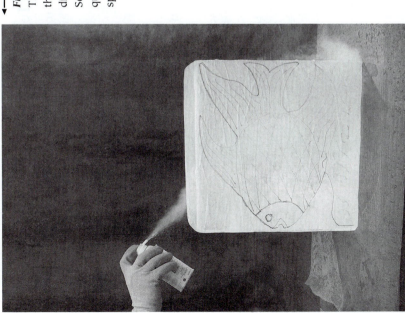

If the ice is 30° F (−1° C) or colder, the paper will not stick on its own because the surface is too dry. This scenario could also be found while working in freezing weather or inside a freezer. In this case, you will need to wet the ice with water and apply the template to the wet surface. Set the template quickly, as the ambient air may soon refreeze the ice's surface, and you won't be able to adjust the template once it's frozen to the ice. It may be helpful to use a hand broom to work out bubbles under the template. (Figure 8-5).

Using Straps

There are times when the freezing method may not work. If you are working outside on a sunny day or in a warm space, secure the template with straps or bungee cords. It is often best to use two cords to secure the template from top to bottom (Figure 8-6).

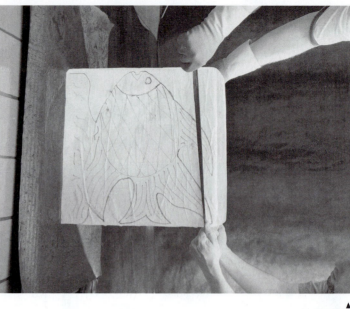

Figure 8-6
A template secured with rubber straps.

Figure 8-7
Tracing the image, with an awl, around a solid cardboard template.

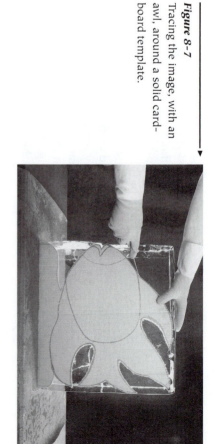

SOLID TEMPLATE APPLICATION

Solid templates are usually made of wood or cardboard and can be used more than once. Many ice carvers prefer solid templates when producing a series of identical carvings. Some also believe that a solid template makes the scratching process easier because the firmer template provides an edge to press against. Solid templates will withstand the exposure to water.

Carver's Note

A template can be applied during the tempering process for the freezing method of template adhesion. This requires experience and practice for the balance of tempering quality paired with timing to the template application. Competitors may find ways to apply a template in any condition. First-time students should follow the outlines listed above.

Applying a Solid Template

Secure the solid template to the ice. Use an awl to scratch the perimeter lines onto the face of the ice. This process is quickly achieved with a solid template (Figure 8-7).

TRANSFERRING THE TEMPLATE IMAGE

Once the template is securely applied, the transfer process can take place. This transfer often starts by dotting through the paper with one of the following tools:

• Six-prong chipper—The six-prong chipper is the simplest to use for this process. When transferring paper templates with a six-prong chipper, a series of dots are passed from the marker lines of the paper to the surface of the ice; the more dots the better (Figure 8-8). The paper is then removed and a perforated image is left, serving as a roadmap of dots (Figure 8-9).

• Awl—The awl is a single-pointed tool that will produce a single dot. Tapping too hard during this step could cause cracking or splitting. It best lends itself to tracing the solid templates or drawing a ruler line. An awl can also be used to rapidly destruct ice blocks into random pieces by piercing directly into the structure.

Connecting the Dots

Once the template has been transferred, it is time to connect the dots by **surface scratching**, followed by a deeper cut to bring the drawing to life.

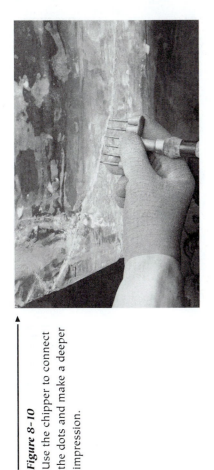

Figure 8-8
The six-prong chipper is used to transfer the lines of the paper to the surface of the ice.

Figure 8-10
Use the chipper to connect the dots and make a deeper impression.

The deeper cut should last through the silhouette cutting phase before melting away.

To Make a Deeper Impression

1. Use the six-prong chipper to connect the dots (Figure 8-10). This starts by scratching along the surface on top of the dots left from the template transfer. Additional lines can be drawn as the ice becomes your canvas for sketching.

2. The angle at which the tool is held depends on the type of line being drawn. The chipper is usually pulled along the surface with light pressure to form a deeper surface scratch. A perpendicular approach to the ice will best form a straight line (Figure 8-11). Sometimes an angular tool position is used to draw curved lines (Figure 8-12).

3. Keep the original scale line drawing nearby for a handy reference. Eventually many carvers are able to sketch the image on the ice freehand with only the line drawing to reference. This skill comes with time and practice.

Now the surface should have a complete impression of the life-size template design. This is a good time to step back 5 feet to see whether the lines are in proportion. Corrections are easy to make at this point because none of the ice segments has been removed.

Final Impression (V–Notch Lines)

Your initial lines won't be deep enough to withstand melting or the buildup of saw shavings. To prevent your lines from disappearing, it's necessary to make a final

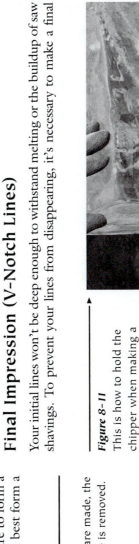

Figure 8-11
This is how to hold the chipper when making a straight line.

Figure 8-9
Once the dots are made, the paper template is removed.

Figure 8-12
Hold the chipper at an angle when drawing curved lines.

impression with a V-notch tool. This tool creates **V-notch lines**, which are angular grooves measuring approximately 1/4-inch deep and which will usually last through the silhouette-cutting phase. The V-notch line is traced over the surface scratch line and is the last step needed before removing segments of ice.

Hand Position

The V-notch tool is held in various positions. Hand placement may vary, as would a chef's hand to an all-purpose vegetable knife.

For the most accurate tracing of the surface scratch, keep one hand close to the tip for guidance and one hand toward the chisel base to provide forward pressure (Figure 8-13). Eventually, the long smooth strokes will create a cleaner line (Figure 8-14). However, the beginner will stay on track better with shorter back-and-forth movements.

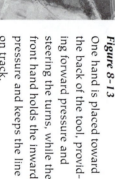

Figure 8-13
One hand is placed toward the back of the tool, providing forward pressure and steering the turns, while the front hand holds the inward pressure and keeps the line on track.

Figure 8-14
A finished V-notched impression over the surface scratch lines of the template transfer.

The pitch angle will determine how deeply the chisel will cut. The bevel of the chisel surface paired with the sharpness of the edge will affect this angle. Only a 1/4-inch line is needed at this point, so apply only enough pitch and pressure to perform this task.

Some experienced carvers skip some or all of the steps and get right to the major cuts. This ability comes with years of practice. This book is designed to teach each step for a beginning carver. Application of the template, its transfer, and its preservation will aid tremendously in making the real cuts.

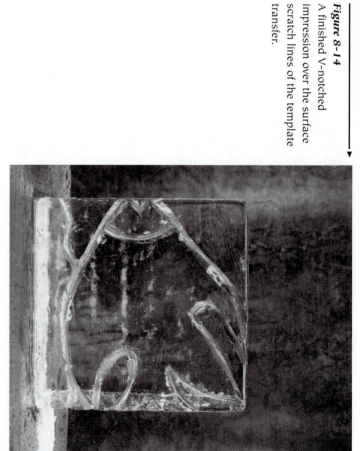

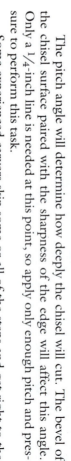

Pro's Corner

Occasionally professional ice carvers apply the paper template, allow it to freeze in place, and use the chain saw tip to either mark their lines or carve through the ice at the same time. This is not recommended for beginners, and most carving classrooms are not suited for such extensive chain saw usage.

SUMMARY

Before ice carving can begin, the template must be secured to the surface of the ice. Once a base size has been established, the template placement is determined. There are several methods of securing a paper template, including the freezing method and using straps. Solid templates are secured with straps. The next step is to dot the ice through the paper template or around the solid template, using a six-prong chipper or an awl. The template is removed and the dots are connected. A final impression that is much deeper is made along the initial scratch with a V-notch chisel. This deeper line won't disappear as the carving melts or becomes covered with saw shavings.

REVIEW QUESTIONS

Short Answer

1. Why should you leave a base out of the ice before you start carving the image?
2. Explain how to adhere a paper template if the ice is kept at 30° F or lower.
3. Under what circumstances would a solid template be preferred to a paper template?
4. Describe the proper tool position when making a straight line with a six-prong chipper.
5. Why is it necessary to make a V-notch line after the surface scratch?

Multiple Choice

6. An ideal base height for a single piece design is
   a. 6 inches.
   b. 12 inches.
   c. 5 inches.
   d. 8 inches.
7. What is a characteristic of tempered ice?
   a. The surface will be dry.
   b. The surface will be wet.
   c. Templates won't stick to its surface.
   d. It will have to go back into the freezer to prevent shattering or cracking.
8. Solid templates are usually made out of
   a. wood or cardboard.
   b. wood or Plexiglas.
   c. cardboard or plastic.
   d. plastic or tin.

9. What tool is preferred for the first step of surface scratching or dotting while using paper templates?
   a. awl
   b. V-notch line
   c. chisel
   d. six-prong chipper
10. Once the dots have been connected by surface scratching, you should
   a. step back about 5 feet from the carving to see whether the lines are in proportion.
   b. secure the template with straps.
   c. put the carving back in the freezer for a resting period.
   d. square the block.

INSTRUCTOR'S NOTES

1. If the refreezing method of template adhesion is used, it can be time productive to make this the first thing the students perform as they arrive for class. The instructor can help the student select their blocks and assist in the refreezing process. Because time may be needed for adhesion, this would be a good time to again review carving safety. Regardless of the schedule, the following should be covered before allowing students to begin their tool work:
   a. Ice tong usage—lifting and lowering full blocks of ice—back safety.
   b. Power tool usage—chain saw, die grinders, disk sanders, etc.—allowing the tool to come to a complete stop before setting down. Avoidance of dangling items in the path of the tools—i.e., clothes, hair, power cords.
   c. Electricity in wet environments.
   d. Proper uniform gear.
   e. Handling the chipper.
   f. Handling the chisel.
   g. Keeping tools stowed when not in use. Not leaving sharp tools on the ground, a hazard.
   h. Keeping the carving area clean of ice, power cords, etc.—to avoid slippage.
2. Consider setting up the initial ice carving area so that students can explore the tools soon to be used. This will be an inspiration to the day to come. As tools are checked out, they are treated as a privilege of possession. Safety first!
3. Instructors may want to reserve one extra paper template as a poster on the wall for future reference.
4. As the first carvers complete their steps, consider gathering all for a demonstration at each step such as dot transfer, surface scratching, stepping away to view proportion, and making V-notch lines.

The Large Cuts—Carving the Second Dimension

9

"A sculpture is just a painting cut out and stood up somewhere."

Frank Stella

Learning Objectives

After you have finished reading this unit, you should be able to:

- Explain how to preserve the template lines through the process
- Demonstrate how to hold the chain saw under control
- Describe the process of tip cutting with the chain saw along the template lines
- Illustrate how to remove a perimeter segment with the straight cut method
- Tell how to remove segments using chain saw bar insertion
- Explain the value of a relief cut
- Demonstrate how to smooth out convex and concave curves with a hand saw
- Show how to remove segments of ice with the six-prong chipper
- Describe how to step away from the carving to identify any remaining work

Terms to Know

compound depth segment
chain saw pushing cut
chain saw pulling cut

chain saw straight cut
chain saw insertion cut
relief cut

convex curve
concave curve

Once you have completed the instructions in Chapter 8, you should have a single face, etched with a template transfer of V-notched lines, positioned on the platform and ready for you to cut the second dimension. The second-dimension segments will be removed in equal proportion from front to back of the template face. As this process takes place, the image starts to emerge from the ice.

In order to demonstrate a variety of basic cuts used to create the second dimension, we will use an angelfish as our design inspiration (Figure 9-1). Imagine that every segment of ice from the front face is discarded and leaves the same exact image as the template line drawing, with voids where unused ice currently exists. Each section to be removed should have the same thickness as it relates to the depth of the block. Ideally, the front and back faces of the block will be identical once these cuts have been made. This result becomes the silhouette image as discussed in Chapter 3 or a sculpture completed to the second dimension.

The one exception in the carving of the angelfish will be where its bottom connects to its base. Naturally, if the lines on the bottom of the fish were cut through the entire block, the design would not have any support. The area where a limited depth is cut to create a relief portion of the design is known as a **compound depth segment** (Figure 9-2).

More-advanced designs may require this second dimension relief image to be created in multiple areas of the silhouette. This component adds difficulty, and it is not recommended for the first-time carving experience. If the second practical carving day is exercised in this class, it may help to then attempt the same angelfish in front of a scene of coral (Figures 9-3 and 9-4).

20"

20"

Figure 9-1   This diagram shows the template lines in bold with an example of the type of inner detail that will be added later.

Figure 9-2
This diagram shows the same template as in Figure 9-1 with the compound depth segment identified in the circle.

20"

20"

Compound
Depth Segment

20"

40"

Figure 9-4
This diagram shows
where the fish will be set
in front of a background
of coral. Note how the
coral supports the fish.
The seven circled areas
represent the compound
depth segments.

Figure 9-3
This diagram shows the
template lines in bold
with an example of inner
detail to be added later.

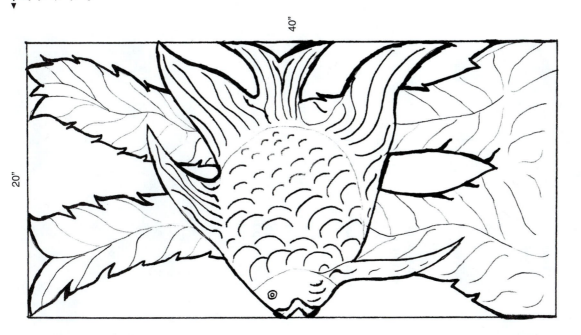

40"

20"

Figure 9-5
Notice how the chain saw cut was made on the outside of the centerline mark, leaving all of the intended sculpture ice.

PRESERVATION OF THE TEMPLATE LINES

Cutting along your V-notched lines will require that you do not remove any ice inside the channel of the groove. As most saws take away a sliver of mass with them, you will need to make your cuts along the slanted portion of the ice segment to be removed. This principle is especially important when using the chain saw, as the cutting blades will remove 1/4-inch of ice. The center line of the channel should remain when the cuts are finished (Figure 9-5).

CHAIN SAW CONTROL

In Chapter 7 we discussed how to make a simple vertical cut along a straight line. As you make cutouts of the silhouette segments, you will need to maneuver the saw in multiple directions, which requires steady control. It is time to review some of the basic tips for using a chain saw.

1. Always keep both hands on the handles of the saw during all stages of cutting. Take note that the left hand will most often drive the pressure while the right hand holds the tool steady. As you practice, you will feel this sensation. (This applies to most saws, as they are usually only available in a right-handed configuration.)

2. While using the saw, observe your surrounding area to be sure no objects, power cords, clothing, or fellow carvers are in the path of the cutting bar.

3. Turn the saw on before touching the ice.

Figure 9-6
The cutting bar is correctly held perpendicular to the ice.

4. Let the blades do the work while you apply only enough pressure to move steadily through the cut. Forcing too much pressure could damage the saw and create loss of control on the line of your intended cut.

5. Keep the bar of the saw perpendicular to the face of the ice at all times. A variance of pitch could result in a dramatic difference in your image on the opposite side of the block (Figures 9-6 and 9-7).

6. Keep the bar pitched in a parallel position. A variance here could again cause the opposite side to vary from the intention of the perfect silhouette image (Figures 9-8 and 9-9).

7. Line your eyes up over the top of the cutting blade as much as possible. Vertical cuts will allow this easily. Angled cuts may require you to tilt your head into a position that observes this principle yet still allows you to remain balanced.

Figure 9-7
An inappropriate pitch of the cutting blade may damage the intended silhouette.

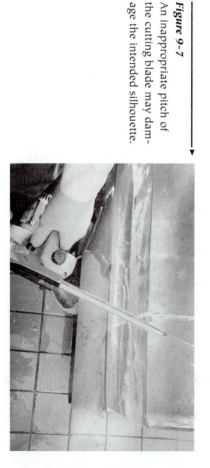

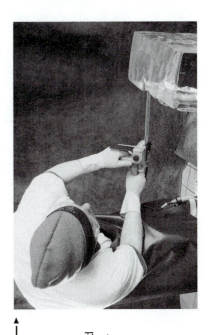

Figure 9-10
The carver cuts a straight line with head and eyes directly over the saw blade. Note that this ice suffered from exterior thermal shock of cracking during storage, although it is still intact enough to carve if care is taken.

Figure 9-8
The cutting bar is held parallel to the ice.

anced on your feet. Horizontal cuts will be more challenging from this view. They will require a steady hand and slow movement through the ice to keep the blade on its mark (Figures 9-10, 9-11, and 9-12).

8. Turn the saw off whenever there is a buildup of ice shavings that resemble snow and it covers the template line. Lay the saw safely down and out of the way. Sweep the excess snow off until you have a full view of the guiding line. This scenario often occurs during a pulling cut.

9. When a segment is about to be completely freed from the main block, be especially careful to observe where and how this segment will fall. In some cases it may be safer to turn the power tool off and set it down. Finish the cut with a hand tool. One hand will be on the tool while the other is available to catch the loose segment.

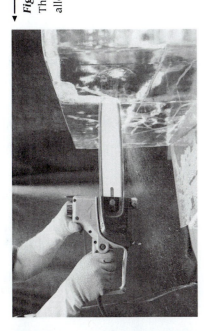

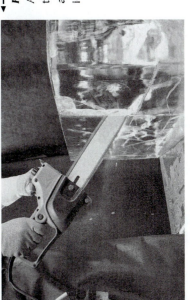

Figure 9-11
The carver cuts an angled line with head and eyes over the saw blade. However, balance is maintained during the cutting process.

Figure 9-9
An inappropriate pitch of the cutting blade may damage the intended silhouette ice.

Figure 9-12
The carver makes a side cut. Notice how the left hand is positioned on top of the handle for a steady grip. The eyes are now over the side of the bar as leaning over sideways would not be a safe maneuver. Extra care is required for these cuts.

Figure 9-13
The top section of the tail fin is cut using a pushing motion.

THE CUTTING PROCESS USING CHAIN SAWS

The process of removing many silhouette segments will follow the same steps as we discussed in Chapter 7 under the heading, "Squaring the Block." It often takes two or more line cuts to remove a section of ice. Interior sections may require the chain saw bar to be inserted straight into the ice from front to back with little or no line other than the height of the cutting bar. Some segments may be removed with the method of curved cutting, which varies slightly from the steps of a line cut. All of these methods can be used alone or with one another to equally remove proportionate segments of the silhouette image. We must also define the difference between a pushing cut and pulling cut for additional reference to this section.

Pushing Cut

When the chain saw cuts from the bottom of the bar or tip, this is known as the chain saw **pushing cut**. This is the most common and safest method to use when cutting ice gravity and particle removal are in your favor (Figure 9-13). Use this method whenever possible.

Pulling Cut

When the chain saw cuts from the top of the bar or tip, this is known as the chain saw **pulling cut**. There are occasional instances in which cutting from the bottom of the bar would be awkward and unsafe. At that time the carver should use the pulling cut, which requires the tip or bar to be driven in a pulling motion. You will notice that the snow emitted from the saw will build up on the

face of the block. This is a setback, as this will cover the line you are trying to follow. Should this happen, you'll need to turn the saw off, set it down, and sweep away the snow to reveal the line. An example of the need to use the pulling cut would be the finishing touch to an upward angled segment, as in the lower tail portion of the angelfish (See Figure 9-14). By using a pulling cut, you will be able to achieve greater accuracy in meeting the lines in the corner of the angle.

Tip Cutting

The tip of the cutting bar is the most-used section, as it tends to do most of the work in this and all of the following cutting methods. Begin by turning the saw on and approaching the line you intend to cut. Insert the tip approximately one inch

Figure 9-14
A pulling motion is used to draw the entire bar precisely into the corner of this angled segment.

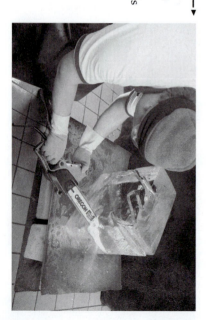

Figure 9-17

The saw has been inserted directly forward into the block.

Figure 9-15

The chain saw tip has cut the initial mark through the first ½-inch of this line on the angelfish's upper tail. Note how the line curves slightly in the design. This gradual insertion cut will follow the curve easily.

into the ice and mark the entire area of the segment being removed (Figure 9-15). This maneuver is best practiced with the insertion cut of an additional inch. The second run will create a guideline to make the rest of the cutting process easier to follow (Figure 9-16). The purpose of this two-step process is to ensure greater accuracy, paired with understanding that the tip is less maneuverable when more of the bar is inserted.

Straight Cut

The **chain saw straight cut** is used to cut a straight line through the ice. Begin with a tip cut, proceed with a half bar cut, and finish with a full bar cut. This process was outlined in the process of squaring the block in Chapter 7. You

should identify that the method used was a straight line cut with a pushing motion. As a review, the student should remember the importance of holding the saw in the correct perpendicular and parallel positions described above. Although this is the easiest and most fundamental movement of chain saw cutting, it is imperative to practice the balance of foot, hand, and eye position for the execution of a perfect cut.

Insertion Cut

The **chain saw insertion cut** is the movement of the bar directly through the ice, which is especially valuable for removing interior segments (Figure 9-17). This cut is also used in a series to separate areas with a sharp curve. A single insertion pierce will cut a section as wide as the bar and chain (approximately 3 inches). In the instance of this single pierce, the bar will be removed in the same fashion as it was inserted. A line cut may be started from the point of the fully executed insertion cut as well. Use the following steps:

1. Turn on the saw before touching the ice.
2. Drive the tip directly into ice, while maintaining a consistent pitch of the cutting bar, until the tip is driven through the opposite side of the block or the intended depth is reached in a compound depth cut.
3. For a single pierce, pull the bar out in the same manner as it was inserted (Figure 9-18).
4. For initiating a line or curved cut, follow the instructions in their respective sections of this chapter. Make a tip cut first to guide your way though the process.

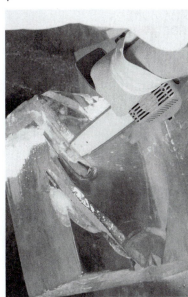

Figure 9-16

The chain saw tip now defines the line by cutting an additional inch into the line just created. This mark will act as a guide for whichever technique is used to remove the rest of the segment.

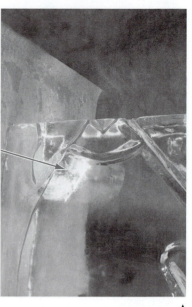

Figure 9-18

The single pierce of this insertion cut has left a rectangular abscess in the ice.

Relief Cut

A **relief cut** is a saw cut made between a segment to be removed and the intended design, thus allowing rapid removal of the unwanted ice without cracking or damaging the body of the sculpture. The straight and insertion cuts described above can be classified as relief cuts as well, yet this term is most often associated with single cuts after which a different tool will remove the excess. This cut will be driven to a very specific point that touches the line of the template design, but no farther. The surrounding ice is taken off with a chipper, chisel, or saw. The relief cut is applied for two reasons:

- The segment to be removed is too concave to be cut with multiple saw cuts.
- A surface area segment needs to be removed. A relief cut can be made from the exterior surface down to the template line to allow hand tools or additional saw cuts from intruding past the intended design.

Figure 9-19

This portion has relief cuts made in the tight area under the tail and lower fin of the angelfish. These cuts will make the unwanted segment easier to remove.

Figure 9-20

Notice how the ice is removed easily with the relief cuts in place. Without such cuts, it might be possible to drive a crack through the entire segment and break off the tail. Use the flat chisel for this procedure.

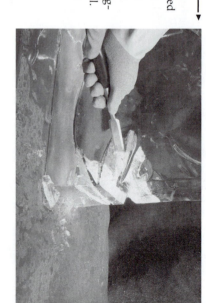

In the case of the angelfish, a relief cut could be used to remove the ice between the lower portion of the tail and base of the design. This is a tight concave area, which could be difficult to remove with a saw. A series of straight cuts could remove most of the segment, but using relief cuts ensures that major portions of the design will not break off when other tools are used (Figures 9-19 and 9-20).

Relief cuts should also be used when the sculpture has a specific line, which should not be breached to avoid damaging the design portion of the block (Figures 9-21 and 9-22). These figures illustrate how the dorsal fin and forehead of the angelfish can be defined through the relief cut process using hand tools only.

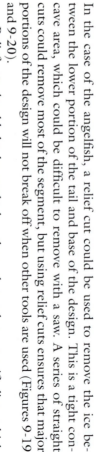

Figure 9-21

This carving is cut so that a straight cut could be used to remove the section above the forehead of the angelfish. A relief cut is made where the dividing line between the dorsal fin and forehead begins. Notice how the cut ends at the point where the template line is drawn.

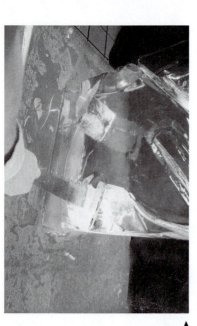

Large Ice Saws

Large ice saws are used to cut through major portions of ice blocks. When a chain saw is not available, it can be of priceless assistance to the carver. Squaring, splitting, and large cuts are easily performed with these larger saws. However, the modern practice of using power tools has replaced the need for this tool with the exception of rare instances such as a hand-tool-only ice carving competition or a chain saw failure.

Pistol-Grip Ice Saws

These smaller saws are used for performing smaller relief cuts and rounding out convex and concave portions of the design. In this section, we will discuss the rounding technique, which is applied in two ways: the **convex curve**, which creates an image that is rounded outward—like the exterior of a sphere or circle—and the **concave curve**, which is rounded inward—like the inside of a bowl (Figures 9-23 and 9-24). Both curves are achieved by pulling on the saw with a twist of the wrist while applying pressure to the surface of the ice.

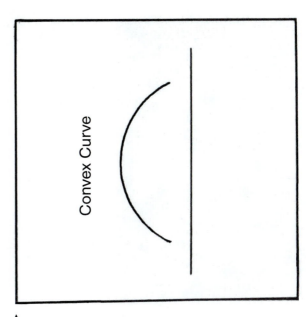

Convex Curve

Figure 9-23
This diagram shows a convex curve.

Figure 9-22
The six-prong chipper shaves away the unwanted ice down to the point of the relief cut. Trying this removal without the relief cut may cause a crack to drive through the entire head of the angelfish.

HAND SAW USAGE

The ice hand saw is a classic tool used in the art of ice sculpture. The chain saw has replaced hand saws in many ways, but it is still recommended that students gain an understanding of how to use hand saws. There may be times when chain saws are not available or not allowed in competitions or when the electricity is off. Hand saws are also useful when both hands are needed when removing large segments. There are two primary varieties of hand saws, which tend to perform separate work: the larger block-cutting saws and the smaller pistol-grip saws. (See Chapter 5 for examples.) As you see in the illustrations, the blades are angled in a fashion that lends itself to cutting in only one direction: pulling. You will discover how the pushing motion removes little or no ice, and the pulling motion of a sharp saw blade rips through the block with speed.

Carver's Note

Some may consider buying a tree-trimming saw, which has matching angled teeth, as opposed to the single-angled type designed for ice. Tree saws do not work well with ice.

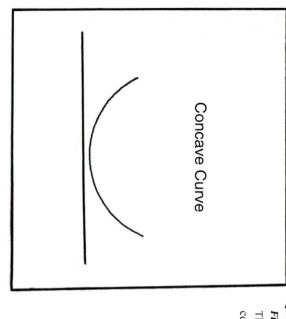

Concave Curve

Figure 9-24
This diagram shows a concave curve.

A rounded area of your template design may be primarily removed through a series of straight cuts paired with other tools, though they require a smoother finish to follow the intended line. A pulling motion, paired with a turn of the wrist, will scratch off a small portion of the surface. This technique is most commonly used for concave curves (Figures 9-25 through 9-30).

Figure 9-25
This tail portion of the angelfish needs to be rounded out with a pistol-grip saw to enhance the concave shape.

Figure 9-26
The hand saw is pulling and turning over the curve to remove unwanted ice and smoothing the curved surface.

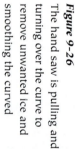

Figure 9-27
The tail has been fully rounded through the pulling and twisting motion of the pistol-grip saw.

Figure 9-28
The dorsal fin has been cut out and needs refinement with the convex motion of the hand saw.

Figure 9-29
The hand saw is pulled and turned to scratch away the unwanted ice.

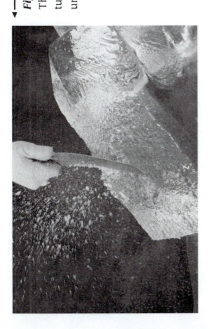

Figure 9-30
The dorsal fin of this angelfish has been properly rounded with the hand saw.

Figure 9-31
The six-prong chipper is shaving down the line of the head section to remove the excess ice. Notice how the tool is gliding over the surface.

can be used as an inexpensive and time conserving supplement to the classroom environment. To use this tool effectively to remove ice segments, follow these instructions:

1. Glide the flat surface of the points across the perimeter segments to be removed (Figure 9-31).
2. Shear away small sections at a time.
3. Avoid forceful piercing of the ice with an excessive perpendicular angle to the ice. This may create an undesired crack (Figure 9-32).

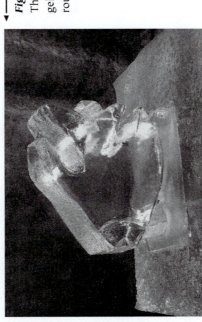

Figure 9-32
This carver may damage the design by stabbing too forcefully into the block. If too much pressure is used along with the pitch shown, the block could split.

REMOVAL OF ICE WITH A SIX-PRONG CHIPPER

The six-prong chipper is the simplest tool to use. Some carvers may even say that a complete ice carving can be sculpted by using this tool exclusively. This is true if a scratchy finish is acceptable. The six-prong chipper has been proven to be the best pencil for the template transfer (see Chapter 8). As a complement, this tool can also remove ice slowly in place of the chain saw. A skilled carver can remove convex angled segments faster with this tool than a dull-bladed chain saw can cut through the same portion. Application of this tool pressure needed to remove small sections at a time to avoid cracking the rest of the block.

4. If an interior section of ice is to be removed, use slow and light pressure while shifting the angle back and forth to the surface ice being pierced (Figures 9-33 and 9-34).

5. With an ice saw, make relief cuts in tandem with the chipper to avoid cracking the sculpture portion of the ice.

STEPPING AWAY FROM THE ICE

Step back at least 5 feet from the carving to see whether all the lines are in proportion. The eyes cannot see such dimension when too close to the sculpture. Use this vantage point to view all angles, curves, and cuts to discover where fur-

Figure 9-33
The area between the base and the fish must be removed slowly with the chipper as there are no entryways for a hand saw to form a relief cut. Apply the tool in one direction, and then switch to the other side to slowly remove the excess ice. Be careful to apply only the

Figure 9-34
The carver has nearly completed the task by removing small bits until the opposite side of the ice has been reached. Once the hole is large enough, the gliding motion of ice removal can be practiced. This illustration is used on the angelfish with coral shown in Chapter 15.

ther work may be needed. Make the appropriate revisions to follow the lines of the template (Figures 9-35 and 9-36).

SUMMARY

The second-dimension silhouette image is a critical step to follow in ice carving. Producing your template lines across the entire block (base and compound depth sections excluded) will be of great benefit in visualizing the next step, the third dimension. But, when given the opportunity, use a chain saw to do most of the work. It is also important to learn the skill of carving most of the ice with hand saws and a six-prong chipper. Use relief cuts wherever possible to protect the design areas. The hand saw is best for relief cuts, and it is used with the scraping technique for

Figure 9-35
The angelfish is nearly finished, though the underside of the dorsal fin and the tail need additional work.

Figure 9-36
This angelfish is completed on the second-dimension silhouette image. All template lines are in proportion, and the carver is ready to go on to the next step, carving the third dimension. Note: This illustration shows an alternate rendition of the same design with use of the same template drawing.

convex and concave curve finishing. Ideally, the front and back faces of the block should be identical once the steps of this chapter are completed.

REVIEW QUESTIONS

Matching

Match the tool to the job (feel free to use a tool more than once).

a. pistol-grip ice saw
b. six-prong chipper
c. chain saw

_____ 1. Pushing cut
_____ 2. Small relief cut
_____ 3. Template transfer
_____ 4. Pulling cut
_____ 5. Concave curve
_____ 6. Tip cutting

Multiple Choice

7. Which word best describes sculpting the second dimension?
   a. flat
   b. convex
   c. silhouette
   d. relief

8. A compound depth segment of a design is best described as
   a. a convex curve.
   b. a limited depth cut to create a relief portion of the design.
   c. a concave curve.
   d. preservation of the template lines.

9. Which of the following tips is *not* given as a way to maintain control over a chain saw?
   a. Make sure there are no objects, power cords, clothing, or fellow carvers in the path of the cutting bar.
   b. Keep the bar of the saw pitched in a parallel position.
   c. Position the blade on the ice before turning it on.
   d. Keep the bar of the saw perpendicular to the face of the ice.

10. When a segment is about to be completely freed from the main block, you should
    a. call "timber" so others in the area will be on the lookout for falling ice.
    b. be careful to observe how and where the segment will fall.
    c. ask for another person's help to catch the falling ice.
    d. run away from the carving area.

11. When a chain saw is cutting from the bottom of the bar or tip, it is called
    a. a pushing cut.
    b. a pull cut.
    c. a tip cut.
    d. a angled cut.

12. Describe the steps taken to produce a chain saw straight cut.
    a. Begin with a tip cut and end with a full bar cut.
    b. Begin with a tip cut, proceed with a half bar cut and end with a full bar cut.
    c. Begin with an insertion cut, proceed with a tip cut, and end with a full bar cut.
    d. Begin with a relief cut and proceed to a full bar cut.

13. Which cut can allow for rapid removal of the unwanted ice without cracking or damaging the body of the sculpture?
    a. relief cut
    b. pistol-grip saw rounding
    c. concave cut
    d. convex cut

14. When using an ice hand saw, which motion will remove the most ice?
    a. pulling
    b. pushing
    c. Pushing and pulling work equally well.
    d. short chops

INSTRUCTOR'S NOTES

1. The angelfish design has been chosen as the model template design for this lesson. However, other simple designs can be used. This sculpture illustrates the basic techniques outlined in this chapter and also molds well into the more advanced design with the same fish set into coral. The first practical day of ice carving should include designs that do the following:

   • Allow the use of multiple tools
   • Can be carved mostly by hand tools
   • Provide a simple enough design so that a student can easily identify what the finished product should look like. Fish designs work well for this.

2. It is recommended to have each student carve the same design. This is a great benefit to the supervision process, and students can follow each others' work.

3. Individual creativity of design could be recommended if a second carving day is scheduled. Keep in mind that each new design practiced by the student will require individual coaching to bring the sculpture to fruition. The instructor's time availability for one-on-one tutoring will play a factor in the diversity of designs allowed.

4. A game plan, depending on your budget and class time, should be devised on the student use of power tools versus hand tools. If only one chain saw is to be used, you will undoubtedly need to plan on making it a hand-tool-only experience for the students. By the time 10 blocks have had their first major cuts, the class will be half over. It is advised to have at least three saws in your arsenal: two for constant use under supervision and one for a spare. More than three, or even one for each student, would be nice, though close supervision is also a key component. Because the physical layout of carving areas vary, it will be up to the instructor to devise the best game plan.

5. Try to give the students exposure to all the major skills. If they finish the entire piece with a chain saw, they will miss out on how to use hand tools to accomplish the same thing. As a minimum, have the student use the chain saw to make a few relief cuts such as over the base on both sides and between the tail and back fin. The rest could be done with the chipper and hand saw. This will give students the feel for a chain saw and keep the program moving.

6. If instructing alone, get the chain saw cuts out of the way and then walk to each station with a hand saw and chipper to guide each carving to progres-

sion. Start a pattern along a template line and let the student finish the concept. This is providing they are feeling stumped and need guidance, which often happens for first-time carvers.

7. During a demonstration moment, take the time to show the value and execution of a relief cut on a block of ice. Once the students grasp this concept, they will progress faster and avoid damaging their design.

8. Demonstrate how the movement of the ice hand saw works in the pulling motion. If a large saw is available, show its capability. With the smaller saw, show the basic straight cut along with curved shaping technique.

9. With a spare chunk of ice, show what happens when the six-prong chipper is properly glided over to remove shavings. In the same demonstration, show what would happen if an ice block were pierced too harshly.

10. Toward the finishing touches of creating the second dimension, demonstrate rounding a curve with the pistol-grip hand saw. This technique will have value throughout the carving process.

11. Demonstrate the movement of looking back 5 feet to identify where additional work is needed. Show how your eyes line up with the lines of the template drawing.

Carving the Third Dimension

"I love sculpture, but I wasn't very good at it and I don't think in a three-dimensional way."

Chuck Close

Learning Objectives

After you have finished reading this unit, you should be able to:

- Use a model or preparatory drawing to visualize the segments to be removed in the third dimension
- Draw lines on the ice where major segments will be removed
- Cut away segments from each side of the ice block, creating the third dimension
- Create the design's image within the base's supporting compound depth segment or the area where the sculpture joins with the base
- Determine what finishing steps are needed

Terms to Know

third-dimension visualization

third-dimension preparatory drawing

carving design model

break-away points

10

The American painter Chuck Close, author of this chapter's opening quote, is known as one of the best artists in the world. He understands the need and the difficulty of visualizing the third dimension. At the completion of Chapter 9 you have a carving that is two dimensional. Ideally, the front and back faces of the block are identical. Now it's time to turn those flat images into a three-dimensional object. This is where the fun truly begins as you watch your flat design come to life and the three-dimensional image emerges. It is during this phase of the carving experience that all remaining major segments of ice are removed. The image

Figure 10-1
The depth of the block is still 10 inches and virtually un-changed in the third dimension.

will be rough and may need additional rounding and shaping by using a variety of finishing techniques, which will be discussed in Chapter 11.

PREPARATION

Follow these steps before carving the third dimension:

1. Begin by getting a clear side view of the ice. This image will leave you with the rectangular shape of your original uncut block, as the entire section is still 10 inches thick (Figure 10-1).

2. The next step is to decide which of the wide and narrow portions should be removed. That can be determined by using a technique called **third-dimension visualization**. Because you no longer have a flat surface on which to apply a template, you must imagine or visualize what must be re-moved. Think about what must be removed and visualize what the ice that is left behind will look like. Do not get discouraged; a few tricks can be used to help the beginning carver proceed through this step.

- One tool is a **third-dimension preparatory drawing**, which is a diagram used to outline the third-dimension segments to be removed. The side-view drawings are often used and a top-view preparatory drawing can also be applied (Figures 10-2 to 10-4). Visualizing the wide and narrow third-dimensional areas of the angelfish in our example, or any chosen design, is a fundamental skill.

- Another handy guide comes with the use of a model. A **carving design model** is a three-dimensional visual aid and replica used to carve the in-tended design. This could be a life-size replica or a smaller version of the design. Smaller-scale models are portable and more often available (Figure 10-5). Some models can guide a carver on individual components of a design, even if the entire sculpture does not resemble the model. An ex-ample for an advanced sculpture might be the muscle structure of a man's chest. The carver may use a warrior toy as a guide to re-create the muscles.

- Many ice carvers take photographs of their carvings so that they can use them as an aid for future projects.

- Copying an identical finished ice sculpture makes an excellent life-size model.

These guiding images will be an asset for those who struggle in visualizing the third dimension.

10"

20"

Figure 10-3

This sketch shows how the two sides of the body will be removed. The tail has been set slightly to the right in this design to provide movement in the sculpture. The upper and lower fins follow the same curve to show the fish as it would be swimming. Note how the marks are shown where the tips of the fin will be narrower than the widest part of the body.

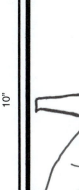

Figure 10-2

This sketch shows how the image will emerge from the ice. Notice the sides of the body, the dorsal fin, and the base with markings to illustrate a narrower portion at the mouth.

10"

20"

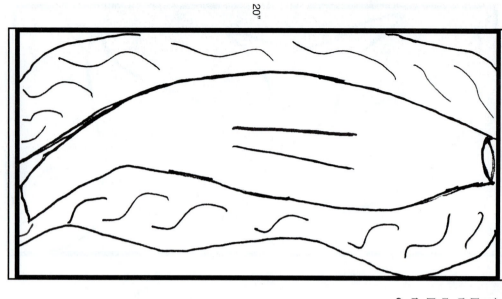

20"

10"

Figure 10-4
The base will be the widest portion for support along with the tapered shape of the mouth and fins. Notice again how the tail fins are curved to display movement in the design.

Figure 10-5   This scale model could be used as a guideline to visualize the third dimension.

Carver's Note

A three-dimensional preparatory drawing or a carving design model is rarely used by most professionals; however, these aids are generally used during competitions. Once the ingredients are memorized, the recipe is much simpler; much like a sauté cook who knows every step of preparing paella by heart. The lack of familiarity with the finished product is directly proportional to the need for a visual aid.

Applying the Cuts of the Third Dimension

Once you have a clear idea of what needs to be removed and can visualize the completed carving, it is time to make the cuts.

1. Before applying the saw to the ice, mark lines on the ice block indicating what areas should be saved and what areas should be removed. The markings are called **break-away points**. The break-away points are applied with the scratches of a six-prong chipper. This concept is similar to the template lines drawn in Chapter 8, though a freehand approach is needed here.

Figure 10-6
Notice where lines have been scratched to indicate the thickness of the mouth section as the narrowest section and the width of the body's center as the widest point of the fish. The exterior segments will be cut away.

Pro's Corner

The experienced sculptor will know these points of reference and begin cutting with a chain saw. Beginners will move step by step by applying the break-away points with a six-prong chipper. The Ice Carving 101 student should practice the skill of cutting these areas with hand tools before moving on to power equipment.

Left-Side Section—Mouth Area

Let's start with the left section of our angelfish sculpture. It will be the mouth area.

1. Use the side-view drawing to apply the same lines on the block with a six-prong chipper. This will mark the break-away points for your cutting. Some places can be more difficult to scratch upon, such as the area in our example where the lower fin meets the base. When applying these marking lines, it is best to notice where certain points of reference are on the visual aid and then apply the same mark on the ice.

- Be sure to keep the base in perspective. Take note of where the mouth of the angelfish is located, in the center of our drawing. This image also shows that the mouth will need to be approximately 3 inches wide on the life-size block.

- Apply this mark by making two swift scratches on each side of the mouth. The portion between the two scratches will be part of your fish, and the exterior portions will be cut away. Next scratch a mark on each side of the top dorsal fin to resemble the widest portion of the body. Add to these marks by scratching a line on the top fin down the mouth to demonstrate the tapered angle of where these lines from these points will meet (Figure 10-6).

2. Begin removing the excess ice segments around the mouth with a six-prong chipper. This can be done with other tools; however, this is the ideal time to learn the art of chipper shaving in this third-dimensional carving process. Use the principles learned in Chapter 9 on shaving with a six-prong chipper and begin removing the sides of the mouth section from top to bottom.

3. During this process, you will need to apply small relief cuts with a hand saw where the bottom fin contacts the base (Figure 10-7). It is best to make the relief cuts when you reach this part of the shaving to avoid cutting too deep. This portion of your work will be complete when both sides of the head portion have been removed (Figures 10-8).

Figure 10-7
A hand saw is applying a relief cut to separate the base from the fish where a segment of the side will be removed. The same cut will be applied on the opposite side as well.

Figure 10-8
The front and mouth area of the fish has been cleared of its primary third-dimension segments. Repeat the procedure on the back side.

Carver's Note

The edges of the sculpture are still cornered and blocky. This is the intention at this point. A beginner may be tempted to continue shaping and forming the detail of the mouth. However, this detail may lose definition from melting by the time the rest of the third-dimension areas are cut. This next step of shaping will be covered in Chapter 11.

Top Section—Top Fin Area

1. Begin this step by marking three sets of points, with the chipper, followed by sketching the break-away lines between the marked points (Figure 10-9). Mark the following points on the dorsal fin:

   - The narrowest point of the top of the fin should be approximately 1 inch wide to allow for melting. Trimming to a point can happen during the shaping step in the next chapter. (This applies to any other carving you may sculpt. Always keep the narrowest point at least 1 inch wide during this initial phase.)
   - The widest area of the fin.
   - The widest area in the middle body of the fish.

2. Make relief cuts, as defined in Chapter 9. The dorsal fin can be rather delicate toward the tip; this is a good time to use the hand saw to cut away major portions of ice. A relief cut down the dorsal fin from the tip to the body on both sides is best used on this movement.

3. Next, use the chipper to follow the line around the top of the body, removing the unwanted ice from the second-dimension image of the dorsal fin (Figure 10-10). Make sure that the tine closest to the dorsal fin does not go beyond the relief cut as not to damage the ice.

4. Continue sketching the guidelines of the top-view drawing by applying the curved shape to the top of the upper tail fin with the chipper (Figure 10-11).

Opposite Side Section—Tail Area

1. Mark the break-away points by following the tail-side diagram. Begin sketching with your chipper where the tail's tip will be located.

2. Use the hand saw to remove the major section on the convex side of the top tail fin in tandem with the chipper to follow your line (Figures 10-12 and

Figure 10-9
This photo shows how the lines of the dorsal fin will taper toward the top along with curving slightly as the body moves to the back of the fin. Create your relief cut with a hand saw along this line as described in step 2.

Figure 10-11
The upper tail fin is sketched with the chipper to match the top-view drawing.

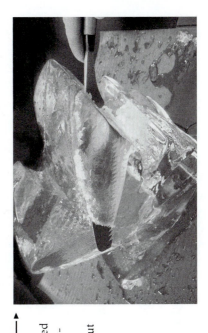

Figure 10-10
The chipper is removing the area on the top of the body to the point where the relief cut was made with the hand saw.

Figure 10-12
The hand saw is being used to cut away the major portion of the convex side of the tail. Notice how this cut is outside of the break-away point.

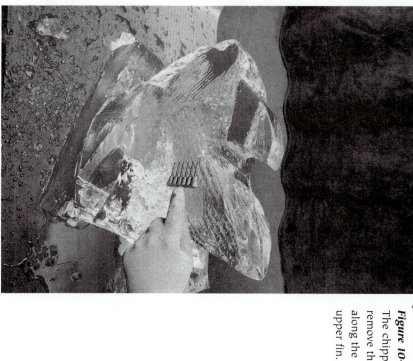

Figure 10-13
The chipper is used to remove the remaining ice along the convex side of the upper fin.

Figure 10-14
The hand saw is used to remove a major segment on the convex side of the middle tail fin.

10-13). The same techniques can be used to form the convex curve of the middle tail fin (Figures 10-14 and 10-15). The concave sides of the upper and middle tail fins will be removed with two cuts meeting in the middle (Figures 10-16 and 10-17). Use the hand saw rounding technique to smooth out the shape of this concave tail section (Figure 10-18).

3. The lower fin will again migrate with the base. You will see how the tail's tip spans out of the base while the center portion becomes a part of the base and supports the entire sculpture. Use relief cuts, made with the hand saw, to separate the base from the lower fin (Figures 10-19 and 10-20). The steps shown in these photos should be followed also on the opposite side. The same shaving and rounding techniques used on the top fin and tail will

take place on the lower tail as well. Completing this step will leave the tail fins carved to their basic form in the third dimension (Figure 10-21).

Carver's Note

The angelfish's tail could also be centered on the side view, similar to the mouth placement. The silhouette drawing used to carve the second-dimension template does not define this point of reference in the sculpture, but, a third-dimension side-view drawing will. One could simply make this fish flat and straight, though this would be boring and lack life in its message to the audience. The design image outlined for this lesson suggests a movement of swimming for the fish.

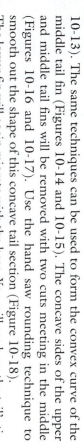

Figure 10-17
The hand saw is used to make a second cut toward the end of the prior relief cut. The major portion of the concave area will fall away once these two cuts are complete.

Figure 10-18
The hand saw is used to round out the lines of the concave portion of the tail fins.

Figure 10-19
The hand saw is used to form a separating line of the convex side of the lower fin. Notice how the saw should stop at the point of the base.

Figure 10-15
The chipper is used to finish the middle fin similar to the technique used for the top fin.

Figure 10-16
The hand saw is used to make a relief cut from the tail to the body toward the break-away point of the line.

Figure 10-20
Cut along your base line to remove the lower tail section. This cut should meet with your prior cut down the side of the fin.

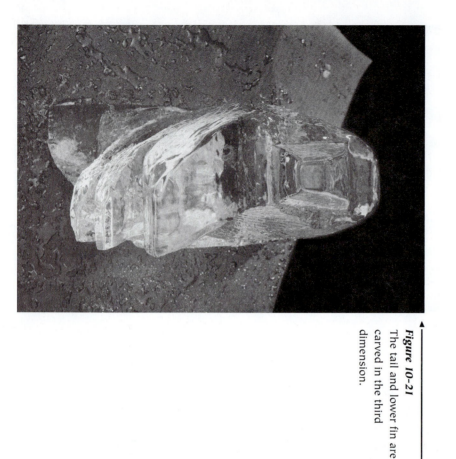

Figure 10-21
The tail and lower fin are carved in the third dimension.

Figure 10-22
A line is drawn to mark the bottom of the fish within the compound depth segment of the base.

BASE SECTION

The compound depth segment of the base is all that remains before we move into the finishing steps. As you examine the preparatory drawings, you will notice how the lower fin emerges from the base. This area is the supporting property of the entire structure. The precise anatomy of the angelfish would yield a narrow section on the lower fin as it meets with the base. Having the support is more important than the symmetry. Therefore, you may need to exaggerate the thickness between the sculpture and the supporting base. Otherwise, this work may result in a lower fin that is unable to support the design throughout the entire display period. This balance must take place from the point of template design and followed though to the finished work of ice.

1. Begin carving the lower fin and base area by marking a curved line into the base that resembles how the front of the fish's lower fin would meet with the base of the carving (Figure 10-22).

Figure 10-23
The chipper is used to scoop out most of the ice in the base that lies in the lower tail portion of the fish.

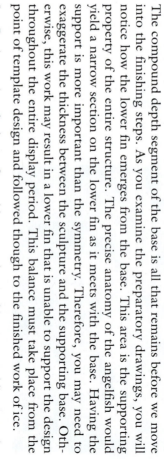

2. Use the chipper to scoop out the meat of the base toward the side of the fish (Figure 10-23). You will not need to remove this entire section to define the line of the fish meeting the base at this point. This defining line will be done later. This step is simply needed to form greater shape in the base.

3. The corners of the base can now be rounded off with the chipper (Figure 10-24). This step will give the water below the fish more shape and prevent a blocky-looking base.

4. Follow the same technique on the opposite side. Once this step is completed, the base will take shape within the design of the fish (Figure 10-25).

5. As a final step in this process, you should step 5 feet away from each angle of the sculpture to see whether all areas match the proportion of your intended design.

Figure 10-24
The corners of the base are rounded off with the chipper.

SUMMARY

The third dimension emerges as ice segments are removed. This step begins by visualizing the areas to be removed with preparatory drawings and possibly a carving design model. Break-away points are drawn on the block, which will determine which areas will be kept in the sculpture and which will be removed. Hand tools are used in this exercise to develop skills. Learning how the hand tools feel as they remove the ice is a key point in this lesson. The carving at this point will be in proportion on all sides, with a rough and blocky surface.

REVIEW QUESTIONS

Matching

Match the term with its definition.

___ 1. third-dimension visualization

___ 2. third-dimension preparatory drawing

a. lines that indicate which ice should be removed and which areas should be saved

b. seeing what the carving will look like once the excess ice has been removed

Figure 10-25   The angelfish with the third-dimension carving step completed.

—— 3. carving design model

—— 4. break-away points

Multiple Choice

5. Which of the following is *not* a tool used for third-dimension visualization?

a. a photograph from a previous ice carving

b. a diagram showing which segments should be used

c. a model of the design

d. a wooden template

6. Break-away point markings should be made with what tool?

a. flat chisel

b. six-prong chipper

c. iron

d. hand saw

True or False

7. A carving "comes to life" during the second-dimensional carving phase.

8. Once the excess ice is removed, the image will be rough and will need additional rounding and shaping.

9. Carving an identical finished ice sculpture makes an excellent life-size model.

10. Don't add the details during the third-dimension carving phase, because the sculpture will lose its definition from melting by the time the rest of the third-dimension areas are cut.

11. Always leave the narrowest point at least 3 inches wide to allow for melting.

12. The supporting property for an entire structure is where the carving meets the base.

c. a replica of the intended carving

d. a diagram that shows which ice segments should be removed

one of the student's blocks. Use the chipper to scratch the marking lines. Choose a student who feels unsure of this step (there could be many) early enough in the exercise to benefit the majority of the remaining carvers.

2. Keep an eye out for students cutting inside the break-away points. Explain how this is essentially damaging their finished piece. Reemphasize how ice can always be removed, but it cannot be replaced in a 3-D relief sculpture.

3. The hand saw rounding technique of a concave area should be demonstrated for students to show how pressure and angular pitch will apply.

4. Look out for carvers who spend too much time applying detail to one particular section, such as the mouth. Encourage the student to move on to the rest of the third-dimension area first.

5. Explain to the students how the curvature of the tail portion provides movement to the design. A natural-looking image is the artistic portion of a sculpture. Use examples in your discussion: A trotting reindeer is preferred over a standing one, and an expression of arms by a human figure is more interesting than a figure standing at attention. This extra step of tail curvature is a basis to how designs should be composed from the point of paper drawing to the point of applying the third dimension.

6. Pay attention to those who are cutting the area next to the base. This area can easily be cut through too far, leaving an undesirable marking impression on the support structure.

7. Take the opportunity to demonstrate how to create the separation of the compound depth segment between the body and the base. Explain how the lower body will be wider in the middle and tapered toward the end to provide supporting structure to the finished piece as it melts on display.

INSTRUCTOR'S NOTES

1. Use the diagrams provided in this book for the angelfish to show how the top view and side views are outlined in the visualization of the third dimension. It is suggested to make a class demonstration of doing this on

Rounding and Shaping

"Whether you listen to a piece of music, or a poem, or look at a picture, or a piece of sculpture, what matters about it is not what it is not what it has in common with others of its kind, but what is singularly its own."

Basil Bunting

Learning Objectives

After you have finished reading this unit, you should be able to:

- Demonstrate how to use a hand saw to further shape the ice carving
- Use flat chisels for shaping and rounding out corners
- Illustrate how to use the V-notch chisel to define separate design segments
- Apply an individual impression of artistry to the base
- Explain how power tools can be used as an alternative to hand tools
- Describe how stepping away from the carving will aid in visualizing proportion

Terms to Know

flat side chisel stroke	design segment definition	die grinder
beveled side chisel stroke	chain saw shaping	die grinder bit
flat chisel shaping	disk sander rounding	die grinder channeling
flat chisel rounding		

It is the shaping and rounding techniques that can begin to turn a templated, cookie-cutter carving into a one-of-a-kind sculpture. Once you have completed the steps in this chapter, you will have a carving that is completely shaped into its final third-dimensional design and ready for the detail finishing work described in Chapter 12.

The steps necessary to sculpt the angelfish will be described in detail for usage with hand tools. We will also include a section on rounding and shaping with power tools.

HAND SAW USAGE

Follow these steps to smooth and round the tail segment:

1. Use the hand saw to redefine the concave areas between the tail segments. Now that the original 10 inches of ice from the silhouette step have been reduced to a lesser thickness, you will be able to make these curves take shape easier and with more precision. Use the pulling motion along with a twist of the wrist to carve a clean curve between the dorsal fin and top tail. Draw the saw upward toward the dorsal fin (Figure 11-1), top fin and tail (Figures 11-2 and 11-3), and tail to lower fin. Notice how the dorsal fin area is wide and round enough to curl through the entire curve with a single stroke. However, the tail areas form more of a point and should be addressed from the top and bottom of the opening and meet at the point of the curve.

2. Next, use the hand saw to define the point of separation from the base and the lower fin. This maneuver will happen by cutting straight in toward the point of separation from both the upper and lower areas of the angle (Figures 11-4 and 11-5). Twisting the wrist is not necessary here. Use light

Figure 11-1
The hand saw is being used to round out the final detail of the curvature between the dorsal fin and the top tail fin.

Figure 11-2
Use the hand saw in a pulling motion with light strokes to define the curvature between the upper back fin and the tail fin.

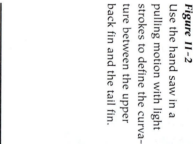

Figure 11-3
Use the hand saw in a rounding technique to define the curvature of the upper tail area for its final finished shape. The curve between the upper back fin and tail fin should now meet closely with the template design of origin.

Figure 11-4
Use the hand saw to define and shape the curve of the lower fin.

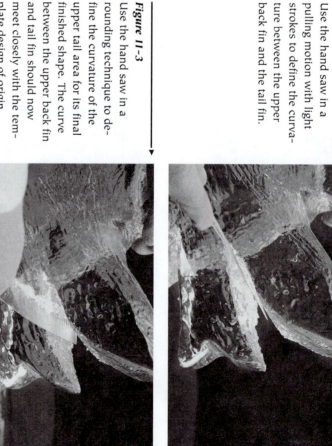

strokes to prevent damage to the intended design, especially toward the point of the angle.

3. Apply this same technique on the front side between the base and the head section (Figures 11-6 and 11-7).

Flat Chisel Side View

▲ **Figure 11-8**   This image shows the distinctive difference between the straight and flat sides of a flat ice carving chisel. All ice carving chisels, regardless of width or shape, will have a straight and a beveled side.

FLAT CHISEL USAGE

The flat chisel will be used in the next steps to carve the dorsal fin, tail, head, body, and base. If more than one size of chisel is available, the choice of tool will depend on the size of the area to be sculpted. In general, a 2-inch blade will suffice for most areas. Larger, flat chisel blades will help to do the job faster in larger areas and narrow-faced chisels will be better in tight, narrow areas.

Before we cut away any more ice, we should discuss the shape and construction of the flat chisel's face. There is a distinctive difference between the flat and beveled sides of the chisel (Figure 11-8). A **flat side chisel stroke** is an application of the flat chisel for shaving away areas of a flat surface or a convex curve. A **beveled side chisel stroke** is an application of the flat chisel for shaving away areas of a concave curve.

The use of the flat chisel is predominantly separated into two functions: shaping and rounding. **Flat chisel shaping** is a process of narrowing an area to its final shape. **Flat chisel rounding** is a process of softening corners to bring two flat faces together.

CARVING STEPS OF THE ANGELFISH

Dorsal Fin

To illustrate the flat chisel methods, we will begin by carving the dorsal fin.

1. If the dorsal fin is still boxy, this is the time to create a point. Start by using the flat side chisel stroke to shape the dorsal fin on both sides to bring the tip to a narrower point (Figure 11-9).
2. Next, round the fin while using the flat side chisel stroke (Figure 11-10).
3. Finish the dorsal fin by using the beveled side chisel stroke to blend the area between the fin and the body of the fish (Figure 11-11). Each of the steps outlined above should be performed equally on both sides of the fin.

▲ **Figure 11-5**
Use a pulling motion with the hand saw toward the base to define the curvature between the tail fin and the base.

▲ **Figure 11-6**
Use the hand saw to finish the area between the head and base.

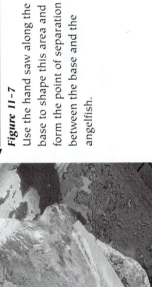

▲ **Figure 11-7**
Use the hand saw along the base to shape this area and form the point of separation between the base and the angelfish.

Figure 11-9
The flat chisel shaping technique is used to carve the dorsal fin into its final shape.

Figure 11-10
The flat side chisel stroke is again applied to create rounded edges of the dorsal fin.

Figure 11-11
The beveled side chisel stroke is applied to smooth out the area between the body and the dorsal fin.

Figure 11-12
The large flat chisel shapes the convex side of the tail to its final form.

Tail

By following the diagrams and directions outlined in Chapter 10 for a curved tail, you should have a curvature that leads to a convex and consequently a concave side.

1. Shape the convex side by using the large flat side of the chisel (Figure 11-12).
2. Use the beveled side of the large flat chisel to shape the concave side (Figure 11-13).
3. Use the beveled side of the medium flat chisel to round the corners (Figure 11-14). Round all corners of all fins to bring the flat surfaces together.

These steps demonstrate the difference between shaping and rounding. The tail should still have enough ice left for some finishing work. Shaping is best described as forming the basic shape of the segment being carved, while rounding is the act of bringing the finished shaped sides together. The fins of an angelfish are round by nature, so they need to be rounded.

Carver's Note

This concept of appropriately using the flat or beveled side of the flat chisel not only applies to the fin of an angelfish. This also is a fundamental understanding of how a flat chisel should be applied to ice.

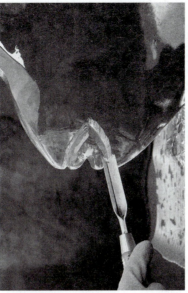

Figure 11-16

Use the V-notch chisel to sketch the curve of the upper lip. Start with the light stroke shown. Repeat by following the same line until the lip is separated from the body.

Figure 11-17

The small V-notch chisel is used again to sketch the same shape to the bottom lip.

4. Next, round off the tail fin areas. The angelfish should have a slightly cornered area where the fins meet the body. The hand saw and ice knife can be used for rounding, while the flat chisel will provide the finishing touches (Figure 11-15). Repeat the same steps on the lower fin area and on the opposite side.

Head

The head area must be shaped and rounded similar to the tail and top portions.

1. Identify where the lips should go. Sometimes the finite details dictate where the rest of the sculpture will go. This is again the time to take out the V-notch chisel. Make the lip segment as big as it would be on the biggest fish you ever saw or hoped to reel in. All this will melt and become less detailed by the minute. This is demonstrated in Figures 11-16 and 11-17. You may want to refer to your original line drawing to follow this

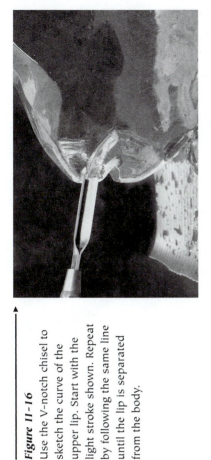

Figure 11-13

The beveled side chisel stroke is applied with the large flat chisel to bring the tail to a point along the thickness of the body.

Figure 11-14

The medium flat chisel is used on the beveled side to round the cornered areas of the tail fin.

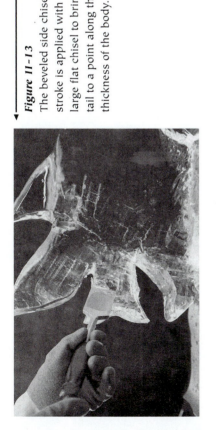

Figure 11-15

The ice knife is used to round out the area where the top fin and the tail fin meet the body.

Figure 11-18
The V-notch chisel has defined a distinctive area between the lips and the body portion of the angelfish. This technique of segment separation is used on all sculptures.

Figure 11-20
The beveled side is used to round off the area between the head and the dorsal fin.

pattern. Use the V-notch chisel, with a deeper impression, to define the design segment (Figure 11-18). The **design segment definition** is the area where particular lines are drawn to create image and definition in the sculpture design.

2. Use the flat chisel to narrow the body area side of the lips to bring out this area for full view (Figure 11-19).

3. Use the flat chisel beveled side again to round off the upper and lower head areas. The top will be rounded to join with the dorsal fin (Figure 11-20). The lower area will join to the base (Figure 11-21). The mouth and lips will need to be groomed to natural appearance. Do this by rounding off the tiny corners of the front lip. This is best done with a narrow flat chisel (Figure 11-22).

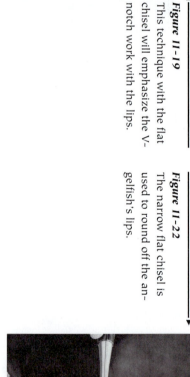

Figure 11-19
This technique with the flat chisel will emphasize the V-notch work with the lips.

Figure 11-21
The medium flat chisel is used to round off the area between the head and base.

Figure 11-22
The narrow flat chisel is used to round off the angelfish's lips.

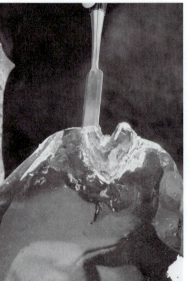

Figure 11-24
The V-notch chisel is used to form a point of separation between the lower area of the fish and the water portion of the base.

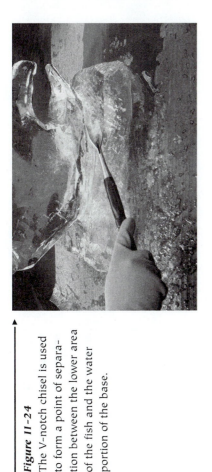

Figure 11-23
Use the flat side chisel stroke to shape the front side of the body.

Body

Once all the appendages, such as the fins, head, and base, have been finished, the body should be brought into its final shape as well. The center of the body is best left as the thickest portion.

1. Use the medium-width flat chisel to give the sides of the body a contour that blends in with the exterior fins, head, and base (Figure 11-23). This step should also remove any rough areas where previous tools may have left a jagged finish.
2. Turn the chisel over and use the beveled side chisel stroke to shape the back side of the body.

Remember that the underlying purpose of the base is for support. Therefore, a solid structure and a wider surface area will need to be in place for the fish to stand on its own. Now the carver should work on the base to make it as wide as possible though possessing as many curves as necessary to make it look natural.

5. Make the midsection of the base into a concave area to form a natural wave (Figure 11-26). This portion of the sculpture holds few boundaries as long as it supports the main portion, which in this case is the angelfish.
6. Continue with the flat chisel around the base to form a water-like shape (Figure 11-27).

Figure 11-25
The medium flat chisel is used to shape the lower area of the body into the groove where the V-notch line separates the base portion.

Base

The base will need shaping as much as the focal point for this angelfish design.

1. Use a V-notch chisel to define the line where the lower fin and the water portion of the base will meet (Figure 11-24).
2. Use the flat chisel to narrow and shape the fish where it meets the base (Figure 11-25).
3. Follow the same concept on the opposite side.

The base area leaves the most open area for artistic impression as it remains an undefined area in most line drawings. Use this opportunity to create the extra credit to your piece and the attention to detail that separates an average sculpture from a great one.

4. Continue by forming the base to appear as a natural body of water.

Figure 11-26
The medium flat chisel is applied to demonstrate how can be performed with power tools. The same work to the middle base can be cut concavely to form a water appearance.

Figure 11-27
The base has been shaped to form a water-like appearance.

Pro's Corner

The shape of the base does not need to wait until the last step, especially in a warm carving area where detail will be lost through melting. The base is often shaped throughout the steps of this chapter, and finer detail areas are saved for last.

Power Tool Usage

We used hand tools to teach the steps of shaping and rounding. The same work can be performed with power tools. It is important for the beginning student to learn the techniques of using hand tools, and that is our focus; first, we will include a brief overview of using power tools.

Safety Note

All power tools must be handled with respect. The speed with which they can deliver results to your sculpture is no comparison to the danger that they represent if they are handled improperly. Be conscious of loose clothing, which can become tangled. Always use GFCI power protection in wet areas. Keep both hands on the tools at all times. Allow the tool to come to a complete stop before setting it down. Use sharp chains and die grinder bits as the application of dull edges can lead the carver to add additional pressure, which could lead to accidents.

Chain Saw

The chain saw can be used for the shaping work. For example, the dorsal fin could be shaped to its final tapered design by cutting with the chain saw along the line the flat chisel left behind. The tip of the cutting bar is often used for tight corners to remove a small portion at a time. The tail area would be an example of tip cutting. **Chain saw shaping** is the carving performed with a chain saw to bring the finished angles and final shape to the design. The beginning carver should become very comfortable with the handling of a chain saw before attempting any finishing work with this tool.

Disk Sander

The disk sander is often used for rounding. **Disk sander rounding** is a process of using a disk sander to smooth out rough areas and corners on the ice. The square corner along the edge of all the fins could be rounded with this tool. To begin using the disk sander, hold the tool with both hands and turn on the power. Apply light pressure to the ice along the corners to be sanded (Figure 11-28). Usually the top portion of the disk is used for rounding. A coarse sanding disk is most often used for ice sculpture.

Figure 11-29
The angled die grinder resembles the shape of a V-notched chisel.

Figure 11-30
The die grinder's angled bit carves the base separation area of the angelfish as the V-notch chisel would.

Figure 11-28
The top portion of the sander's surface is used to round off the top of the dorsal fin.

The disk sander is also handy for flattening out rough surfaces. If the sides of the fish are still rough from the cuts made during the three-dimensional phase, they can be smoothed over with this tool. A flat chisel can perform the same function, though it may take a little longer.

SAFETY NOTE

The disk sander can throw particles of ice in many directions, so the operator should use protective eyewear. The particles can also strike others standing nearby. Be conscious of those standing near you when using the disk sander. Always allow the disk to come to a full stop before setting the tool down.

Die Grinder

The **die grinder** is a high-speed rotary tool that shears the surface of the ice to form a channel. The shape of the channel is determined by the bit. A **die grinder bit** is a removable attachment used to cut channels of various shapes and sizes. **Die grinder channeling** is the act of using a die grinder tool to form a groove.

The angled V-shaped bit will form a channel similar to that of a V-notched chisel (Figures 11-29 and 11-30). The 1/4-inch straight bit will carve a channel that can be used as a relief cut in an area to be defined, such as the lips of the

angelfish (Figures 11-31 and 11-32). The end mill shearing bits (available in straight and tapered designs) are used for rounding off corners and cleaning out small tight areas (Figures 11-33 and 11-34 along with Figures 11-35 and 11-36). The die grinder is also used for detail and scroll work, which will be covered in Chapter 12.

Figure 11-31
This diagram illustrates the narrow channel and shape of the ¼-inch die grinder bit.

Figure 11-34
Notice the four-sided cutting edge of the tapered end mill shearing bit.

Figure 11-32
The ¼-inch straight flute die grinder bit is used to separate the lip area from the body. This bit can be used for many other points of separation.

Figure 11-35
The straight-sided end mill spiral bit is used to finish the curvature between the upper back fin and the tail fin. This action is similar to the hand saw work described earlier in this chapter.

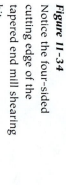

Figure 11-33
A straight-sided end mill shearing bit. This would likely be used in place of the hand saw for rounding out tight corners.

Figure 11-36
The tapered three-flute large conical spiral end mill shearing bit is used for rounding the corners, as would the beveled side of a flat chisel.

Carver's Note

Some may think of the die grinder as another version of a standard drill or a power screwdriver. These tools are not qualified substitutes as they do not have the revolutions per minute (RPMs) to cut the ice efficiently. The average drill rotates at 1,000 to 2,000 RPMs, while most die grinders turn at over 20,000 RPMs.

Pro's Corner

Carbide die grinder bits are often worth the extra expense as they tend to stay sharp far longer than do standard steel bits. Die grinder bits are not easily sharpened, and sharp tools are key to forming a clean channel in the ice. Always dry your bits off after usage and store them in a dry place to prevent rust.

_____ 3. Smoothing out the concave areas between the tail segments

_____ 4. Shaving away the flat surface

_____ 5. Shaping the curve of the upper lip

_____ 6. Concave curve

_____ 7. Convex curve

c. flat chisel (beveled side)

d. V-notch chisel

Short Answer

8. Explain the difference between a flat side chisel stroke and a beveled side chisel stroke.

9. List four suggested safety precautions when using power tools in general.
   1.
   2.
   3.
   4.

10. List two safety precautions that should be heeded when using a disk sander.
    1.
    2.

INSTRUCTOR'S NOTES

1. Demonstrate the light stroke usage of the pistol-grip hand saw. This technique will illustrate the difference between a strong cutting and pulling stroke used for a relief cut versus the light scraping stroke used for rounding out a curve.

2. Demonstrate the finite details of flat chisel usage. The best time for its use is during the shaping phase. Emphasize the advantages of the flat side and of the beveled side.

3. The V-notch chisel will be used primarily in the next chapter. Use this segment to reintroduce this tool for purposes other than the tracing step followed in the template transfer section. Rather than detail, this is the time to relate the lines of the original drawing to the finished piece. If a student is losing the way in the vision, have him or her transfer the line drawing to the ice for basic lines. This concept starts with the area where the fish meets the base. The head is next, and the body line to the tail fins could be last. The students who read this book should know what to do, although some students may need this process to be done for them.

4. The base area design is one of the areas best left to individual artistic ability. As long as the angelfish still has the support necessary for display, this part can't go wrong. Allow the students to express their own image of what

SUMMARY

Once the steps of this chapter are complete, the only sculpture work remaining will be the fine details to be discussed in the next chapter. All the steps of shaping and rounding can be achieved with a hand saw, flat chisels and a V-notch chisel. As with every step in the process of ice carving, it is advised to step away from the sculpture to view its form for any imperfections. Corrections to shape and rounding should take place before moving on to the detail. The angelfish should have its final shape, along with its base, when this section is complete.

REVIEW QUESTIONS

Matching

Select the suggested tool to the job. Tools can be used more than once.

1. Body
2. Marking the point of separation between the lower area of the fish and the water portion of the base.

a. flat chisel (flat side)

b. hand saw

water should look like under a fish. Rest assured, every sculpture will look different at the base. This book of ice carving is not meant to turn all students into fine artists but to assist those who have the interest. An evaluation of artistic ability is also a fair judgment for a student ice carver. Many of the steps to carving a single design are defined in this book. The base could best outline individual expression and attention to detail for a grading element.

5. Power tool usage and coverage will depend on the battery of equipment available to cover this subject area. If all of the tools listed in this chapter are available, their usage should be demonstrated. In most cases, a tool is not available for every student. Therefore, a format for finishing the piece for a first-time student is covered in detail. However, these tools are often used in the professional industry. Make an effort to demonstrate these tools if the facilities are available.

6. Once a sculpture is finished with the rounding and shaping portion of the ice carving process, take a step back to evaluate its proportion and preparedness for the next step of detail. This may be a good exercise for all students to observe.

The Finishing Touches

"I sometimes wonder if the hand is not more sensitive to the beauties of sculpture than the eyes."

Helen Keller

Learning Objectives

After you have finished reading this unit, you should be able to:

- Visualize the finished sculpture
- Reference a model, line drawing, or the imagination to apply the finishing touches to a carving
- Use hand tools to apply the finishing touches
- Discuss how power tools are used to apply the finishing touches
- Identify areas where detail will melt faster on display
- Prepare the base for finishing detail with or without lifting handles
- Describe how to clean the sculpture with water or heat when needed

Terms to Know

visualization
detail visualization
fine shaping detail
decorative lines
groove detail line
gouge chisel

channel detail line
detail model
detail line drawing
allowance for melting
sculpture cleaning
hand broom

air broom
heat gun
water washing
die grinder finishing
end mill die grinder bits
base lifting handles

The finishing work breathes life into the sculpture. Once you have completed the steps in this chapter, you will have a carving that is finished and ready for storage or display. The details on how to properly store or display your finished ice sculpture are outlined in Chapter 13.

This chapter will outline the finishing steps for the angelfish or any other ice carving project. The chapter will also discuss the use of hand tools in finishing work for beginning students and power tools for an alternative approach. The final step to be covered is cleaning the piece once it is completed.

VISUALIZATION

In prior chapters, we discussed the concept of visualization. **Visualization** is the basic practice of examining the ice and formulating an idea of what the sculpture will look like after a carving step is completed. Visualizing the entire process from the basic uncut block to the finished sculpture can be overwhelming. This is especially true for a beginning carver. The progression of this book has taken the whole process of the project and broken it down into logical steps. Visualization can be simpler when a carver focuses on one segment during a single carving step. For example, shaping the tail fins is simplified when the second dimension is followed by the third dimension and then completed by shaping and rounding. Visualizing the finished tail from the initial point of the solid block would require more experience. On occasion, through the step-by-step process, the carver will still need to step away from the block to examine how all the segments are flowing together to form the entire sculpture.

Detail visualization is the practice of formulating where the fine shaping details and decorative lines will be carved. The **fine shaping detail** is the smaller segments left for the end of the carving process to avoid excessive melting. A combination of V-notch and small flat chisels are often used for fine shaping detail. Facial features are often left for the fine shaping detail portion of the carving process. This book's color insert illustrates a Styrofoam detail model of the angelfish.

Decorative lines are a combination of grooves and/or channels, formed by various tools, to highlight the detail of the original design. For example, the lines carved on the tail fins of the angelfish add detail and will enhance the carving's overall appearance.

A **groove detail line** is a decorative impression, drawn along the surface, to form a single-angled V-notch shape with the V-notch chisel or a concave curved line with the gouge chisel. The **gouge chisel** has a curved blade. The gouge has either an interior or an exterior bevel, and it is available with various curvatures. See Chapter 4, Tools of the Trade, for further explanation. The gouge is one of the least used tools, compared to the flat and V-notch varieties, though its use

still adds another component to your carving abilities. Some carvers using power tools may choose to use a die grinder with an angled or rounded bit to form groove detail lines.

A **channel detail line** is a decorative impression, drawn through the surface, to form a double-cornered line within the ice. This type of line is most commonly carved with the tip of a chain saw or with a straight die grinder bit. Both the groove detail and channel detail lines are methods commonly used by ice sculptors. Each practice has its own benefits. A channel detail line will hold its shape better during the melting process than will a groove detail line. A groove detail line is typically more visually appealing, as the surfaces within the groove are easier to see and will be enhanced if display lighting is to be used.

Detail visualization is best followed through the use of a **detail model**, which is a life-size or scale version of the carving design used to guide the sculptor in visualizing the fine shaping or detail lines to be carved. These models are very handy for the third dimensional detail visualization such as the lip structure of the angelfish.

Detail line drawings can be used instead of a detail model. **Detail line drawings** are sketches used for visualization that demonstrate the areas where detail lines will be drawn on the ice. Line drawings showcase the areas where groove lines should be placed. Such detailed drawings will also help with the placement of detail shaping, though some use of imagination will still apply when shaping the third dimensional areas. The detail line drawing is best stored in a clear plastic sheet protector with tape sealing the open end to prevent water damage.

The best example of a model would be to have a life-size finished sculpture to copy. Another detail model option would be a smaller version of the design, which demonstrates the detail lines you intend to follow in a permanent medium such as wood or plastic. Such models are not always available for each design a carver intends to sculpt. Therefore, a detail line drawing is an economical and handy substitute. In many cases, the carver will revert back to the original template line drawing. When the drawing was used for building a template, only the perimeter lines were needed. For detail work, the interior lines on this drawing can be used for the detail visualization. Refer to Figure 9-1 for the half block angelfish.

Figure 12-1   The V-notch chisel is used to make the groove detail line between the fin and body portion.

THE ANGELFISH DESIGN

We will continue using the angelfish as our example.

Body

The finished detail of the body will depend on the tools applied. A set of grooved detail lines can be applied with hand chisels. The channel detail lines are applied with a die grinder or the tip of a chain saw.

A student using hand tools will apply the V-notch chisel to follow the lines of the model or template line drawing supplied. The illustrations in this book will leave a finished appearance using hand chisels. Power tools are discussed further in Chapter 14, Advanced Skills.

Begin by carving a groove around the back fin area from the top to the bottom (Figure 12-1). Follow these lines on the opposite side as well.

1. The scales of the angelfish can be detailed in multiple ways. We will demonstrate two methods, known as the curved diamond shape and the curled scale method.

Figure 12-2   The V-notch chisel is drawn across the body to form the curved diamond shaped scales.

2. The diamond curve is usually easier and faster as it can be drawn with curved lines made from the V-notch chisel (Figure 12-2). This pattern also follows the template line drawing provided in this book. The curled scale method is formed by a series of brisk strokes paired with the twist of the V-notch chisel to make individual scales on the body of a fish (Figure 12-3).

3. The opposite side of your sculpture should match the choice of scale pattern carved on the front. Continue by detailing the scales on the opposite side.

Head

Finishing the head is simple. Draw a curved detail line behind the eyes and lips at a point that separates the head from the body.

1. Use the template line drawing as an example of this curved line placement. A medium to large V-notch chisel is best for forming this line. Be aware, this is a good time to start in the middle of the line placement (directly behind the mouth) and take upward strokes for the top area and then carve the lower area with a downward stroke from the center. This principle of two-stepping a

Figure 12-3   The V-notch chisel is applied with a brisk twisting stoke to form a pattern of individual curled scales.

detail line is commonly practiced when the position of your body, or the angle of the chisel, is difficult to achieve by carving from one end to the other.

2. Finish the head area by carving a few short strokes below the mouth to produce the gills.

3. Continue by following the same steps on the opposite side.

Fins

1. Use the medium flat chisel to bring the fin tips to a narrow point. Remember, a sharp point is not required, as the melting process will do this for you. The finished product should be natural and meet within a 1-inch thickness. Again, the allowance for melting shall apply.

2. Use the detail line drawing as a tool to visualize where the fin lines will be carved. A V-notch chisel is best used for carving these grooves with hand tools. As the fins are rather delicate, use light pressure while starting from the body and working your way toward the tip of the fin (Figure 12-4). Also

Figure 12-4   The V-notch chisel is used to carve the groove detail lines of the dorsal fin. Notice how the lines pull out of the ice before the tip of the fin is reached.

note that these lines are best finished before the tip of the fin is reached. Otherwise, the fin tips will have an unappealing zigzag shape. This motion of carving will put the sharpness of your chisels to the test. If your chisel is dull, you may be forced to apply added pressure, resulting in a broken fin.

3. Continue with the same steps on the opposite side.

Some carvers using power tools may choose to create channel lines with the chain saw tip or a die grinder. This choice may not leave as clean of an appearance, though it is often quicker.

Lips

To finish the lips, use a model, detailed line drawing, or your imagination. To compensate for melting, always exaggerate the size of the lips. This concept of the **allowance for melting** is a skill obtained through experience with anticipation of what will happen to the ice as it melts on display.

The process of melting should always be a consideration, depending on the arena for display. The average revenue sculpture for a four-hour display will

Figure 12-7
The exterior beveled gouge chisel cuts out the interior of the mouth.

Figure 12-5
The small flat chisel is used as a rounding tool for the lips.

require some thickness of structure, while a competition piece in a freezing environment will have a delicate detail for judging upon completion. Rather than cut to the point of no return, the student should lean toward the principle that ice will always melt away.

1. To finish the lips, redefine them by using the V-notch chisel to outline the lip formation.
2. Create the same detail on the opposite side.
3. Use the narrow flat chisel to round and shape the lips (Figure 12-5). If you have an interior beveled gouge chisel, the same shape could be applied with a finer rounding effect (Figure 12-6).
4. Use an exterior beveled gouge chisel to open out the interior of the mouth and provide definition to the lips (Figure 12-7). This technique can be applied to the upper and lower portions of the mouth's interior.

Eyes

The eyes of the angelfish can be carved in a variety of ways. A simple method is to simply drill a round hole where the eye belongs. For the sake of artistic impression, we will carve an eye socket while leaving a ball in the center.

1. Begin carving the eye socket with a small V-notch chisel. Form a round circle about 2 inches in circumference. The circle should also leave a round dot of ice in the center to represent the eyeball (Figure 12-8). Because this maneuver requires a sharp twisting movement, it is best to start with a shallow groove, which establishes your line. Then make the groove deeper by tracing over the circle a few times until it is deep enough to leave a lasting impression. This method of tracing a shallow line followed by a deeper one is practiced on many chisel strokes.
2. Follow the same steps for the opposite eye.

Figure 12-8
The V-notch chisel carves the circle of the eye while leaving a dot in the center for the eyeball.

Figure 12-6
The interior beveled gouge chisel is used to provide a rounded shape to the lips.

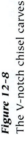

Carver's Note

A perfectionist may be tempted to round off the eyeball with a small flat chisel. This step is unnecessary, as the melting process will round it off quickly. The only exception may be when a carver is working in a freezing environment and the sculpture will be displayed in a freezing area as well.

Base

Most single-block carvings will incorporate a base structure under the design of the sculpture. Some exceptions may apply for advanced compositions that incorporate the base as a portion of the primary design. This book focuses on the beginner's concept of learning the art of ice sculpture. Therefore, the carving student should plan a supportive base for all sculpture designs.

In a similar respect to the value of artistic impression, the base should be decorated and finished in some way or another. All too often this area is left untouched by novice carvers. This lack of attention leaves an unappealing square and blocky segment on an otherwise finished sculpture.

In the case of the angelfish design, we have encouraged the student to form a body of water under the fish. The basic natural shape, which could nearly be any shape at all except square and blocky, should be rounded and shaped at this point to resemble some form of curvature. The image of water in the finishing process can be carved with a variety of tools. The hand tools would involve a V-notch chisel and/or a gouge chisel.

For the angelfish base, one could follow the flow of water with a movement and a wave toward the back. The water can be created by using both the V-notch chisel and the gouge chisel (Figures 12-9 and 12-10). This area could be expressed in nearly any form and still look good as long as the fish takes shape and the sculpture has the support it needs.

Figure 12-9
The base is being carved with the V-notch chisel for the wave area in the rear.

Figure 12-10
The gouge chisel is used to carve the rolling water toward the front.

A Final Look

Now is the time to step away from the sculpture one last time to see whether anything was missed. All the steps of detail should be applied by this point, and look again to see that each segment flows from one to another. There may be a need to touch up a fin line or reshape an eye that has melted a bit while the rest of the carving was being finished. Go ahead and set the lines a little deeper if needed. In some cases, the hand saw may need to be applied in light strokes between the base and the body or even the opening of the mouth. This last look, on all sides, is your project's test of completion.

Sculpture Cleaning

Once all the details have been applied and the sculpture work is finished, there may still be ice shavings scattered over the carving. The final step before storing or displaying is to perform these unsightly fragments. The base is most likely to have

form **sculpture cleaning**, which is the process of removing unwanted ice fragments from the finished sculpture by use of water, air, heat, or broom sweeping. If the temperature in the carving area is above freezing, the large piles of ice shavings are easily removed with the hands or more often with a **hand broom**, which is made of straw or nylon.

In a freezing carving environment, an air broom could be used to remove the fragments, as the surfaces will be dry and fragments can easily be blown off the surface. An **air broom** is a power tool emitting a high-velocity concentrated airflow to clean dry ice shavings from the surface of a finished sculpture. It can be as large as a shop vacuum used with reverse air flow or a more commonly used commercial tool that resembles a hair dryer without heat. Air brooms are available from suppliers listed in the appendices.

A freezing environment may also call for the use of a heat gun to loosen unwanted shavings that have fused to the sculpture. A **heat gun** is a commercially built power tool used to throw a concentrated flow of heated air onto the ice. It can also create controlled melting, which may be desired to soften the surface. This practice is often used in outdoor carving venues where the conditions are freezing and the sculpture will be displayed right away in a freezing area. Heat guns often are used in winter ice carving competitions.

SAFETY NOTE

Electrical shock could occur with use of a standard household hair dryer. Such hair dryers are not recommended for use as an air broom or a heat gun because the insulation usually not suitable for working in wet environments.

The final touch of most sculpture cleaning is to perform **water washing**, which is the step of cleaning an ice carving to leave a smooth and sparkling finish. This should be done with cold water to prevent excess melting. This step will wash away most remaining ice fragments and leave a clean appearance. A garden hose could be used, ideally with a spray nozzle. A simple bucket of water and cup to splash the carving is another choice. A squirt bottle or even a spray bottle would be another option. Be aware that this will rapidly melt away detail, so the water should be applied sparingly.

At this point, the sculpture is finished (Figure 12-11). Now is the time to either store the carving in a freezer or to move it rapidly to the display area.

Figure 12-11   The finished and cleaned angelfish ice sculpture.

Figure 12-12
A straight shaping die grinder bit is used to detail the base.

POWER TOOL USAGE
FOR THE FINISHING TOUCHES

As discussed throughout *Ice Carving 101*, the focus of study for the first-time ice carver is to understand the application of hand tools. A large classroom venue may lack the resources of power and equipment to allow each student to finish a sculpture with power tools. The element of safety and supervision is also a concern for schools or any other learning environment. As a point of reference for self-study and practice experience, the optional use of power tools is reviewed to complete the content of this book.

Die Grinder Finishing

Die grinder finishing uses a die grinder fitted with various shaped bits. These bits are used to create channels, grooves, shaping, or rounding in the application of finishing detail (Figures 12-12, 12-13, and 12-14).

All of the detail lines for the angelfish could have been carved with a die grinder. The use of a V-shaped bit would leave a groove similar to the shape of the V-notch chisel. The use of a straight bit would leave a channeled detail line.

When using a die grinder, always keep both hands on the tool and follow the pattern illustrated in the detail line drawing. Some professional carvers use **end mill die grinder bits**, which are straight or slightly conical for shaping or rounding. Unlike the V-bit, they are not often applied by piercing into the ice. Instead, the side of the bit is pressed against the sculpture to shave away ice, similar to the use of a flat chisel. The straight shaping bit is used more for shaping and is especially handy for carving interior curves. The conical shaping tip can be used for rounding. This tip can also be used to create the scales by making a backward

Figure 12-13
A conical end mill shaping die grinder bit is being used to shape the lips of the angelfish.

C shape over the body of the fish (Figure 12-15). Try overlapping Cs for different type of scales (Figure 12-16). Occasionally, a conical shaping bit with a narrow tip may be used in a similar fashion to the straight bit of a V-bit to leave a groove line.

Chain Saw Finishing

The chain saw can also be used for some of the finishing work. Many professionals may use this method in the interest of saving time. However, the beginner should avoid using the chain saw for detail finishing.

The tip of the bar can be used to form channel lines on the fins, the diamond pattern of the scales, and the water lines in the base. Although this method can carve the detail work often faster than hand tools and possibly even a die grinder, the cut is usually a crude form of detail. The lips and eyes could also be shaped with precision handling of the chain saw tip. Yet, this would require a fine touch with a bulky tool meant for larger work.

Figure 12-14
The die grinder V-bit is used to form detail lines on the tail.

The chain saw channel lines will form an acceptable finishing detail for some designs. Experience will dictate when the chain saw may be applied for finishing detail.

BASE LIFTING HANDLES

The half-block angelfish outlined in the book will be light enough to lift and move easily. The area between the base and the lower sides of the fish also provide a sturdy area in which to cradle and grip the carving while moving or positioning it. Larger sculptures may be heavier. Some designs may also lack a handy area to grab for a sure grip while lifting the sculpture into place. An example would be the swan design (Figure 12-17). The neck

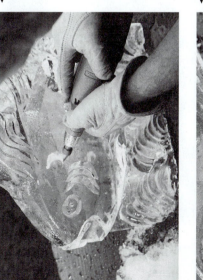

Figure 12-15
The conical end mill die grinder bit is used for creating the scales.

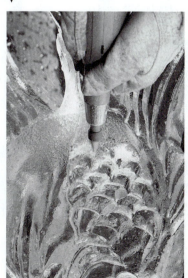

Figure 12-16
Overlap the shapes to create realistic scales.

Figure 12-17   The swan demonstrates how it would be difficult to pick this sculpture off the ground as there is nothing sturdy to grab on to. The neck may break off it were used as a handle.

Figure 12-18   The chain saw is used to cut handles into the base.

Figure 12-19
This photo shows the base handles at the bottom of the base.

is one of the few areas to grab, but this area is far too delicate to support the weight if it were used for a lifting handle. The technique of lifting sculptures onto display will be covered more in depth in the next chapter.

A common practice in the industry is to carve **base lifting handles**, which are rectangular holes cut into the base with a chain saw to allow the hands to slip into the structure, allowing the carving to be easily lifted.

1. To cut the base handles, insert the tip of the chain saw blade approximately 3 inches into the base.
2. Remove the saw and then repeat with another insertion right next to the first. These insertions may need to be repeated, though a 1 inch × 4 inch hole should be left behind.
3. This process is typically applied to the four corners of the base to allow a scenario in which two people can easily lift the sculpture onto a display table (Figures 12-18).
4. Another method would be to insert holes into the underside of the base. This is best done during the beginning stages of the carving process (Figure 12-19).

Pro's Corner

The base handles are not always necessary. Some carvers feel the holes leave an unfavorable look to the base. The decision to cut base handles will depend on the qualifications of the staff expected to display the sculpture along with how much of the base will be seen.

SUMMARY

Once the steps of this chapter are complete, the sculpture is ready for storage and display. The finishing begins by visualizing where the detail lines will be by using a detail line drawing or a detail model. All the steps of the finishing touches can be applied with hand tools. The V-notch chisel is used as the primary decorating tool. A gouge chisel can be used as well for a detail effect, such as the water in the base of the angelfish. The allowance of melting should be understood to avoid overcarving a detail area. Power tools can be an option for finishing details, and their usage was reviewed. As with all steps throughout the carving process, taking a moment to step away from the sculpture to ensure that all areas flow with one another is done for one last time. Cleaning the sculpture of ice shavings and fragments with air, sweeping, and water is the last step in preparation for storage or display.

REVIEW QUESTIONS

Matching

Match the word or phrase to its definition.

____ 1. Detail line drawing

____ 2. Visualization

____ 3. Base lifting handles

____ 4. Gouge chisel

____ 5. Allowance for melting

____ 6. Die grinder finishing

____ 7. Fine shaping detail

____ 8. Groove detail line

a. process of using a power tool, fitted with various bits, to finish the sculpture

b. final shaping done at or near the end of the carving process

c. decorative impression made with a V-notch or a gouge chisel

d. holes cut into base for ease in lifting the ice onto a display

e. added structure thickness to extend the display time of the sculpture

f. a sketch used for identifying where detail lines are carved on the sculpture

g. carving tool with a curved shaped blade

h. formulating an idea of what the sculpture will look like after a carving step is completed

Short Answer

9. Explain the visualization process and the best way for beginning carvers to implement it.

10. Why is it important to compensate for melting once the sculpture is on display.

11. Describe the purpose of cleaning the completed sculpture.

INSTRUCTOR'S NOTES

1. The best subject for visualization of detail would be a life-size sculpture. If a demonstration sculpture were carved prior to the practical carving day, this would make a great option. Keep in mind that such a life-size model is ideal to have around throughout the entire carving process. If the carving venue is a warmer area, the detail lines may have melted away by the time the students get to the finishing points of the exercise. Management of detail preservation may be a concern. Keep the piece out of sunlight and elevated at eye level.

2. Another option may be to have a second, identical angelfish carved to the point of shaping. This second carving would be brought out first for the initial portion of the carving session. The finished detail piece would be displayed as the first students are beginning the detail portion of their sculptures. At this point, the first shaped piece could be used as a class demo for carving detail lines.

3. Whether or not you have a three-dimensional model, each student should still have a detail line drawing to reference. This principle is important to understand as this preparation for visualization will often be the only tool available for future designs the student may choose to carve.

4. Consider taking a moment as the class shifts to the finishing step to perform a demo. This would be a good time to review the visualization concepts described in this chapter. Talk about the allowance for melting. For repetition purposes, demonstrate how the V-notch and gouge chisels are applied to the ice. Showcase how pitch and pressure will dictate the way the chisel moves through the ice.

5. Occasionally, when the ice has been exposed to hot weather or direct sunlight, the ice may have sharded and no longer lends itself as a good subject for detail finishing as large chunks may break off when the chisel is pressed through the ice. In this case, sharper chisels will perform better than duller ones. Another option would be to use the die grinder as it will not displace as many shards as will the hand tools. If class time allows, the ice could be

placed back in the freezer after the shaping portion. This step would adhere the shards to a stronger structure, though they would still exist in the harder frozen state. As a last resort, allow the student to place a few simple lines and accept it as a finished sculpture without fine grooves of detail. This concept of ice degradation through exposure time and the environment will dictate how to plan ahead for creating the ideal setting for an ice carving session.

6. Explain the need for applying base lifting handles and determine whether the angelfish, or whichever design you are demonstrating, will need this extra step.

7. Use your discretion paired with your power tool budget and level of safety supervision to allow students to use power tools for finishing work. For first-time carvers, it really isn't necessary to have every student practice this, especially because they will be far less likely to have a die grinder when the time comes for them to practice their carvings on their own. Incorporating exposure to power tool finishing can make a nice subject for a class demonstration.

8. Some carving instructors may debate the reason why carving the base was discussed after the finer detail areas such as the eyes. This was done for the simple purpose of listing the order of importance on finishing principles and reading retention. You may choose to have the students detail the base first and essentially work in the reverse order of this chapter's progression as it relates to detail lines.

9. Be prepared with the water and other cleaning tools as the students wrap up their sculptures. If the tap water is especially warm, combine the water with a bucket of ice or create an ice bath with a stockpot of water to use for water washing. Using hot water during this step can rapidly degrade the detail work of the sculptures.

10. Have the students who finish first become teammates for the closing details. The first finishers can assist in either displaying or storing other students' finished sculptures. Additional teams could assist in cleaning the common carving areas. Class time is often critical for this exercise, and teamwork will make the closing routine go by much faster.

Storage and Display

"Art must be enjoyed first and analyzed later."

Kristine Kathryn Rusch

Learning Objectives

After you have finished reading this unit, you should be able to:

- Describe the technique of transporting finished sculptures
- Identify the sensitivities of storing finished sculptures
- Explain the various display methods for ice sculptures
- Describe how to fix repairable damages to a broken ice sculpture
- Identify various lighting techniques for displaying ice
- Outline the sensitivities to photographing ice sculptures

Terms to Know

lifting crane
display tray

ice reassembly
single-break fracture

snow-filled repair

Like most artists, ice carvers find great satisfaction of seeing their finished work properly displayed for others to admire and appreciate. No professional would find it acceptable for a master to have all his or her labor destroyed at the end by improper handling. Respect and care should be taken in the handling of any high-quality work of art, especially ice sculpture, due to its fragile nature.

Before an ice sculpture can be enjoyed, it first must be stored properly and then set up for display. This unit will give the student a greater understanding of how to transport, store, display, and photograph a finished ice carving. Photographs give the ice carver a record of his or her work. This chapter will also include tips for repairing a damaged sculpture. Those who need to display an ice carving, though not necessarily carve one, should also read this chapter for a greater understanding of "what to do." All management involved with displaying ice sculpture will find pertinent information in this section.

TRANSPORTING THE FINISHED SCULPTURE

A finished sculpture must be moved to a freezer for storage or to a vehicle for transport. Two types of dollies can be used to move a sculpted block of ice. A flatbed dolly with four or more wheels can move the sculpture in a gentle manner. A hand truck dolly can also be used for moving a finished ice sculpture, although the ride will be bumpier. Once the dolly is secured, it must be lined with some form of padding to handle the momentum and bumps. A padded blanket, cardboard, foam, or other suitable liner should be used on the surface of the dolly. Pad all metal parts and secure the dolly from heat or impact. A hot metal dolly can be an accident waiting to happen without proper protection.

The sculpture itself should also be wrapped in a thermal blanket with securing straps or a large plastic bag as a minimal protection (Figure 13-1). Many completed sculptures will include fragile details, so the protective cover should be added before transport.

Depending on the location of the event, a car, truck, or payload-style golf cart may be used to transport the finished sculpture. The same respect to impact and temperature shock as described with movement on a dolly will apply. Additional considerations may apply for the time out of the freezer and security of placement in the vehicle. Padding is again suggested, and prevention of sunlight exposure is required. Securing straps may be needed to prevent any tipping or moving during transport in a motorized vehicle.

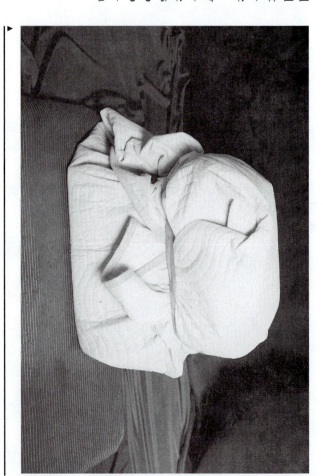

Figure 13-1   This carving is padded for transportation to the display site.

STORAGE

A block of ice must be stored frozen for it to remain preserved. That seems like an obvious point, though one would be surprised how many times a spectator will ask, "How do you keep it from melting?" There are many colorful answers to this, though the most common is to say, "We store it in the freezer." The exception to this rule applies if you are carving in freezing weather.

Freezer storage has a few sensitivities. Some of these notes of concern involve airflow, possible breakage, and cumbersome adhesion. A work of art must remain as such, or the labor of your work may be sacrificed.

The damage from airflow in a freezer will vary depending on the carving's location and the type of freezer used. Ideally, the best environment for an ice sculpture is no air movement at all. This is usually only available in a cold-walled conduction chest freezer, which is rarely used for storing sculpture ice. Most modern freezers maintain their temperature through convection. The defrost cycle of such freezers will create a slight melting period on your ice if not protected. Long-term storage in a convection freezer will slowly yield a deterioration of detail. The best prevention from this damage is to keep the sculpture thermally wrapped in a blanket or only store it temporarily within a day or so from display.

Breakage can happen when a delicate portion is left in the line of hazard. An innocent worker may bump into a sculpture located near the door. Placement under the ice cream shelf may result in a tub being dropped by one in a hurry. The most unused portion of the freezer is usually the best storage position.

A wet melting sculpture will still be melting at the moment you deliver it to the freezer. Ice adhesion to foreign objects may create a cumbersome chore when it is time to remove the ice for display. Breaking the sculpture away from a foreign object may result in damage. If the carving is placed on metal, it will emboss the shape of that metal on its resting surface and possibly freeze in place. If this bottom surface is the base structure of the ice, this may not be a problem, as this area will not be seen. A precision segment of ice may suffer damage from direct placement on the floor of the freezer. If placed on an absorbent surface, such as cardboard, the ice will melt and then fuse together with the cardboard. The best initial surface for melting ice is an insulated platform, such as extruded polystyrene insulation. Once the ice is dry from the cold air, it should be wrapped in padded protection and stored away from hazards until ready for display. Always keep sanitation in mind, as ice sculptures are usually displayed near food.

LIFTING FOR DISPLAY

The final step in the transportation of a finished sculpture is to lift it up onto the display tray. There are many ways to achieve the feat. Both the safety of the staff doing the lifting and the sculpture itself are important considerations.

A small half-block carving may weigh as little as 50 to 100 pounds. In this case, an individual could use a couple of hand towels and lift the block into place. It is always recommended to have an assistant nearby just in case. When lifting heavy objects, it is suggested to wear a back-support harness. Always bend the knees more than the back during heavy lifting to prevent injury. Begin by tilting the block slightly to the side to allow a towel-covered hand to slide underneath the base. Terry cloth towels will offer the best grip on wet ice. Continue by gripping the rest of the base or a sturdy portion of the ice design with the other hand and lift slowly. This should always be done close to the display tray. Finish by gently setting the base in place.

Always lift from the base when possible. Portions of some carvings may appear to have convenient handles, such as a swan's neck built into the design. There are two critical problems with lifting from such an area. The most obvious will be the high potential for breakage as the segment being gripped may not be sturdy enough to handle the weight of the entire block. The other con-

sideration comes from realizing that the swan's neck may seem easy to hold while on the ground or dolly, but this segment will often be far above your head once it is lifted high enough for the average display tray. This overhead weight-bearing position is very awkward and also unsafe. Some carving designs will allow base lifting handles to be used. See Chapter 12 for further details on base lifting handles. In this case, use the handles with an assistant to lift the carving into place.

Most full block sculptures will weigh at least 100 to 200 pounds. Remember that the raw ice block weighs around 300 pounds. A heavy sculpture should never be lifted by one person, although a macho individual may try this and possibly even succeed. This is not only a dangerous safety hazard for both the lifter and the carving, but it also leads others to believe they should be doing the same. Always plan the lifting to take place with two or three people. The use of towels and back support, as mentioned before, apply to the heavier sculptures.

The best scenario for lifting is to put three qualified people on the task. Two will be the primary lifters, lifting from the underside of the base, gripping the base handles, or occasionally using the trick in which a sturdy table cloth is cradled under the carving and the two ends are twisted to make handles for lifting (Figure 13-2). As many sculptures are top heavy, the third person will steady the center during the lifting process (Figure 13-3). The third helper should also be the navigator to guide the carving into place (Figure 13-4). Once the carving is in place, any towels used for lifting will need to be removed by tilting the sculpture slightly and pulling the fabric out from underneath. This also requires a steady grip on the bottom and center of the block and is best performed with a team of three.

Always determine where the sculpture will be placed before moving it. The edge of a display tray should be within 1 foot of the table's edge. Make sure you will have a clear and safe access to the position of the display tray. An elevated placement in the center of a 72-inch round table might seem like an impressive centerpiece to a cold food or pastry table. However, be sure to think through how you will plan to lift the sculpture into place. Such a round table option may leave you needing scaffolding over the table, as no one will be able to reach the display tray. In the extreme cases of show quality and budget, many things are possible, though the practical elements of planning usually prevail.

Another option exists with the use of a lifting crane. See Chapter 4, Tools of the Trade, for details of this equipment. The **lifting crane** is a manual or mechanically operated lifting device used to elevate heavy objects. A platform can be lowered to the floor level and then raised to the height suitable for ice display and rolled into position for movement onto the display tray. The expense of the crane and the storage and movement requirements may be worth it, as a lifting crane will eliminate the need to have the staff do the heavy lifting.

DISPLAY TRAYS

A **display tray** for ice sculpture involves a sturdy base and a pan capable of capturing melting water. Some models come with a drain tube, which is very handy. The display trays with a drain tube will require a water reservoir large enough to hold the entire runoff during the display period. A five-gallon bucket will usually suffice for a single block sculpture during a four-hour display period at room temperature. Larger vessels may be needed for multiblock designs.

Display trays come in all shapes and sizes. They are also available with a lighted base. The style chosen will depend on the size of the sculpture and the budget for display equipment. The size of the pan must be larger than the carving's base structure as the display tray must hold the ice within its barriers. A

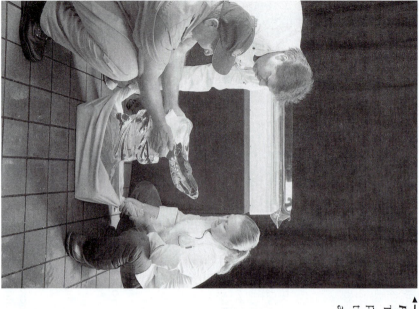

Figure 13-2
The ice carving is lifted into place by one carver while two people hold the ends of a tablecloth.

Figure 13-3
Two lifters move the carving while a third helper navigates the placement and holds the upper portion of ice steady.

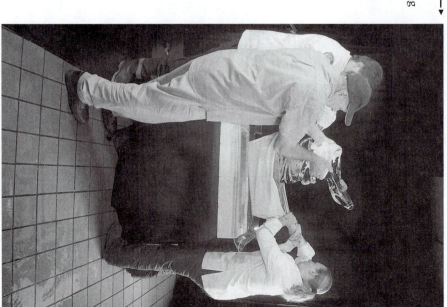

24 × 24-inch tray will easily hold an upright block, while a 44 × 24-inch tray will hold a horizontal carving design. Other sizes and shapes are available for larger or smaller designs, though those two dimensions listed above are the most popular.

Economical options may consist of a roasting pan or even a kiddie pool. Either can be lined with a tablecloth to look more appealing. However, this choice will require the manual salvage of water as it builds up in the pan. Any water-draining display pan will suffice if large enough for the carving.

Once the carving is in its final display position, it should be secured with ice cubes around the empty area of the tray. Filling in this empty area not only holds the sculpture in place, but it also often creates a chilled bed for additional foods

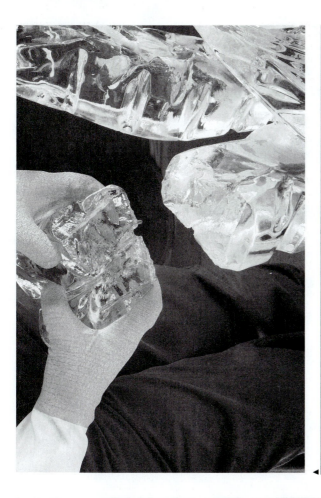

Figure 13-4
The third carver navigates the carving into place.

or garnishes to be added such as a raw bar display. Ice cubes are not always needed when the display vehicle incorporates a stabilizing element, such as an underlying towel or a textured surface. The latter option of avoiding ice cube security is taken when the ice will be displayed without food on its perimeter and the lighting is generated from points other than the base. When the ice cube security method is practiced, it is common to hold these cubes in place with salt. See the Faults of Salt Application section later in this unit for a greater understanding of salt and ice.

MANAGING DAMAGES

Unfortunately, the handling of a fragile material, such as ice, can result in accidental breakage. These types of accidents can happen at any stage of the sculpture process including during carving, transporting, storing, or displaying. There are a few tricks to aid in the repair of breakages, though sometimes a multiple fracture may result in losing the work altogether. Repairing such fractures may require **ice reassembly** skills, which is the practice of attaching two separate segments of ice together to form an adhesive part of the intended sculpture.

Single-Break Fractures

A **single-break fracture** is a point of ice breakage where only one point of severance has taken place on the broken segment. A **clean break** is a term used for a single-break fracture when no additional chips or shards have severed from the broken area (Figure 13-5). This type of break can be repaired by moving all segments back to the freezer for hardening followed by reattachment.

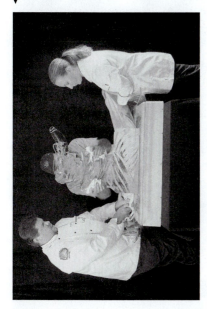

Figure 13-5   This photo shows a clean break where the two surfaces to be repaired can be easily reattached for repair.

Reattachment will take place by holding the cold frozen clean-break surfaces against each other while dribbling water over the break to form the fusion (Figure 13-6).

It may not be possible to return an ice sculpture that is already on display to a freezer. When this is the case, use a freeze spray, along with iced water, to form a repair to the fracture. This is done by lightly spraying both of the fracture surfaces with the freezing spray to make them colder. In a quick motion, the surfaces should be reattached while adding a few drops of iced water above the cracked surface to allow a weld to form. Hold the ice in place until a fusion has formed. Certain breaks may require a snow-filled repair.

Snow-Filled Repair

A **snow-filled repair** is a slush of ice shavings that will sometimes be applied for a patch when the clean break weld does not hold on its own. This type of snow is best created with the shavings thrown from a chain saw or die grinder. Capturing such shavings is done by having a helper hold a bucket in the line of snow spray as a scrap piece of ice is being machine cut (Figure 13-7). Once this snow

Figure 13-6   Hold the break in place and dribble a little water on the surface to weld it in place.

is captured, it should be hydrated slightly with a few drops of water to form slush. (A warm weather condition will create this naturally.) This slush will become a healing element to a fracture, and it is best applied in a freezing environment like the freezer, though it can also be applied at the display table (Figure 13-8). Freshly formed snow is always easier to mold because it is loose. One can save the snow throughout the carving process if the carving weather is freezing. However, a snow reservoir left in the warmer conditions for a few minutes will become a solid cake when stored in the freezer for later use. It is best to save the scrap ice segments for possible snow formation when needed at the last minute.

Follow these steps to form a snow-filled repair:

1. Chill the broken surfaces by placing them in the freezer or with an application of freezing spray.
2. Position the fractured surfaces together and apply a few drops of cold water into the seam.
3. Apply the slush to the exterior of the fracture, along with filling in any open areas that may have broken off. Tap the slush lightly into place with either the fingertips or entire hand.

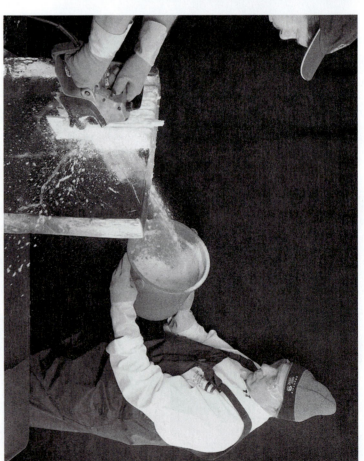

Figure 13-7   A helper captures snow from a scrap block of ice being cut by chain saw.

4. Hold the broken segment in place until the fusion takes place. This may take seconds or up to a minute or two depending on the surfaces as well as the ambient air temperature. A freezing spray can expedite this process.

Carver's Note

Using a snow-fill slush is always a quick fix and never a plan, though it is a skill needed by experienced ice carvers.

LIGHTING

The lighting of an ice carving has its sensitivities. Illumination is best from the back or from under the base. Remember, as was mentioned in Chapter 2, that ice can form a prism and refract light. Sometimes this comes as an advantage when used for display, and sometimes it is a hindrance for photography. A lighted base is a great way to set off an ice sculpture. A colored gel light filter (a tinted plastic sheet placed between the light and the ice) can enhance the carving to another dimension.

An ice sculpture can be illuminated with track lighting provided at the display venue or with clip-on lighting attached to the table. Always illuminate an ice sculpture from the rear to showcase its qualities. Lighting from the front will detract from the desired prism effect.

Always position the lights in a direction from a point other than your current view, such as from underneath or behind the ice. A dark backdrop is best for the background. If the sculpture is illuminated from the base, the backlighting is best pointed into the dark backdrop to provide a softer and more appealing display. This practice will best enhance the sculpture (Figure 13-9).

Pro's Corner

Another way to add color to a clear ice sculpture is with colored battery-powered insert tabs. These would be placed in precise sections. See Appendix B for a list of suppliers.

PHOTOGRAPHY

Photographs of completed ice sculptures become the most important record for future use in advertisements and marketing materials such as Web sites, e-mail, and brochures. They also serve as an objective means of measuring skill improvement. As one advances in carving technique, a visual record notes refinement of style. Those photos may also be used as a guide for future similar carvings.

Some of the most difficult subjects to photograph well are transparent. Clear glass objects and clear ice, being essentially invisible, require specialized

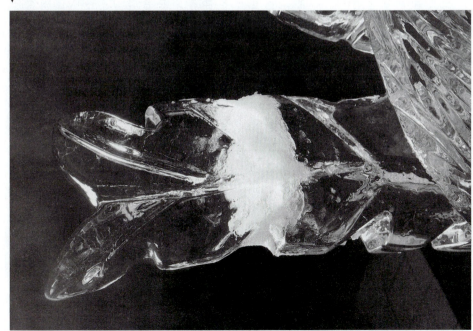

Figure 13-8

The snow is used to create a patch for the broken segment.

Faults of Salt Application

The use of salt for ice carving has been a misconception for many culinarians. Some believe it can be used for repairing fractures or that it has some other benefit to clear ice. This tale is far from the truth, as salt degrades the molecular structure of ice and lowers its melting point. Hence, the use of salt on icy roads to prevent slippage over the frozen surface. Salt should never be used on an ice sculpture and has no place in any step of the carving process. The only exception may be for sprinkling over the ice cubes on a display tray, as mentioned earlier in this chapter.

Figure 13-9 This carving is lit appropriately for display and photography.

techniques for satisfactory results. This chapter will reveal simple-to-use "secrets" that professional photographers use when photographing ice. The authors wish to thank Michael Pizzuto, CCE, NICA Ambassador at Large, noted carver and photographer, for his assistance in writing this chapter.

Getting Started

The nature of the subject determines which type of lighting must be used, and how the light is controlled is the most important thing to keep in mind before taking any picture, especially of glass or ice. Here we will consider the type of camera and settings, display location of the ice, special effects, and lighting. Because most ice carvers are not professional photographers and simply desire a good image of their best work, we will discuss basic equipment that can perform reliably and be cost effective and easily purchased.

While film has been the common medium for a century, digital cameras now dominate the market. Digital cameras provide immediate results, and they are extremely user-friendly at practically no cost per image. Once equipment is purchased, there is very little expense in producing a finished picture. While using a digital format is the basis of this section, owners of film cameras can follow the same guidelines.

Equipment

The best type of camera is a single-lens reflex (SLR) capable of using interchangeable lenses. Modern technology has made taking photographs and processing easier than ever for cameras with autofocus, built-in light metering systems, and many other variable functions common in consumer-level cameras. "Point-and-shoot" cameras do not yet produce results good enough for sales and marketing production and are not discussed with this lesson.

A digital camera of at least six to eight megapixels should be used for any pictures intended for expansion or publication. A three to six megapixel camera would suffice for a personal collection of your work. Lenses specific to digital capture are of different quality than those for film and can be purchased with the camera. Prices at the time of this publication range from $500 to $1,000 for a higher-quality camera. Depreciated against the income for five ice carvings at $200 each, the expense is easily justified for the initial outlay of cash and it doesn't melt!

Lens capability should be of the zoom type and have a range between 28 and 110 millimeters. Most ice carvings can be photographed from 8 to 15 feet away; zooming allows full-frame to close-up shots from one position.

Tripods or some other solid base, such as a table or column, should be used to stabilize the camera. Ignoring this advice will invalidate all other information about photography, as freehand holding of a camera will not produce a clear image. Most ice displays tend to be in moderate to dimly lighted rooms, and cameras require longer open-shutter times in order to absorb enough light for proper exposure. Hand holding a camera will often result in a blurred photo.

Camera Settings

Consult the camera owner's operating manual for recommended settings for best image sharpness. However, the procedure for shooting ice sculptures may be summarized in one phrase: depth of field. Simply explained, this refers to the area front to back of any object or scene that is in clear focus. The depth-of-field concentration is controlled by how wide the lens opening (aperture) is set at the moment of pressing the shutter release button. The aperture can be adjusted manually or with automatic settings on the camera to produce the ideal degree of focus.

Background

Use what professionals call the "dark field" method to accentuate the ice. This means that the background or area behind the ice should be as dark as possible. That provides the contrast necessary for the transparent ice to stand out and become the center of attention. A white or light-toned background will blend into the ice's shape and lose visual impact, and thus creating a poor photograph.

Special Effects

Special effects such as colored gels, floral displays, and other decorations may enhance ice carving photos if added moderately and do not distract the view of the primary object.

Photographic Lighting

Lighting can produce a spectacular display or diminish the unique characteristics of an ice carving. When photographing ice, the main light source should be placed directly below or behind the ice. Forget any form of front light, as it is nearly useless with clear ice due to the reflections it will cause.

Most high-quality ice display vessels provide a clear plastic tray and a drain tube. The best also have built-in under lighting. This satisfies many of the special effects previously mentioned because colored lighting gels can be inserted between the bottom lights and tray to create more contrast and highlights.

Every appropriate digital camera has an automatic white balance feature. This greatly simplifies the confusing need for any number of light filters required for

film cameras. Many lighted display bases use fluorescent tubes. Used either alone or with colored gels, digital color balance virtually eliminates off-color problems. Intense spotlights are unnecessary. Refraction, which is the scattering of light within the ice, makes it possible to use low-wattage bulbs. Avoid using direct, front flash or lighting as doing so will bounce light reflections exactly back into the camera lens for a totally overexposed white photo.

One last consideration can be made. If the ice is displayed in front of a window with daylight coming in (not direct sunlight) and the camera is correctly set for such backlighting (review the manual), diffused light can be especially effective in revealing facets of the ice's surface.

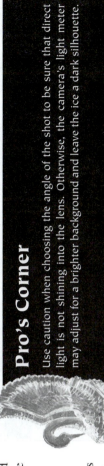

Pro's Corner

Use caution when choosing the angle of the shot to be sure that direct light is not shining into the lens. Otherwise, the camera's light meter may adjust for a brighter background and leave the ice a dark silhouette.

Taking the Photo

1. Set the camera on a tripod at the distance required. Fill the viewfinder with the ice carving by zooming in or out. Remove nonessential items from the picture.
2. Set the aperture at a wide opening of $f5.6$ or $f4.0$. (The background will be blurred.)
3. Most modern cameras automatically adjust the shutter speed for the available light.

In review, there are four steps for taking a high-quality photograph.

1. Use a dark background.
2. Mount your camera on a tripod or set it on a hard, stable surface.
3. Use proper camera settings.
4. Place the lights correctly.

The camera's operating manual and supplementary books from any bookstore's photography section can provide further details concerning ISO (sensitivity to light) settings, shutter speeds, and use of flash.

Photo Labeling

Photos should be properly filed for easy recovery. A digital file or a manual file should include the title of the sculpture along with the date of the work. Also record the size of the carving, as this will often be hard to detect from a photograph.

Pro's Corner

To provide an added touch for future business, consider bringing the proper backdrop, lighting, and photographic equipment to the display. Take a good picture and send this record with your invoice.

Summary

The lessons of this chapter will prepare you to properly display a finished sculpture, ready for the intended audience. Transportation to the display site must be handled with care. Lifting the carving onto a display tray will require skill and safety precautions. Preserving your work through photographs is the best way to allow the work to be remembered for the years to come. Proper lighting will aid in the display and photographic quality of ice. An ice sculpture requires planning throughout the carving and display process. Observation of the storage conditions, transportation, and display technique are critical components to the art of ice sculpture.

Review Questions

True or False

1. The best freezer environment for an ice sculpture is one that has no air movement at all.
2. Always bend the knees more than the back when lifting an ice sculpture.
3. Raw blocks of manufactured ice weigh 200 pounds.
4. When photographing an ice sculpture, the main light source should be placed directly below or behind the ice.
5. Freehand holding of a camera is strongly recommended.

Multiple Choice

6. Most modern freezers maintain their temperature through
   a. thin walls.
   b. ice-cooled chambers.
   c. blast systems.
   d. convection airflow.

7. Ice sculpture adhesion to foreign objects occurs when
   a. a display tray is too small for the sculpture.
   b. a snow-filled repair forms slush.
   c. sunlight is too bright.
   d. a melting sculpture is placed in the freezer.

8. It is best to use _____ qualified people when lifting a full-block sculpture.
   a. two
   b. four
   c. three
   d. five

9. The edge of a display tray should be within
   a. 2 inches of the table's edge.
   b. 1 foot of the table's edge.
   c. 4 feet of the table's edge.
   d. 5 feet of the table's edge.

10. The display tray is needed to provide a sturdy base for the sculpture and
    a. to capture the melting water.
    b. to aid in moving the sculpture.
    c. to hold any broken fragments.
    d. to provide a track for backlighting.

11. Another name for a clean break in ice carving terms is
    a. a simple fracture.
    b. a single-break fracture.
    c. a shard.
    d. a fusion break.

12. Salt degrades the molecular structure of ice and
    a. lowers its melting point.
    b. raises its melting point.
    c. doesn't affect the melting point.
    d. None of the above

13. An ice sculpture is best when viewed with
    a. backlight or light from under the base.
    b. backlight only.

c. light from under the base only.

d. lights pointing forward on the ice.

INSTRUCTOR'S NOTES

1. This chapter represents an ideal instruction manual for the display staff. Those who are only concerned with setup and display should be made aware of the lessons in this section.

2. Movement of the finished sculpture should be illustrated in the form of a demonstration. Use the students to create the scenario of lifting a sculpture onto a display table. Qualified lifting candidates are required for safety.

3. Demonstrate how lighting will play a factor for display and photography.

4. Explain how keeping a record of ice carving, along with all other culinary accomplishments, will enhance a professional chef's portfolio.

5. Bring a camera to the class to show students how to record their work. Demonstrate some of the tips for enhanced photography as discussed in this chapter.

14

Advanced Skills

"I recently took up ice sculpting. Last night I made an ice cube. This morning I made 12. I was prolific."

Mitch Hedberg

Learning Objectives

After you have finished reading this unit, you should be able to:

- Explain the basic fundamentals of logo and scrollwork
- Discuss human proportion
- Identify the utilization of a functional design of ice sculpture
- Demonstrate the techniques of flat welding, gravity adhesion, and peg and notch fusion
- Describe how an ice sphere is sculpted
- Outline the advantages of participating in ice carving competitions

Terms to Know

scrollwork
front-filled scrollwork
back-filled scrollwork
sand-fill technique
three-dimensional logo
functional ice carving design

multiple-block designs
computer-assisted design (CAD)
computer numerical control (CNC)
ice fusion

flat welding
metal-plate fusion
gravity adhesion
peg and notch fusion
ice sphere

For many students, a one-time ice carving experience merely whets the appetite for future carving sessions. Once you have completed the instructions in this chapter, you should have a greater understanding of the advanced principles of ice carving. Students will be introduced to logo design, ice reassembly, and carving a sphere, as well as ice carving competitions. The skills learned from this unit will help a novice carver move above and beyond the basics toward advanced and professional carving.

LOGO CARVINGS

Carvings bearing a logo are in high demand for corporate events. A logo design will often incorporate the need for **scrollwork**, which is a design technique that involves filling an engraved channel with a cloudy snow to create a contrasting image within the ice. A clear block of ice will best showcase the internal craft of scrollwork as the block must be transparent for a contrasting image to be seen. Scrollwork images are most commonly placed on perfectly flat surfaces of ice. This requires the preparation of flattening with a metal plate, similar to the method of flat welding illustrated later in this chapter. The die grinder must be used with a router bit of various sizes to form a channel of the design. The snow, from either a natural resource or the spray of a shearing power tool, is used to fill in the channel and form the contrasting image (Figure 14-1).

A **front-filled scrollwork** carving incorporates an image placed on the front of the ice block. This is done by channeling on the front-view side of the ice and filling the channel with snow (Figure 14-2). The front-fill technique is the easiest form of scrollwork as it can be as simple as using power tool penmanship to create the desired channeling needed for the design. However, placing a template over the ice is often advised for accuracy, rather than attempting the image in a freehand style (Figures 14-3 and 14-4).

Pro's Corner

Because ice carvings usually have an expected display time of at least four hours, the channel of scrolling should be carved at least 1 to 2 inches deep. The snow used to fill this area should be packed in with the fingertips and applied two or three times.

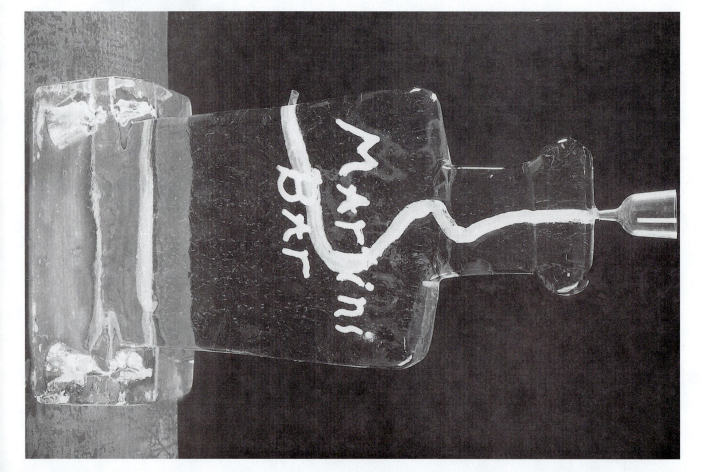

Figure 14-1 Front-filled scrollwork is used to apply lettering in this design.

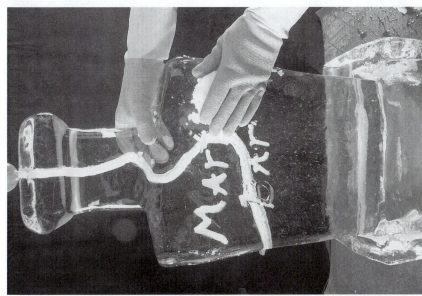

Figure 14-2
The scrollwork of the die grinder is packed with loose snow to fill in the channels.

A **back-filled scrollwork** carving is produced by creating a negative image on the backside of the ice. When viewed from the front, it appears in its normal perspective. From the backside of the carving surface, the channeling will reflect a reverse format of the intended design. An effective method to reverse a scrollwork template design would be to scan a positive image design with a computer. Most photo editor programs can easily transform a design into a negative format. Another method requires the use of an overhead projector. The image is printed onto a transparency and the transparency is turned over onto an overhead projector. The projected image will be an accurate negative image of the scrollwork design.

A back-filled scrollwork design can also incorporate the use of sand filling to create various colors. Any addition of colors will require the channel to be

Figure 14-3 A scrollwork logo design uses the front-filled technique. A template is utilized to accurately transfer a scrollwork image.

cleaned thoroughly with an air broom, water, or any means necessary to remove all the white snow remaining from the machining process. The **sand-fill technique** is achieved by pouring a layer of colored sand at the bottom of a back-filled scrollwork channel. A plastic foodservice squirt bottle is ideal for this sand application. The sand is then locked into place by dribbling small amounts of water into the sand and allowed to freeze. The remaining voids of the channel are packed with snow to secure the sand image (Figure 14-5). Another method of applying color to a channel involves using a colored gelatin mixture in place of the sand. Either method is suitable for highlighting color to bring out the image within the ice.

Figure 14-4 A die grinder is used to carve the channel of a scrollwork template into the face of an ice block.

Pro's Corner

Snow must be used to secure a sand-filled channel. Filling the entire channel with water after the sand-fill step will cause shattering as the water expands during freezing.

Figure 14-5 This photo demonstrates the image of a back-filled scrollwork design using the sand-fill technique.

Logo carvings can also be carved in three-dimensional shaped designs. A **three-dimensional logo** is a design with the ice sculpted into a formation of letters or a specific artistic image where the carving portrays the full-size image of the logo.

Additional Advanced Sculpture Designs

Occasions will arise for a professional to create more intricate sculptures that require advanced carving skills. This demand may involve the human figure,

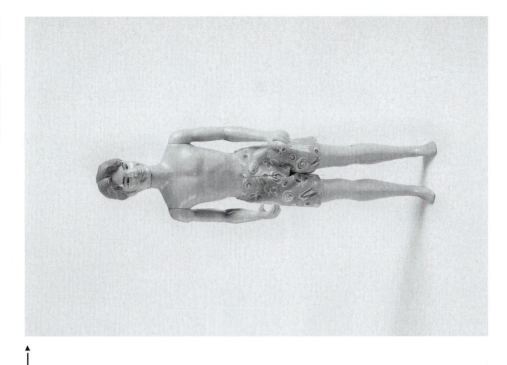

Figure 14-6
Doll shows the human image of a man in its upright position.

exotic animals, functional designs, and even multiblock creations to perform a specific purpose. The sky is the limit to the challenges created by those who are willing to create a unique carving. The beginning carver should only focus on simple sculptures for a basic buffet or cocktail party display. However, the professional and competitive sculptor will explore the advanced possibilities of ice design.

HUMAN FIGURES

The human figure is often considered to be the most difficult composition of all sculpture designs. This is an oddity as there are so many humans on our planet and they all have distinctive characteristics. It would seem that it would be simple to create a version of a man or woman in sculpture. One of the problems associated with carving human figures is that we have a discriminating audience who has a trained eye for what a human's muscle tone or facial structure should look like. A model or figurine is best to view when identifying the anatomical sculpture needs of the human body. A toy doll is often the best model to use for the basic human shape as well as for the muscle structure and movement poses (Figures 14-6 and 14-7).

The human face is usually the most difficult as there are so many shapes to define in such a small area. The element of ice as it melts also creates a factor when it comes to keeping the definition of the intended design. A cartoon or character image is usually easier to sculpt than any realistic human face. Because the ice melts while on display, it is best to overemphasize a few features to keep the design looking good over time. A larger-than-life nose or the lips with an opening into the mouth are good examples.

Showing the muscle tone of the man or woman in a natural state is also complex. The look of human muscles changes depending on the posture. An example might be how the man's bicep will be bulged when the arm is curled, while the same muscle would appear flat in a stretched pose. The abdominal area will either show muscle tone or a big belly, depending on the design. The characteristics of a warrior versus a cherub are examples of this principle. Gender-specific details must also be considered when carving a male or female.

Many art reference books give good tips for carving human figures. Some would argue that drawing a human in a two-dimensional form is more difficult than sculpting a three-dimensional figure. Only the artist can decide. Both have their artistic value.

Human Dimension

It is important that ice carvers working on human figures understand a few facts about human dimension:

- The head is usually proportionate to seven or eight times the height of a standing human body.
- The chest is located one head from the base of the head (using eight heads to measure the body).

Figure 14-7
Doll is shown in a form of movement and the muscle tone serves as a pattern to follow.

Face

- The space between the eyes is equal to the width of one eye.
- The base of the nose is as wide as the space between the eyes.
- The size of the face is equal to the size of a human hand.

Shoulders

- Shoulders measure the length of two heads or a little longer if the figure has broad shoulders.

The elements of cultural background, race, gender and genetic qualities may vary. However, this principle of proportion will often apply when it comes to a normal sculpture design (Figure 14-8).

Arms

- Arms are close to three heads long.
- When arms are down at the sides, the wrist is even with the hips.
- The elbow is aligned with the waist.

Hair is also difficult to define in ice, as its finer detail can be difficult to display realistically. It is often better to create an overall shape of hair structure and then create a few defining lines to represent the flow of the hair. The parting of the hairline is a good example of a defining line.

A human image wearing clothes is usually the easiest to sculpt, as the garment will cover up the muscle tone. A face can be left simple with a nose and basic eye and mouth structure.

ADVANCED ANIMAL DESIGNS

Animal designs will also require research or familiarity with the anatomical structure of the design at hand. Again, there are many art books as well as nature books that can become a valuable tool for the carver. *How to Draw Animals*

- The waist is one head from the chest.
- The hips are located one head from the waist.
- The knee is one head from the hips.
- The calf is one head below the knee.
- Another head will measure to just above the knee.
- The final head measures to the bottom of the feet. The leg area is the most common variable for proportion in height to equal seven or eight heads.

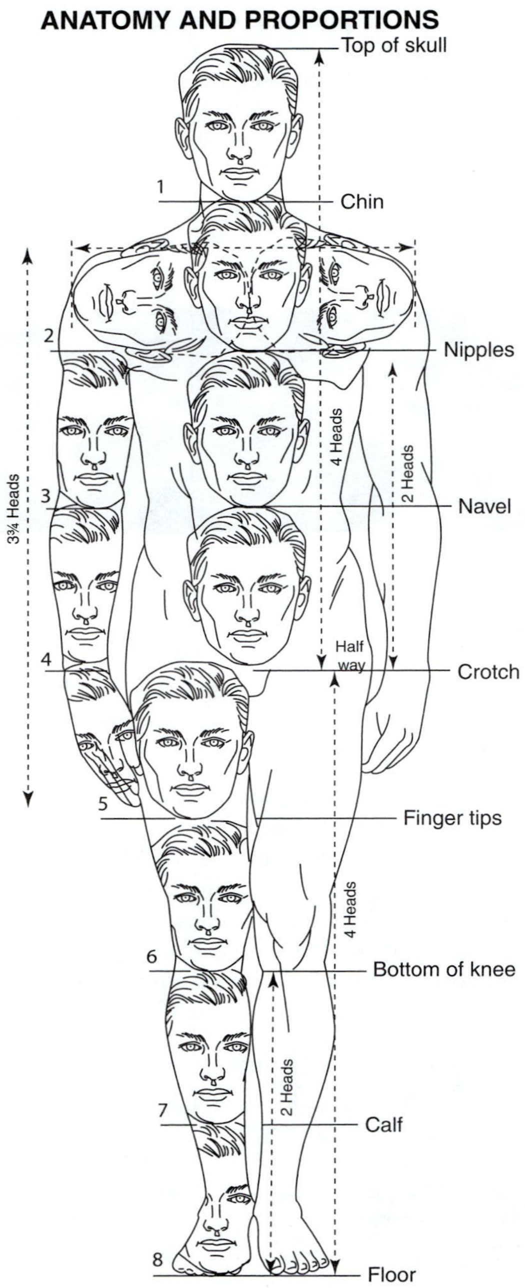

Figure 14-8   The height of one head equals seven to eight times the height of a standing human.

by Jack Hamm is a great book for learning how to draw animal figures. Once a carver can draw an image paired with the knowledge of how to go about the principles of sculpting from this book, he or she will adapt the skills necessary to create a three-dimensional sculpture. The angelfish used in this book is an original design from the author of this book. However, the design is similar to many common renditions of an angelfish carving. As a sculptor develops his or her own talents, original designs will become commonplace.

Functional Designs

Many ice carvings are functional, above and beyond being used as a centerpiece. **Functional ice carving designs** serve a practical display purpose. They can hold or display food or beverages. On a larger scale, functional ice carvings can serve as a bar, a piece of furniture, or an archway. Raw bar presentations of a boat or seashell, or shot luges used for beverage stations, are examples of functional designs. A bartender's ice station and even a full-size castle for spectators to walk through are functional. The sky is the limit.

Multiple-Block Designs

Multiple-block designs are sculptures that incorporate more than one block of ice to create the display. Such carvings can incorporate some or all of the advanced techniques listed in this chapter. *Multiblock* could be applied to a few segments within one standard carving block or to the formation of several carving blocks to create the finished design. Multiple segments of ice, which come together to form the sculpture, will compose a multiple-block design.

Computer-Assisted Design

A computer can aid in the work of carving away the ice by offering **computer-assisted design (CAD)**. The software is learned though a specialized method, and the hardware consists of a **computer numerical control (CNC)** machine. Ice carving CNC machines are available from many manufacturers (Figure 14-9). A CNC machine can produce specific designs with amazing accuracy. CNC works on an axis point of X, Y, and Z, representing all three

ANATOMY AND PROPORTIONS

Figure 14-9
A CNC ice carving machine available on the market.

Flat welding is a method of adjoining two flat surfaces of ice. It is carried out through making two surfaces touch with a flat surface for adhesion. The flat welding technique is performed through metal plate fusion or gravity adhesion in a planned format for ice carving. A flat plate of metal will create a perfect surface for flat welding, regardless of the angle of fusion. The more perpendicular the design is to the ground, the more difficult an ice fusion will become.

Metal-Plate Fusion

Metal-plate fusion is the act of fusing two segments of ice by creating perfectly flat surfaces with a metal plate. Use the following steps when fusing two segments using the metal-plate fusion technique:

1. Prepare the ice to be welded by applying a flat metal plate to the surfaces that will touch. A slightly heated plate is better. This is done with exposure to warm ambient temperatures, which can be accelerated by placing an iron in a dry area or other heating device on the plate. It is important to avoid getting the plate too hot as thermal shock may damage the ice. The plate should feel warm to the touch, but not singe your hands. A surface temperature of 100° F (38° C) to 200° F (93° C) degrees is preferred.

ICE FUSION

Ice fusion is the act of joining two segments of ice to become one. The process of ice fusion is often performed through flat welding or the peg and notch method. The clean-break repair is also a form of ice fusion, as discussed in Chapter 13.

dimensions of sculpture. Professional ice sculpters will utilize a CNC machine to reduce labor time for logo work or even primary segment removal on figure-based designs.

7. Put the two surfaces together to begin the fusion process. This is a good time for a helper. One person should take the majority of the weight and the other should align the surfaces. Check to make sure that a flat seam is evident. If not, consider removing the segments and applying the metal plates until the surfaces appear seamless. While holding the ice in position, trickle small amounts of the chilled water above the seam to allow it to fill in the gap. A colder surface area will bond faster than melting ice and the use of colder water will help the fusion process along. Eventually, the ice will fuse itself for a fine display of a flat welding technique. For the trickier fusions of angles defying gravity, it will be necessary to hold the segments until the bond is solid.

Pro's Corner

Placing small chunks of dry ice over the seam during the bonding process will speed up the fusion time.

SAFETY NOTE

Dry ice should never be touched with bare hands, as extreme freeze burning can occur, especially with wet hands. Dry ice can be nearly −94° F (−35° C) below zero. Always wear protective gloves when handling dry ice.

Gravity Adhesion

Gravity adhesion is the fusion of ice through gravity stacking and often using a saw, nail board, or even a metal plate to bring the adjoining surfaces to a flat seam. Gravity adhesion takes place by assembling two segments of ice in a vertical stack for display or as a part of a multiblock design. Such designs involve stacking two or more flat segments, which are parallel to the ground or center of gravity. This happens often in many designs of either simple or advanced composition. A simple pedestal to raise the height of a basic sculpture is a good example of where gravity adhesion is practiced.

Figure 14–10
The base section of the clamshell functional carving design is flattened by a metal plate to prepare for metal-plate fusion. The level is used to ensure that the area of the joint is level.

2. Apply the flat metal plate to the adjoining surfaces to be fused (Figure 14-10).
3. Press the opposite segment with the heated metal plate to form a matching flat surface (Figure 14-11). The two parts of a clamshell are an example of this effort.
4. Once the surfaces have been flattened, they are ready to be put in the freezer or be displayed. A colder surface is always better for adhesion.
5. For assembly, have a squirt bottle of chilled water nearby, as this will be needed to fill the seam. If the seam is parallel to the floor, gravity will hold the fusion easily. If the angle defies gravity, more measures will be needed to ensure a quick and solid fusion.
6. The segments can be placed in the freezer to chill the surfaces, or a chill spray can be applied to the flat surfaces to form a quicker bond. Care should be taken with chill sprays as they can also create cracking through thermal shock. Hold the can about 12 inches away and pass it quickly over the ice in several motions.

Figure 14–11
The top section of the clamshell is flattened to prepare the fusion onto its base.

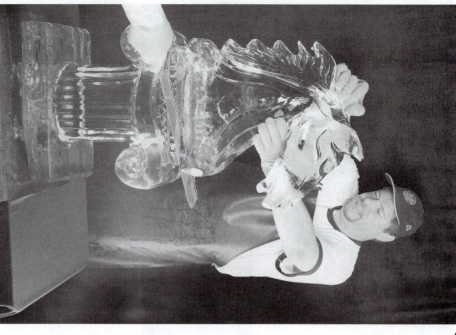

Figure 14-12
A hand saw is used
to bring the seam
between the upper
and lower segment of
ice to form a stronger
bond of fusion.

Figure 14-13
The nail board is
used to flatten the
surface of the base
structure for the
sculpture, which it is
about to support.

Place the two segments together in a stacked finished display. The seam may be even or it may not. Use the suggested tools to bring this seam to its final resting point. Flatten surfaces with a nail board or metal plate or by running an ice saw through the adjoining point to create a fusion. The welded seam will require an even surface for flat welding. The nail board or flat-plate method will be exercised while the segments are still separate. The saw method happens when the segments are stacked and the saw is driven through the seam to flatten the surfaces together (Figure 14-12). A nail board can also be used on the base section to create a level surface (Figure 14-13).

Peg and Notch Fusion

The peg and notch method for ice sculpture fusion has been practiced in the past and is still used in some designs. **Peg and notch fusion** involves a section of the adjoining segment having a peg, or a male section of protruding ice beyond the intended design, along with the opposite female segment, having a void to match the shape of the peg (Figure 14-14). The seam of the design should come together as one as the peg and notch join together (Figure 14-15). This format is most often used when the law of gravity works against the design.

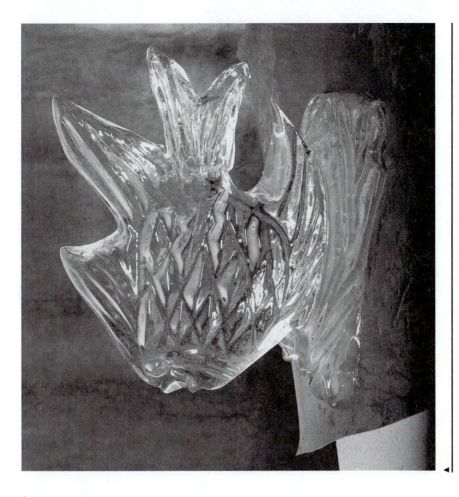

Figure 14-15   The tail is in place and the seam is hardly noticeable.

Figure 14-14
The tail of the fish is about to be attached to the body using the peg and notch method.

Pro's Corner

A clean-looking ice sculpture will have as little cloudy slush as possible. Clear is always better, and slush leaves a messy appearance. Use the flat welding technique, whenever possible, for a cleaner looking design.

The peg and notch method is difficult to master, though it becomes a standard when advanced ice design is at hand. A peg and notch formation that is perfect will join with little help of slush. However, it is common to use a little slush inside the notch to help form a good fusion. Some slush can also be used in the seam, but this is difficult to match perfectly without the ability to flatten it with a plate or other means. Securing the seam is important for a good fusion and strength. For a review on how to make slush, refer to the Snow-Filled Repair section of Chapter 13.

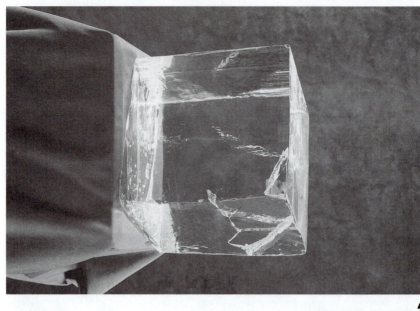

Figure 14-16
This ice cube will be the starting point for carving a sphere.

Figure 14-17
The top of the cube is near completion for the first step in adjoining the side portions to form the sphere.

CARVING AN ICE SPHERE

Carving a sphere, or ball, is a technique that can be incorporated into advanced designs or even the simpler compositions. An **ice sphere** is a three-dimensional ball carved from a cube of ice. A crystal ball in a mystical design is a good example of how a sphere is used in ice carving.

Follow the steps below for carving an ice sphere:

1. Begin by creating a cube (Figure 14-16). Note that the cube must be slightly larger than the intended size of the finished ball.

2. Secure the cube on a sturdy carving surface and use the flat chisel or six-prong chipper to work out the center area from the top to the side while leaving the corners intact (Figure 14-17). Continue this step on all four sides.

3. Turn the cube onto its opposite side and perform the technique as described in step 2. The center point of each side should be left in its original girth, while the center sections on each side will have ice removed to form a convex curve to its adjoining side in the cube. The result will leave a ball set within eight corner sections (Figure 14-18).

4. Form the ball shape by removing each corner section, one by one, while keeping the convex curve consistent to match each side (Figure 14-19). Note that the last few corners will only leave a curved surface as the base. It is advised to use an absorbent liner on your work surface to keep the ice steady during carving.

5. The fully shaped ball may have a few flat surface points. Use the flat side of the medium flat chisel to round off any of these flat surfaces to form a better ball shape (Figure 14-20).

6. The ball may require additional smoothing to become perfect in shape. This smoothing step is performed by submerging the sphere in a tub of water while rolling and rubbing it with the hands. This step will involve rapid melting of the finished ball's diameter, and this is why starting with a cube larger than the intended design is necessary (Figures 14-21 and 14-22).

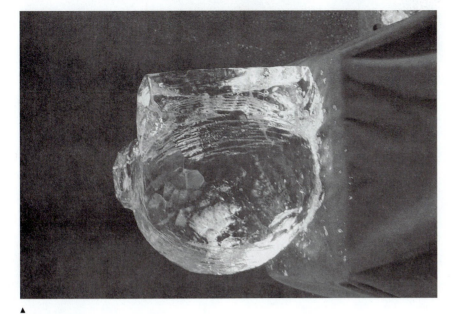

Figure 14-19
The corners are shaped from a cube to a ball.

Figure 14-18
The sphere is now taking shape as all sides have been carved.

COMPETITION ARENA

The competition circuit of ice carving can offer the most educational development among skills and new design possibilities. This concept applies to all facets of the culinary arts. The "Work of the Masters" creates new ideas and a fundamental goal pursuit toward the art of this book. A beginner should consider what it would be like to enter a competition and additionally accept the idea that you're not there to win, yet present to learn.

Preparation is the key to completing a competition in its required format. This preparation includes your design formation, preparatory drawings, templates, a list of required tools, and practicing enough times to complete the work within the time limit. Competing says you're ready for the next level. If you're a winning competitor, this is an even greater accomplishment of your study.

Competition ice carvings are often judged on 10 areas of carving ability. These competencies will include the following areas of judgment: first impression, utilization of ice, technical skill, attention to detail, finished appearance, structural technique, proportion and/or symmetry, design and composition, creativity, and artistic impression.

Figure 14-20
The medium flat chisel is used to round off any flat uneven surfaces.

Figure 14-21
The nearly perfect ball is submerged into a water bath for smoothing and shaping into its final shape.

The most recognized entity for ice carving sanction is the National Ice Carving Association (NICA).

"The National Ice Carving Association is a professional association of ice sculptors. The association was formed to develop standardized judging criteria and offer training to students and professionals through seminars and articles. NICA also creates public awareness of the art of ice sculpting as an art form through carving events world wide. The association encourages the use of ice sculpture as a marketing tool as well. This organization provides a forum for the exchange of ideas, techniques and encouragement among sculptors," says Alice Connelly, executive director of the National Ice Carving Association.

The American Culinary Federation (ACF) also has sanctioned student and professional competitions.

These organizations have regulated the rules and criteria for ice carving competition longer than other organizations. If you can win the NICA championship, you are destined to be a world gold medalist in your craft of ice sculpture. The World Olympics would become the next oyster of your ability if this title should be earned.

Figure 14-22
The finished ice sphere
made from a cube.

REVIEW QUESTIONS

Multiple Choice

1. Scrollwork is an ice carving design technique that
   a. incorporates the scrolling of a spherical ball.
   b. incorporates more than one block of ice.
   c. is used to fuse two segments of ice together.
   d. involves filling an engraved channel with a cloudy snow to create a con-
      trast image within the ice.

2. The _____ is the tool of choice to form a channel in a logo carving.
   a. V-notch chisel
   b. awl
   c. die grinder
   d. scroll bar

3. The sand is locked into place when using the sand-fill technique by
   a. using the gravity adhesion technique.
   b. using a peg and notch fusion technique.
   c. pouring clear sand and allowing it to freeze into place.
   d. packing snow on top of the sand and letting it freeze into place.

4. Because ice melts while on display, it is best to _____ facial features.
   a. underemphasize
   b. overemphasize
   c. avoid carving
   d. none of the above

5. The human head is usually _____ to _____ times the height
   of a standing human body.
   a. 9 to 10
   b. 7 to 8
   c. 8½ to 9½
   d. 5 to 6

6. CNC machines are used to produce
   a. very specific designs.
   b. ice fusions.
   c. template transfers.
   d. template adhesion.

7. The following is *not* a technique used to fuse two segments of ice
   together.
   a. scroll adhesion
   b. metal-plate fusion

SUMMARY

The mission of *Ice Carving 101* is to provide the initial tools for learning the
art and science. By practicing the fundamentals in this book, a beginner will
learn how to reason and formulate the process of carving new and more difficult designs. Winning competitions will come as carvers learn the fundamentals
and gain higher learning, paired with perseverance and desire to achieve a
higher goal.

c. gravity adhesion

d. peg and notch fusion

8. The following is the final step in carving an ice sphere.

   a. Use the medium flat chisel to round off flat surfaces.

   b. Rub diamond-coated sandpaper all over the ball.

   c. Submerge the sphere in a tub of water and rub it with your hands.

   d. Allow it to stand at room temperature for an hour and then go over the surface with a warm, wet towel.

Short Answers

9. What does the acronym *NICA* stand for?

10. Describe a method for creating a reverse scrollwork template design that is used when doing back-filled scrollwork.

11. Explain how to determine the size of a person's face.

12. List three types of functional ice carving designs.

13. Describe how the peg and notch fusion technique works.

14. Give an example of when an ice sphere might be used in the hospitality industry.

INSTRUCTOR'S NOTES

1. Describe what scrollwork is and where it takes place in ice sculpture.

2. Explain how a logo becomes a salable value in ice carving.

3. Illustrate how the human figure can be the highest-valued and among the most difficult to carve in sculpture. This lesson should show respect for the art of sculpture along with any tips to achieve such greatness in artistic talent.

4. Outline the meaning and purpose of a functional design. Offer examples from personal experience and/or the designs in this book.

5. Explain how fusion and ice reassembly works as it pertains to ice carving. Show the tools and provide examples on ice if the means are available. If time allows, show the flat-plate method paired with gravity fusion and the peg and notch method.

6. Explain how computer technology is available for foodservice and include ice carving from the design aspect to the availability for ice carving.

7. Provide a demonstration on how a sphere is made from a cube of ice. This presentation will prepare students for the sphere on the hand design included in this book.

8. Provide the materials available for competition participation. List personal experience in competitions.

Additional Designs

15

"Art in ice is a treasure. Look away and it will change. Look far and it will reappear in your memory."

Michael A. Jasa

Learning Objectives

After you have finished reading this unit, you should be able to:

- Create an angelfish on sea coral
- Carve the head of the horse
- Transform the horse head into a beverage luge
- Sculpt a Roman column base pedestal
- Carve a swordfish in ice
- Sculpt a martini bar shot luge
- Carve of a spherical ball in hand
- Formulate a functional clam shell
- Orchestrate the process of carving a flying swan in ice

Figure 15-1
The template is applied to the ice.

Figure 15-2
The silhouette portion of the ice has been cut away. Notice where the compound depth segments are located. This stage has all areas with a 10-inch depth.

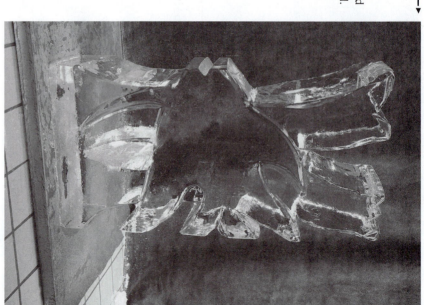

The previous chapters in this book have taught the fundamentals of ice carving using a basic angelfish as the example. This unit will cover additional designs for a carver to explore as he or she continues to hone carving skills.

ANGELFISH ON SEA CORAL

Ice required: Full-sized block of ice.

This exercise takes the basic angelfish to a new level by using a full block and adding sea coral to the design.

Steps:

1. Apply the template (Figure 15-1).
2. Create the outline for the silhouette image using the template transfer method.
3. Remove the segments of the silhouette two-dimensional image. Notice how this design contains a few compound-depth segments, such as where the coral touches the back body of the angelfish. For this step, all portions for the second dimension will be cut away (Figure 15-2). The angelfish and the coral will be defined later in the third-dimension segment removal.
4. Cut away the third-dimension segments to form the basic design (Figures 15-3 and 15-4). Notice how some areas with compound depth segments

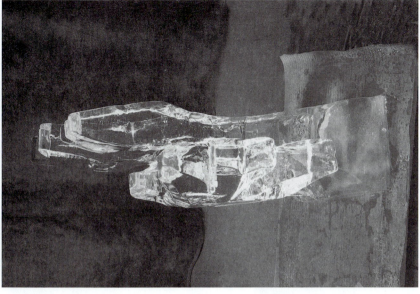

Figure 15-3

This photo illustrates what the head side view looks like after the major third-dimension segments are removed. Notice where the coral is primarily in the back of the design and the fish is in the front.

Figure 15-4

This photo illustrates what the tail side view would look like after the major third-dimension segments are removed. Notice the curvature in the tail and the shape of the coral toward the top of the carving.

Carver's Note

Notice how this third-dimension step also illustrates creating basic shape in the curves of the coral. Having each strip flow in the opposite direction, at the top, demonstrates flow and movement. If they were left as straight vertical strips, the image would appear less alive. This concept should be practiced with all ice carvings, and this ability to sculpt movement into a design is a mark of a better sculptor.

are cut separately from other portions. An example of this would be how the coral is defined on the backside and how the angelfish is defined on the front side. This will involve the technique of making relief cuts to separate the areas to be removed. Then use a chipper, flat chisel, or even a chain saw to cut away the three-dimensional segments to be removed. The backside of the carving will also require a channel area to be removed between the two strips of coral. The compound depth segment of where the fish is located will be around 5 inches deep. Cut through the entire block of the lower area. This lower area removal is possible with a chipper, though much easier through chain saw insertion cuts if the tool is available. A utility cutting die grinder bit, such as the shark tooth end mill, can also be handy on this task.

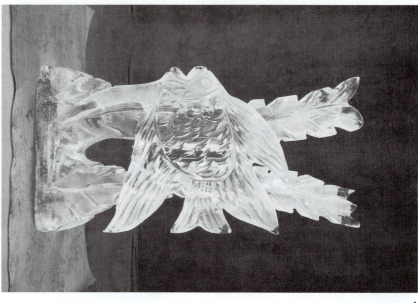

Figure 15-5
The completed angelfish on sea coral.

5. The next procedure after removing the large third-dimension segments is the rounding and shaping step. Various flat chisels, or a chipper, are used to refine the shape of the fins, the head, and the corners of the coral. The leaf separation cuts on the coral should also be performed. This step will be complete when the entire design is in its finished shape and only the detail lines remain.

6. Finish this sculpture by following the line drawing and the image drawn in the final finished sculpture (Figure 15-5). The V-notch chisel is used to place lines on the fish as shown in the drawing and similar to how the primary angelfish design of this book is detailed. Decorative lines should also be carved onto the coral. Defining the lips, mouth, and eyes is best saved for last.

HORSE HEAD

Ice required: Square-cut half block.

Steps:

1. Apply the template (Figure 15-6).
2. Create the outline for the silhouette image using the template transfer method.
3. Cut away the silhouette image segments (Figure 15-7). On this design, you can visualize how the hair on the mane will be far narrower than the origi-

Figure 15-6
The application of the template.

Figure 15-7
The silhouette image should resemble this photo.

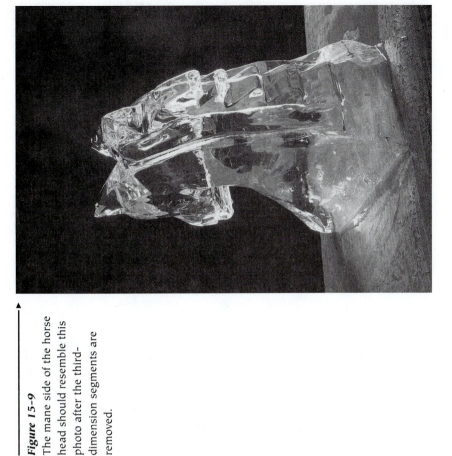

Figure 15-9
The mane side of the horse head should resemble this photo after the third-dimension segments are removed.

nal 10 inches in the silhouette-cutting step. This is mentioned for the reason that time could be saved by simply marking the curves of the mane. Little detail is needed on the front and back areas of the ice because this will be cut away during the third-dimension step. Cut the silhouette entirely to perfection before moving on to the third-dimension cuts. With experience, you'll learn what areas require more time to follow this detail, along with the sections requiring such attention later in the carving process. The curvature of the mane will gather more attention in the shaping and rounding portion of the work.

4. Follow the silhouette stage by cutting the third-dimension areas (Figures 15-8 and 15-9). The most difficult area will be the mouth and contours of the elongated head. Observe where the jowl protrudes in the jaw. Also note how the forehead is at its widest in the eye area. Additional tips on shaping

the head of a horse can be gotten from a 3-D carving model or by reading the section on horses in reference books, such as Jack Hamm's *How to Draw Animals*, listed in the appendices.

5. Continue shaping the sculpture with various flat chisels. Take note of leaving a bulge where the eyes are placed. Observe how the chin protrudes down a little more under the mouth. Now is the time to place a finished curvature in the mane. The socket area of the ears can either point forward or toward the side, as both are a natural position on a horse.

6. Finish the details of the horse head by following the lines shown in the preparatory drawing and observing the photo of the finished design

Figure 15-8
The mouth side of the horse head should resemble this photo after the third-dimension segments are removed.

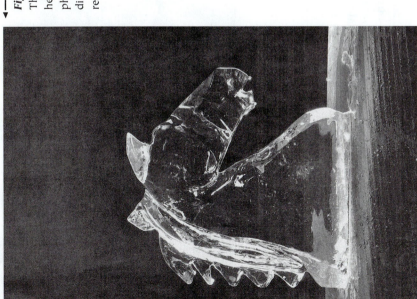

Figure 15-10
The carver adds the final touches to the horse's head.

Figure 15-11
The ½-inch elongated drill bit is slowly boring a hole from the mouth to the top of the head.

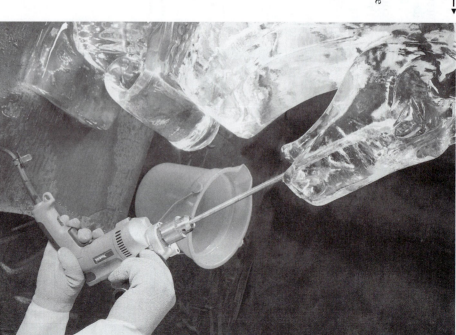

(Figure 15-10). V-notch chisels will do most of the work. Leaving a little ice over the top of the eyeball cut will serve as an eyebrow section. A die grinder with a straight fluted bit is good for boring out the holes in the nostrils.

HORSE AS A BEVERAGE LUGE

Nearly any carving design, including a horse head, can be transformed into a beverage luge by boring a hole from one end to the other with a long drill bit (Figure 15-11).

Steps:

1. Use a clear vinyl tube with the same outer diameter as the drill bit. A ½-inch hole is used in the picture. Apply the bit at a very low speed and repeatedly pull the bit out to remove the shaved ice. This effort and patience will reduce the pressure which may cause possible breakage.

2. Attach the cup to the tube and insert into the ice. Always start with a little extra tubing and then trim it to the perfect length once inserted. If the cup should be tilted too much after insertion, reposition to a

Figure 15-13
Apply the template for the column.

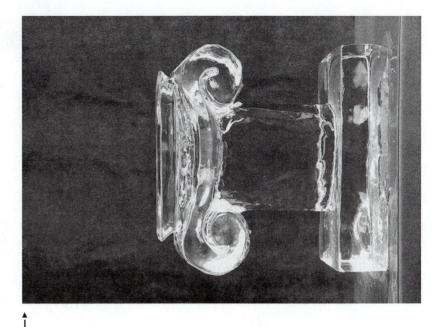

Figure 15-14
Cut out the silhouette image.

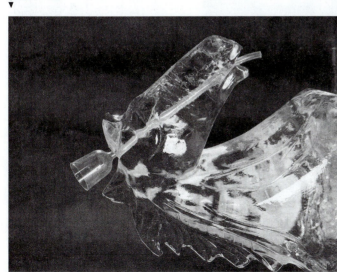

Figure 15-12
The completed horse head shot luge.

more upright angle and then pack a little slush to hold it in place (Figure 15-12).

ROMAN COLUMN BASE PEDESTAL

Ice required: Square-cut half block.

Pedestals are practical carvings. They can be used as a base for other ice carvings as illustrated with the horse head design stacked on top of the column base.

Steps:

1. Apply the template (Figure 15-13).
2. Create the outline for the silhouette image by using the template transfer method.
3. Cut the third-dimension shape (Figures 15-14 and 15-15). Both sides should look identical.

Figure 15-15
This side view illustrates how the third-dimension cuts are made. The opposite side should be identical.

6. The channeling of the spirals can be done with a V-notch chisel. However, a conical end mill bit on a die grinder performs this task very well.

7. Complete the base pedestal design with placing vertical lines on the round column. This can be done with a V-notch or gouge chisel. Keep the distance between lines consistent. It is best to carve the front and back lines first and then make up for any inaccuracies on the sides, where the lines are less visible. This base carving can be used to support many types of other sculptures (Figure 15-16).

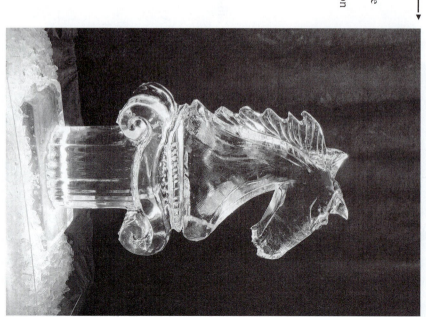

Figure 15-16
This photo provides an example of where the base pedestal could be used to highlight the horse head on display.

4. Form the round shape of the column around the entire carving. Notice that about 1 to 2 inches of ice are left on the top as the flat plate on which other ice will be stacked. It is likely that this flat section will need to be leveled once placed on display. Having a little ice to trim away later, without breaking into the column structure itself, is the intention.

5. Finish the shaping of the curved top sections with flat chisels, hand saw strokes, or even a disk sander. The base is left alone in this design to bring more attention to the column itself and the featured design. Only the top perimeter of the base is smoothed over by rounding the top edge.

Figure 15-18
The silhouette stage of the carving is completed.

MARTINI BAR SHOT LUGE

Ice required: L-cut half block (a full block can also be used for this design)

Steps:

1. Apply the template (Figure 15-17).
2. Create the outline for the silhouette image by using the template transfer method.
3. Cut away the silhouette image (Figure 15-18). Reserve the side sections of the bottle without excessive breakage. These pieces can be used later for making snow.

Figure 15-17
Apply the template.

4. Remove the third-dimension segments (Figure 15-19). Both sides should look identical. This design alone can be one of the most simple carvings to create in ice. Transformation into another function will involve additional steps. Adding a label is a great canvas for practicing scroll work.
5. Shape the bottle with a flat chisel, hand saw strokes, or a disk sander.
6. Create the shot luge design by adding the tube and cup. Begin by using a die grinder bit that has the same outer diameter as your tubing. A 1/2-inch tube and grinder bit are used in this example. Turn the die grinder on and

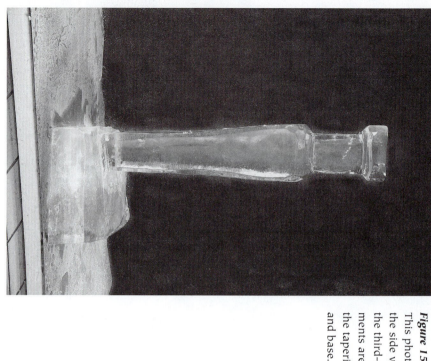

Figure 15-19
This photo illustrates how the side view will look after the third-dimension segments are removed. Notice the tapering of the neck and base.

Figure 15-20
The die grinder is used with a 1/2-inch bit to channel a groove where the shot luge tube will be inserted.

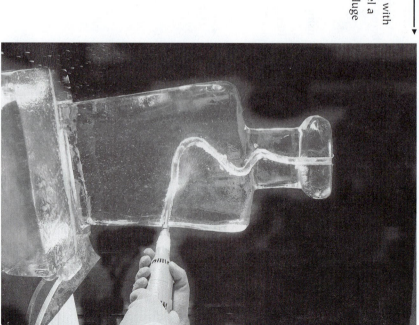

mark a channel from the top of the bottle toward the side of the bottle (Figure 15-20). A few curves will add to the festive nature of the design. Once the line is marked, continue by boring into the channel approximately twice as deep as the tube is wide. For example, the 1/2-inch tubing will need a 1-inch channel.

7. Clean the channel of snow.
8. Assemble the tube and cup and place them in the channel (Figure 15-21).

9. Complete the carving by packing wet snow behind the tube to lock it into place (Figure 15-22).
10. One of the finishing touches will be to add letters or a logo to the front of the ice by using the front-filled scrollwork method described in Chapter 14. Apply a separate template for this scrollwork design and freeze in place with a little water and freezing spray or simply place the sculpture back in the freezer for approximately 10 minutes. Once the template is secured, use the die grinder with a straight fluted bit to channel out the letters

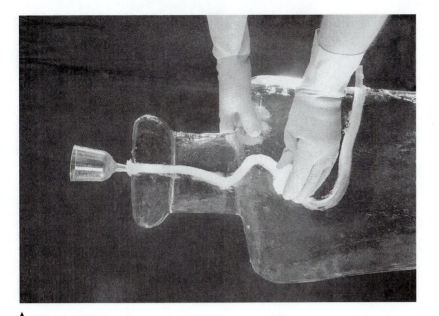

Figure 15-21
The tube is attached to the cup and inserted into the groove.

Figure 15-22
Snow is packed over the tube to secure it.

(Figure 15-23). The size of the bit will affect the size of the letters. This design uses a $1/4$-inch bit. Turn the die grinder on before applying to the ice. Hold the tool at a slight angle and begin marking the lines by intruding by $1/2$ inch. Then follow through the channels one or two more times to form a deeper impression. You will need to bore through at least 1 to 2 inches for the letters to last for hours while on display. Remove the paper template once the channels are complete. If the paper is still frozen, use a little water warm on the surface. Check to see that paper flakes no longer remain in the channels.

11. Fill the channels with snow. Produce fresh snow with the chain saw from a scrap piece of ice or from the segment reserved from the silhouette phase of the carving.

12. Rub the snow into the channels (Figure 15-24). Using your fingertips, press the snow deeply into the channels. Repeat the snow rubbing process until the entire channel is densely packed. Air pockets left inside the channels may cause premature melting during display.

13. Perform the cleaning steps to complete the martini bar shot luge (Figure 15-25).

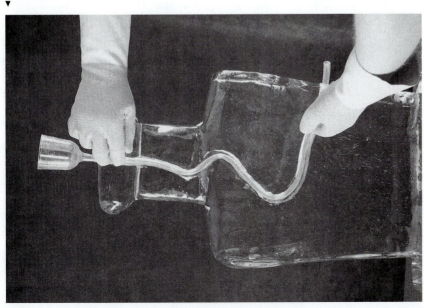

Figure 15-23
The die grinder with a
1/4-inch straight bit is used
to channel out the letters
through the template
paper. Notice how the tool
is held at a slight angle to
the ice. Once the letters
have been transferred,
make the channels deeper
for a longer-lasting display.
A 1-inch depth would be a
minimum.

Figure 15-24
Freshly made snow is
packed into the channels to
highlight the letters. Remember the importance of
packing this snow in with
the fingertips and repeating
this step at least two times.

Figure 15-25
The completed martini bar
shot luge.

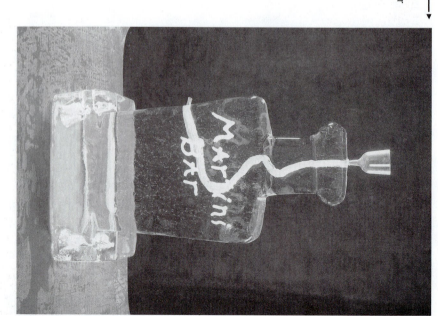

Carver's Note

The snow will be dry if it is fresh and you are working in a cold area.
Adding a few drops of water can moisten the snow. If working in a
warmer area, it will become naturally slushy within a few minutes.

SWORDFISH

Ice required: Full-sized block or an L-cut half block

Steps:

1. Apply the template (Figure 15-26).
2. Create the outline for the silhouette image.
3. Cut away the silhouette image (Figure 15-27). The concave curve between the tail and the body will be one of the tougher areas to remove. It is

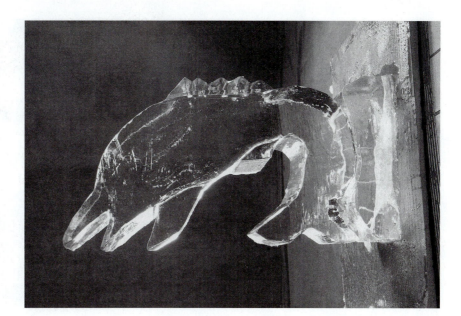

Figure 15-27
The silhouette image ice has been removed.

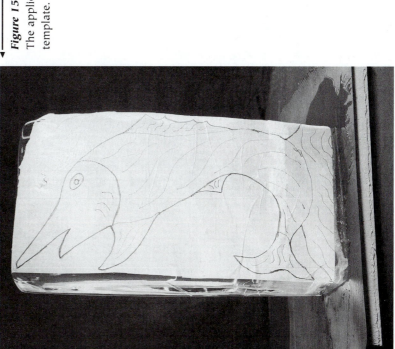

Figure 15-26
The application of the template.

Pro's Corner

There are many techniques to making a great shot luge. The one provided in this book is one of the simpler methods. Other methods may include splitting the block in half, inserting a tube through a carved channel, adding a printed logo on paper or a transparency sheet, and welding the blocks back together. The logo will appear to be in the center of the ice with this method. As shown in the photographs, the tube can conflict with the logo or design qualities within the clarity of the ice. This example shows how the two channel formations could combine, though still be a part of the functional design.

acceptable to leave this in a rough form until later in the process. The same goes for the curves in the dorsal fin.

4. Cut away the third-dimension area (Figures 15-28 and 15-29). Notice how there is a slight curvature to the tail to add movement. Also, leave a good amount of ice between the fish and the base to provide a sturdy structure.

5. Form the rounding and shaping with flat chisels and hand saw strokes. Now is the time to clean up the concave curve of the tail, along with the curves of the dorsal fin. Leave the pair of head fins on the thick side as these tend to melt quickly on display.

6. Finish the detail as shown in the preparatory line drawing (Figure 15-30). Using a sharp V-notch chisel will prevent breakage on the tail. Too much pressure may cause it to snap off and become a difficult repair. A die grinder may be used for detail lines as well. The base should be decorated to look like water or a coral rock to add to the finished look of the design.

BALL ON A HAND

Ice required: A full block of ice can yield two sculptures of this design if desired. This is a two-part process of carving a sphere combined with carving a hand.

Figure 15-28
The head side of the carving will resemble this illustration after the third-dimension segments are removed.

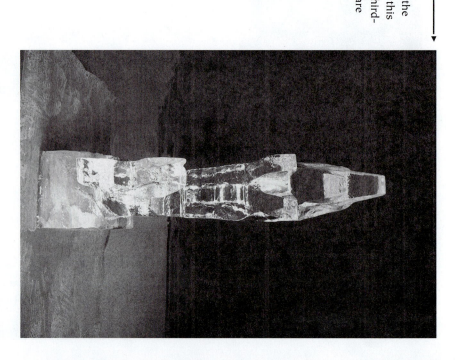

Figure 15-29
The dorsal fin side of the carving will resemble this illustration after the third-dimension segments are removed.

TEMPLATE DESIGN WORKSHEET

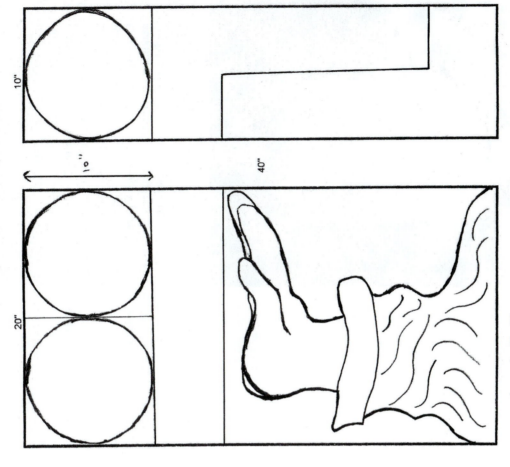

10"

10"

20"

40"

Legend: 1" = 5"

▲ **Figure 15-31**   This preparatory drawing illustrates where the block will be split into a 10-inch section and a 30-inch section. The 10-inch section will be split in half to allow the carving of two spheres. The 30-inch section can be carved into one hand or split into two L-cut half blocks.

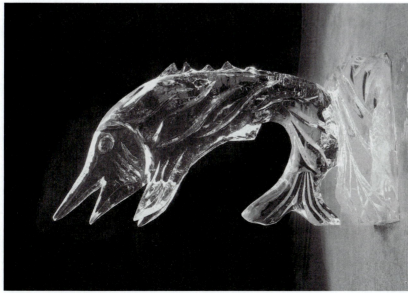

▲ **Figure 15-30**
The completed swordfish after shaping and detail have been applied.

The Ball

Refer to the section in Chapter 14 on the methods required for carving a sphere.

Steps:

1. Follow the outline drawing (Figure 15-31).
2. Cut a 10-inch section from one side of the block.
3. Cut this rectangular section into two 10-inch cubes. Carve the spheres out of these cubes and reserve in the freezer until displayed.

The Hand

Steps:

1. Divide the remaining 30-inch section into two L-cut half blocks.
2. Apply the template (Figure 15-32).
3. Create the outline for the silhouette image using the template transfer method.
4. Cut the silhouette image (Figure 15-33). Note how the wrist appears to be coming out of a jacket with a cuff. This design is much simpler than sculpting the entire arm. This technique is common in ice sculpture design.
5. Cut out the third-dimension (Figure 15-34). The index finger is defined by making it shorter than the middle finger. The thumb is also curved inward as if the hand is cupped to hold the ball.

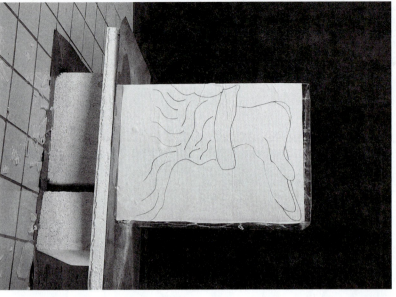

Figure 15-32
Apply the template of the hand as shown.

Figure 15-33
The hand will resemble this image after the silhouette image has been removed.

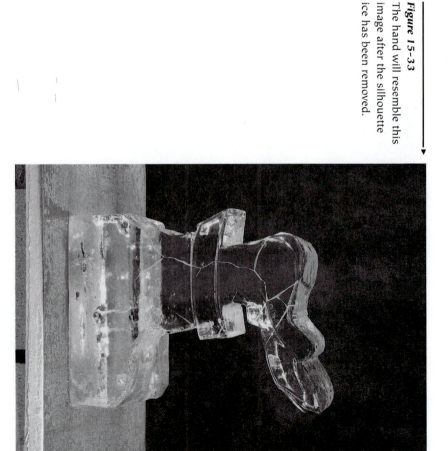

Carver's Note

For shaping the hand, one of the best carving models is your own right hand. Hold it in the air and apply the same shape to the ice. The base and clothed forearm can be abstract as long as the cuff shows a clear separation from the wrist.

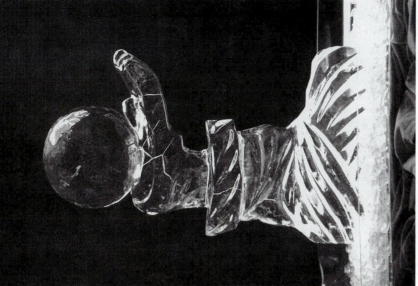

Figure 15-35
The completed ball on a hand.

Figure 15-34
The fingertip side of the carving will resemble this photo after the third-dimension segments are removed.

6. Add the detail lines as shown in the preparatory drawing and as illustrated in Figure 15-31 (Figure 15-35).
7. Add a cup-shaped impression to the palm of the hand to hold the ball. Use the gouge chisel to scoop this section out.

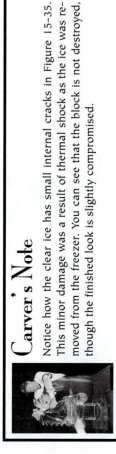

CLAM SHELL

Ice required: Square-cut half block, which will be split in half to form the two sides of the clamshell

This carving can serve as a functional serving piece filled with crushed ice and seafood as a raw bar.

Steps:

1. Apply the template (Figure 15-36).
2. Create the outline for the silhouette image using a template transfer method.

Carver's Note

Notice how the clear ice has small internal cracks in Figure 15-35. This minor damage was a result of thermal shock as the ice was removed from the freezer. You can see that the block is not destroyed, though the finished look is slightly compromised.

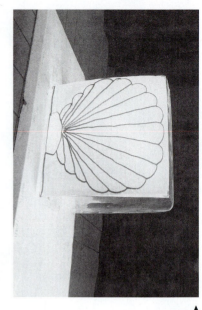

Figure 15-36
Apply the template.

7. Apply a finished detail look by creating groove lines with a V-notch chisel from the hinge to the outer rim.

8. Once all the shaping and groove lines are completed, prepare the hinge by flattening it with the metal plate. This will make it easier to set up for display. Store this sculpture as two separate pieces for ease of transport, then attach them at the hinge when placing the sculpture in its final position (Figure 15-39).

as shrimp cocktail. Use the flat chisel to refine the curved areas on the exterior rim.

3. Cut the silhouette image (Figure 15-37). The exterior of the shell can be either symmetrical or abstract. The image carved for this book is more on the abstract side, as the exterior part of the shell was left uneven to project a weathered look.

4. Split the silhouette shell in half with a hand saw or a chain saw (Figure 15-38).

5. Remove the third-dimension segments by adding curvature to the shell.

6. The shaping will involve scooping out the interior area with a gouge chisel. Be sure to leave the back hinge area flat on the lower shell to allow a bonding surface for the top shell during display. Scooping more ice out of the lower shell will also create more volume to hold food such

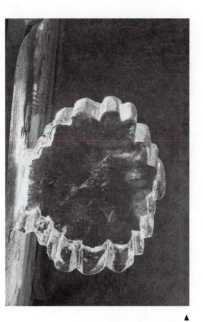

Figure 15-37
The silhouette stage will appear as shown. Note that the curves of the edge do not have to be perfect at this point. Refinement will come later.

Figure 15-38
The chain saw is used to split the shell in half.

Figure 15-39
The completed clam shell. Attaching the halves will be much easier if done on the display table.

FLYING SWAN

Ice required: A full block of ice

The swan is a very popular design in ice carving, though often it is mistakenly chosen as one of the first sculptures to carve by beginners. The elongated neck and wings can be difficult to manage, especially when carved too thinly. A little more experience or close guidance is recommended when carving the swan.

A chain saw will be handy for segment removal during the initial steps of this project, especially between the wings and the opening of the neck.

Steps:

1. Apply the template (Figure 15-40).
2. Create the outline for the silhouette image.
3. Cut the silhouette image (Figure 15-41). The area between the head and neck can be the most difficult to remove. This area can be left rough at this point to prevent breakage.

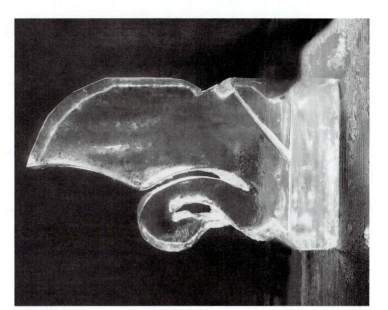

Figure 15-41
The silhouette image will resemble this illustration.

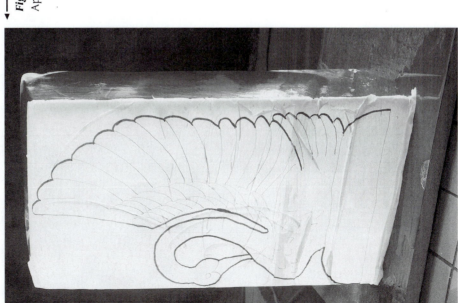

Figure 15-40
Apply the template.

Pro's Corner

If the shell is designed to hold food in the lower shell, bore a drain hole through the bottom so that melting water will not build up and drown the products intended for display.

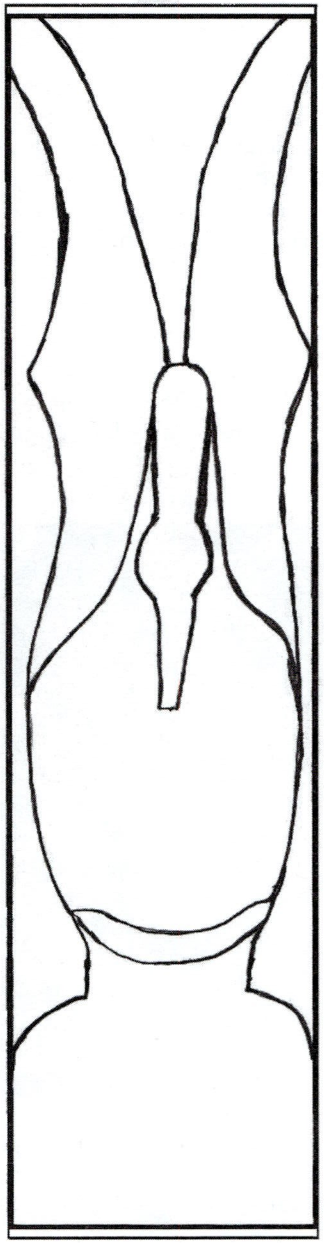

40"

10"

▲ *Figure 15-42*
Compare this diagram to the photo shown for an example of how to follow the third-dimension procedures on the head portion of the swan design.

4. The area between the neck and wings should be only slightly separated with a saw. Too wide of a gap may distort the shape of the neck or wings. A chain saw is recommended for these difficult areas.

5. Carve the third-dimension segments to resemble the side-view drawings and the illustrations (Figures 15-42, 15-43, 15-44, and 15-45).

6. To create the head and neck, start by drawing scratches with the six-prong chipper to identify where the thinnest part of the neck will be at the top of the curve, then marking the widest part of the head, and then again marking where the body will join the neck. Cut lines should run from the

Figure 15-43
The head side of the swan will resemble this image after the third-dimension segments have been removed.

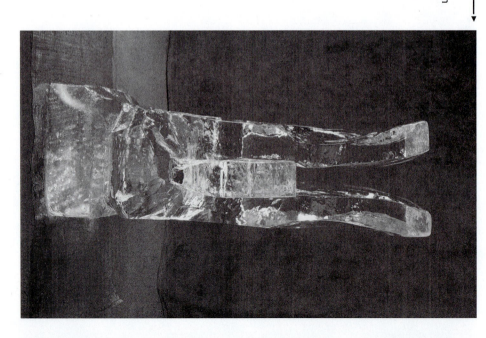

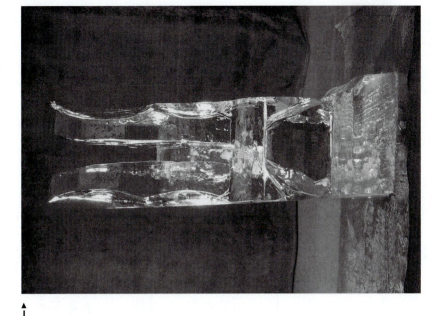

Figure 15–45
The tail side of the swan will resemble this image after the third-dimension segments have been removed.

Figure 15–44
Compare this diagram to the photo shown for an example of how to follow the third-dimension procedures on the tail side portion of the swan design.

narrowest necklines toward the width of the body. The middle scratch lines for the head should be respected and cut secondarily after the first segments are removed.

7. The back area will form a curve in the tail. The separation of the wings will be the primary skill. If the relief cuts are made properly, this still leaves a good portion of ice connected between the removal segment and the top of the body. Removing this section after the side cuts are complete is best done with a strike of the flat chisel to crack the segment from the body. It is advised to have a helper ready to hold the middle segment so it doesn't fall and break the wing segments.

8. Shaping and rounding will take place on the neck, body, base, and tail. The head will take the most attention in this phase to keep the jowl intact; form a beak that is both sturdy enough to last through display yet delicate to

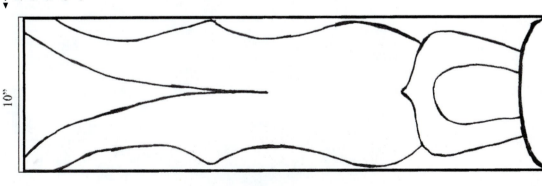

10"

40"

represent the gracefulness of a swan. Notice how the beak is left in contact to the body on this design. This attachment allows for more sturdiness for placing detail lines. Too much pressure on a softened separated head structure could result in the head's breaking off, a catastrophic result. A separated head design on a swan will require a very sharp decorative chisel or a die grinder to avoid breakage.

Carver's Note

A common mistake is to overcarve the wings. The wings are highly susceptible to breakage during carving, transport, storage, and display. The wings should be smoothed over to remove rough edges and left bulky enough to sustain the rigors of transporting and display.

Finishing Touches

Wings

The wing lines are graduated from a small feathered row near the bone line to outer plumes. The first row is placed along the lower joint of the wing to follow the bone line. This is followed by a secondary interior set of feathers. The outer plumes will be deeper and span from the top of the prior two rows of feathers down into the body as it meets the tail. All lines are carved with graduating V-notch chisels or creative die grinder usage.

Body

The body is separated by the breast area and the tail section. The tail is highlighted through deep solid V-notch lines. The middle body and breast are best accented through small curves of a V-notch chisel or an angled bit of a die grinder.

Head

The head is finished with an eye-marking detail and the lines to form the beak detail. Note that the beak should be left attached to the breast for stability. A final move involves taking the notorious five steps back to see whether the proportion and detail are finished. The standard cleaning, storage, and display techniques apply (Figure 15-46).

Figure 15-46
The completed flying swan.

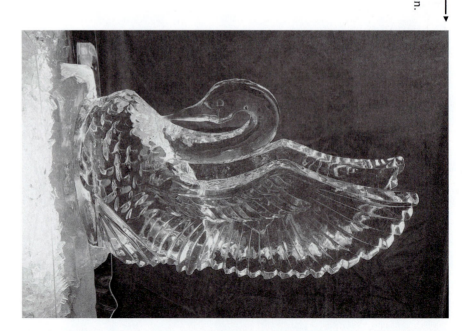

Summary

The lessons of this chapter will prepare you for additional designs of ice sculpture. The angelfish, which is the primary lesson in this chapter, is expanded into a full-block sculpture with a background of coral. Other wildlife are illustrated to showcase additional simple and functional designs. The purpose of a base pedestal is demonstrated through the column. The advanced carving techniques of spheres or bird wings are offered in a design format tailored for the first-time carver. These designs, along with additional offerings in the references provided in the appendices, will create inspiration for students, instructors, and professionals alike to pursue the world of sculpture.

INSTRUCTOR'S NOTES

1. The designs offered in this chapter are examples of additional material to allow the first-time carver to explore beyond the class lesson of fundamental learning and the angelfish. Many other designs are available.

2. The diversity of designs presented to the students should be in direct proportion to the class time and supervision level available. As an extreme example, it would be very difficult to coach 20 different designs on a single day with only one instructor. Figure that about seven designs per mentor will keep the third day flowing in a five-hour class. This allows for the hour spent in setup and breakdown with a carving time of more than three hours.

3. The lecture portion of the first day should include notes about additional designs beyond the angelfish, especially if a two- or three-day format is used.

4. Use the ball carving lecture in a separate format if time allows.

5. Explain how the progression of additional carving designs in the career will take time and practice.

Templates

10"

5"

35"

L-CUT BLOCK – SIDE VIEW OF FULL BLOCK

L-Cut Half Block Diagram

TEMPLATE DESIGN WORKSHEET

20"

10"

40"

Legend: 1" = 5"

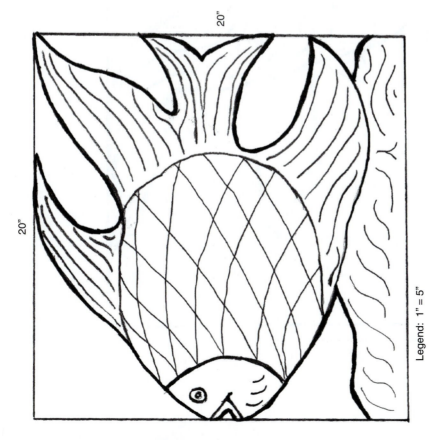

Design 1 Angelfish Template

20"

20"

Legend: 1" = 5"

Design 2 Angelfish on Full Coral Block Template

20"

40"

Legend: 1" = 5"

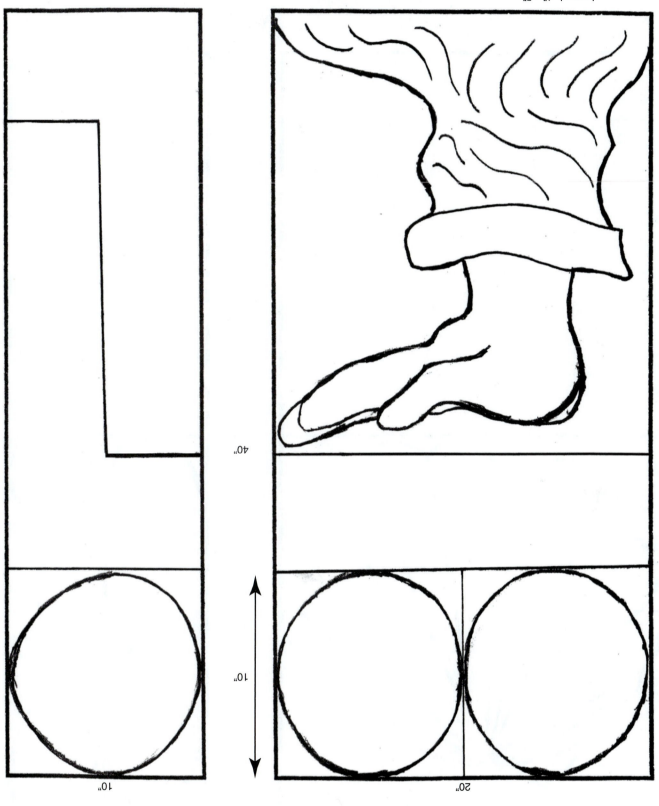

Legend: 1" = 5"

40"

10"

10"

20"

TEMPLATE DESIGN WORKSHEET

Design 3 Ball on Hand Template

TEMPLATE DESIGN WORKSHEET

20"

10"

40"

Legend: 1" = 5"

Top   Bottom

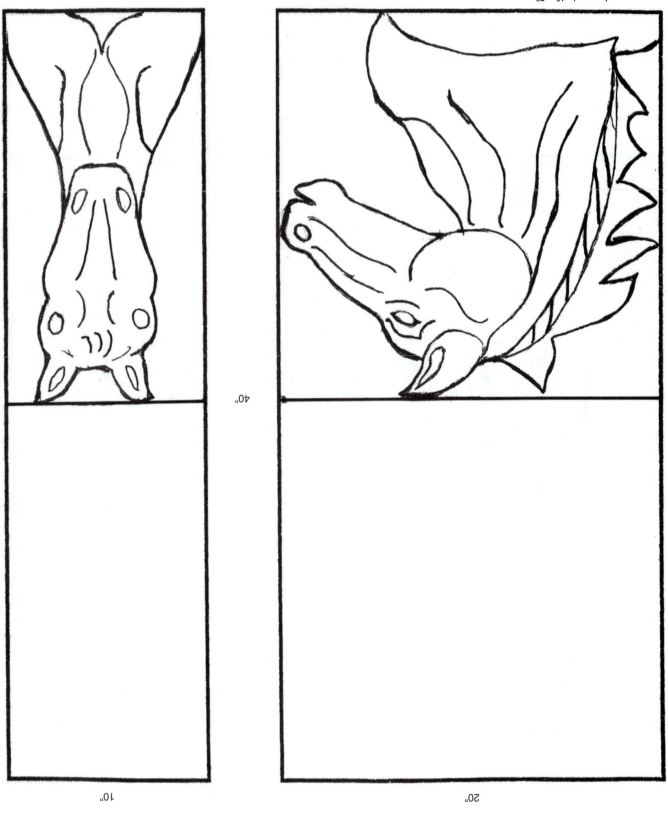

Legend: 1" = 5"

40"

20"

10"

TEMPLATE DESIGN WORKSHEET

Design 4 Clamshell Template

TEMPLATE DESIGN WORKSHEET

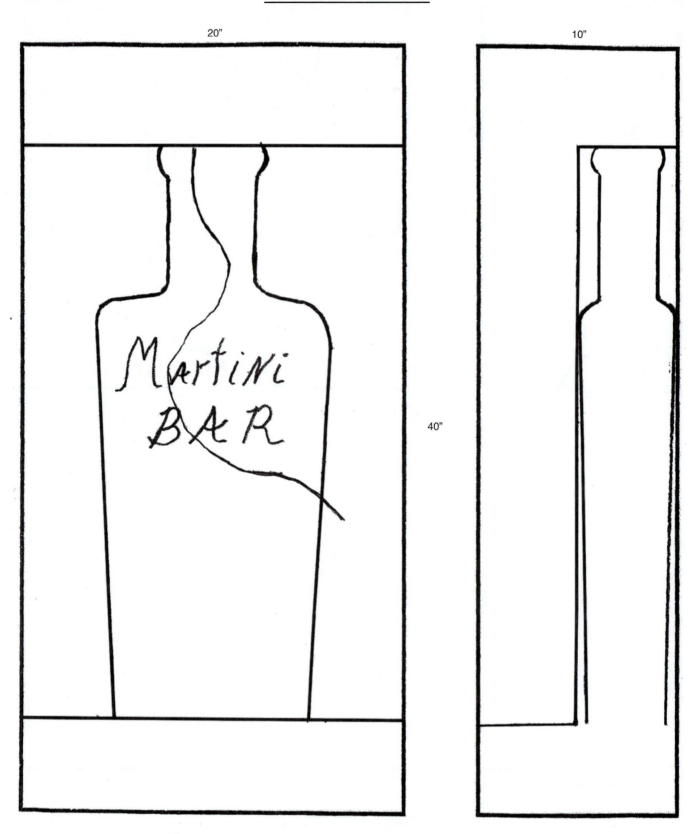

20"

10"

40"

Martini BAR

Legend: 1" = 5"

Legend: 1" = 5"

40"

20"

10"

TEMPLATE DESIGN WORKSHEET

Design 6 Martini Bar Shot Luge Template

TEMPLATE DESIGN WORKSHEET

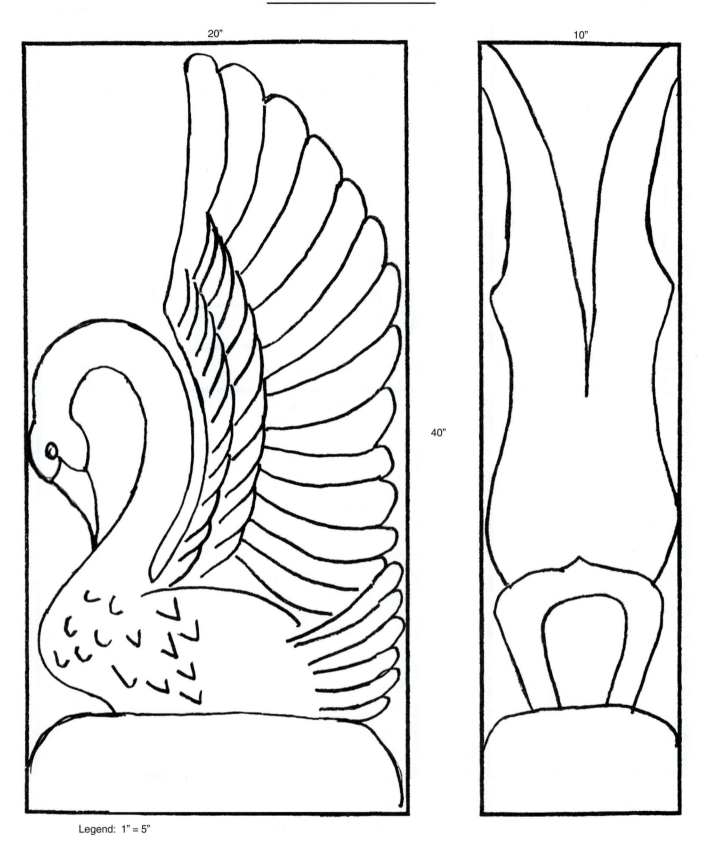

Legend: 1" = 5"

Legend: 1" = 5"

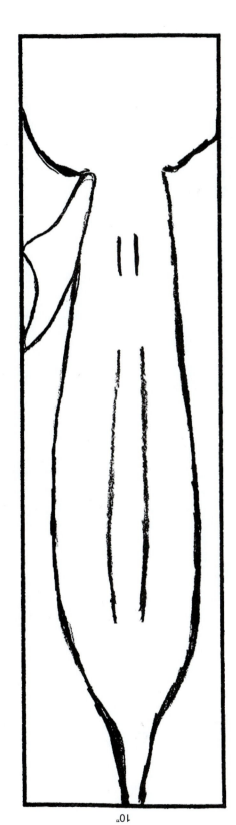

40"

10"

20"

TEMPLATE DESIGN WORKSHEET

Design 8 Swan Template

APPENDIX B

Sources for Tools and Supplies

INFORMATION AND CONSULTATION

Culinary Artz LLC
Michael Jasa, CEC
www.culinaryartz.com
email: ChefMJ1@aol.com
954-757-5649

ICE CARVERS CLOTHING

RefrigiWear (clothing, gloves, boots)
www.refrigiwear.com
PO Box 39, Dahlonega, GA 30533
800-645-3744

ICE MAKING EQUIPMENT

Clinebell Equipment Company
www.clinebellequipment.com
890 Denver Ave., Loveland, CO 80537
800-699-4423

ICE CARVING TOOLS

Ice Crafters (full line)
www.icecrafters.com
PO Box 2664, Glen Ellyn, IL 60138
630-871-0739

Makita Power Tools
www.makitatools.com
1-800-4Makita

JB Prince (chisels, power tools, saws, tongs, chippers, sharpening stones)
www.jbprince.com
800-473-0577

I-Sculpt (CNC carving machinery) by Dean Carlson
West Palm Beach, FL
561-795-1151
Available for purchase through Ice Crafters

TEMPLATES

Duende Ice Division
www.duendeicedivision.com
The Racquet Club of Memphis, Special Events Office
5111 Sanderlin Ave., Memphis, TN 38117
901-765-4400

Ice Crafters
www.icecrafters.com
PO Box 2664, Glen Ellyn, IL 60138
630-871-0739

MOLDS

Ice Crafters
www.icecrafters.com
PO Box 2664, Glen Ellyn, IL 60138
630-871-0739

DISPLAY EQUIPMENT

Glo-Ice by Engineered Plastics
www.gloice.com
336-449-4121

Ice Crafters
www.icecrafters.com
PO Box 2664, Glen Ellyn, IL 60138
630-871-0739

JB Prince (display trays)
www.jbprince.com
800.473.0577

L.E.D. Effects, Inc. (lighting)
www.ledeffects.com
11390 Sunrise Gold Circle, Suite 800, Rancho Cordova, CA 95742
916-852-1719

Sparktacular (fireworks for displays)
www.sparktacular.com
4101 Ravenswood Rd., Suite 126, Dania, FL 33312
877-792-1101
954-792-1101

LIFTS

Ice Crafters
www.icecrafters.com
PO Box 2664, Glen Ellyn, IL 60138
630-871-0739

T&S Equipment Co.
www.tseq.com
2999 N. Wayne St., Angola, IN 46703-9122
260-665-9521

EQUIPMENT REPAIR/SHARPENING

NuCut Grinding (sharpening service for all carving tools)
www.end-mill-sharpening.com
38 Manhattan St., North Tonawanda, NY 14120
716-694-7950

Samurai Chisel Sharpening by Michael Pizutto
Golden, CO
303-423-6560

APPENDIX C

Industry Organizations

American Culinary Federation—ACF (Culinary association supporting ice carving; organizes competitions)
www.acfchefs.org
800-624-9458
904-824-4468

American Hotel and Motel Association
www.ahma.com
202-289-3100

Friends of Sculpting (organization devoted to promoting the art of ice carving)
www.snow-ny.org

International Caterers Association
www.icacater.org
877-422-4221

National Association of Catering Executives—NACE
www.nace.net
410-290-5410

National Ice Carving Association—NICA
www.nica.org
630-871-8431

Professional Chef's Association—PCA (culinary association supporting ice carving)
www.professionalchef.com
970-223-4004

World Association of Chefs' Societies—WACS
www.wacs2000.org

World Ice Sculptures Alliance—WISA (10 companies working together to raise level of the ice carving profession)
www.icesculpturesltd.com
616-458-6005

Sample Release Form

This form is provided as an example to follow in formulating one's own waiver of liability document. This page is not intended to be photocopied or reproduced in a word-for-word format. Instructors and/or event organizers should seek advice from their own legal council to generate their own individual legal documents.

RELEASE FORM
ICE CARVING
LIABILITY AND INDEMNITY

I, _____, realize that participating in the ice carving portion of this class, or event, will require the use of tools (including chain saws) and equipment to carve ice. I agree to follow "Safety First" behavior while participating in this activity. I also understand that the blocks of ice used in ice carving often weigh in excess of 300 pounds. By signing this release form, I acknowledge that I am doing this activity at my own risk. I am releasing the school, event organizers, its officers, and instructors from all liability that might be incurred relative to the carving activities held within this class.

Carver's Name

By signing this agreement, I am stating that I am fully aware of the responsibilities and possible hazards that might occur in relationship to my participation in ice carving.

Name of School: _____

Date: _____

Student or Guardian Name (printed): _____

Signature of Student or Guardian: _____

Bibliography

Amendola, Joseph, and Larry Malchik. *Ice Carving Made Easy*, 2nd ed. New York: John Wiley & Sons, 1994.

Bayley, Julian. *Ideas That Work*. Hensall, Ontario, Canada: Author, 2002.

Durocher, Joseph F., Jr. *Practical Ice Carving*. New York: CBI/Van Nostrand Reinhold, 1981.

Garlough, Robert, Randy Finch, and Derek Maxfied. *Ice Sculpting the Modern Way*. Clifton Park, NY: Delmar Learning, 2004.

Hamm, Jack. *Drawing the Head & Figure*. New York: Putnam, 1963.

Hamm, Jack. *How to Draw Animals*. New York: Putnam, 1969.

Hart, Christopher. *Human Anatomy Made Amazingly Easy*. New York: Watson-Guptill, 2000.

Hasegawa, Hideo. *Ice Carving*. Carlsbad, CA: Continental Publishing, 1974.

Hogarth, Burne. *Dynamic Anatomy, The Revised Edition*. New York: Watson-Guptill, 2003.

Peck, Stephen Rogers. *Atlas of Human Anatomy for the Artist*. New York: Oxford University Press, 1982.

Shimizu, Mitsuo. *The New World of Ice Sculpture*. Japan: Shimizu Ice Carving Academy. (Japanese)

Shimizu, Mitsuo. *The New World of Ice Sculpture, Vol II*. Japan: Shimizu Ice Carving Academy, 1982. (Japanese)

Winker, Mac, and Claire Winker. *Ice Sculpture: The Art of Ice Carving in 12 Systematic Steps*. Memphis, TN: Duende Publications, 1989.

Glossary

Air broom–power tool emitting a high-velocity concentrated airflow for cleaning ice shavings from the surface of a finished sculpture

Allowance for melting–technique used by carvers to compensate for display melting; it usually involves exaggerating the size of the features of an ice sculpture

Ambient air environment–determined by the temperature, wind velocity, and lighting of the carving area

Amortized value of your equipment investment–expense to your business equal to the amount you would need to charge to pay off your investment in tools and supplies

Arthur's law (thermal ice degradation)–a solid state of water (H_2O), as ice, will deteriorate from heated thermal shock in direct proportion to the change of its temperature environment

Back-filled scrollwork–channeled design produced by creating a negative image on the backside of the ice

Base lifting handles–holes cut into the base with a chain saw to allow the hands to slip into the structure, allowing the carving to be easily lifted

Beveled side chisel stroke–application of the flat chisel, which is used for shaving away areas of a concave curve

Break-away points–lines on the ice block indicating which areas should be removed

Carving design model–three-dimensional visual aid used to carve the intended design

Carving platform–surface that supports the ice as it is being carved

Casting sculpture–image created by pouring a liquid into a mold; it cools and solidifies into the shape of a sculpture

Chain oil–oil that is suitable for the oil pump, chain, and bar sprocket of a power saw

Chain saw insertion cut–piercing the block straight through the ice; especially valuable for removing interior segments

Chain saw line cutting–cut that follows a straight line through the block of ice

Chain saw pulling cut–cut made when the chain saw is cutting from the top of the bar or tip

Chain saw pushing cut–cut made when the chain saw is cutting from the bottom of the bar or tip

Chain saw shaping–carving performed to bring the finished angles and final shape to the design

Chain saw straight cut–a chain saw cutting method used to cut a perfectly straight line through the ice

Chain saw tip cutting–technique of inserting the first inch of the saw blade to mark a line

Chain sharpening–method used to keep the links of a chain saw sharp and ready for use

Channel detail line–decorative impression, drawn through the surface, to form a double-cornered line within the ice

Compound depth segment–area where a limited depth is cut to create a relief portion of the design

Computer-assisted design (CAD)–computer program application used to design and manufacture products, in this case ice carving

Computer numerical control (CNC)–precision machine used to produce very specific designs with accuracy

Concave curve–rounded inward, like the inside of a bowl

Convex curve–rounded outward, like the exterior of a sphere or circle

Corner balanced position–point where the ice is standing on its lowest corner and secured by the grip of the tongs and the torso of your body

Decorative lines–combination of grooves and/or channels, formed by various tools, to highlight the detail of the original design

Design segment definition–area where particular lines are drawn to create image and definition in the sculpture design

Detail line drawings–sketches used for visualization that demonstrate the areas where detail lines will be drawn on the ice

Detail model–life-size or scale version of the carving design used to guide the sculptor in visualizing the fine shaping or detail lines to be carved

Detail visualization–practice of formulating where the fine shaping details and decorative lines will be carved

Die grinder–high-speed rotary tool that shears the surface of the ice to form a channel

Die grinder bit–removable attachment to a die grinder used to cut channels of various shapes and sizes

Die grinder channeling–using a die grinder tool to form a groove of various depths within the ice

Die grinder finishing–using a die grinder fitted with bits of various shapes to produce the finishing touches

Disk sander rounding–using a disk sander to smooth out rough areas and corners on the ice

Fine shaping detail–smaller segments left for the end of the carving process to avoid excessive melting

Flat chisels for ice carving–hand tools designed to be driven through ice and water

Flat chisel rounding–process of softening corners to bring two flat faces together

Flat side chisel stroke–application of the flat chisel for shaving away areas of a flat surface or a convex curve

Flat chisel shaping–process of narrowing an area to its final shape using a flat chisel

Flat welding–method of joining ice by making two surfaces touch with a flat surface for adhesion

231

Freehand drawing–practice of sketching a design on a blank sheet of paper

Front-filled scrollwork–carving that incorporates a channeled and snow-filled image

Functional ice carving designs–carvings that serve a purpose other than as a centerpiece

GFCI–ground fault circuit interrupter, designed to protect the carver from severe or fatal shocks

Gouge chisel–ice carving chisel with a curved blade

Gravity adhesion–fusion of ice through gravity stacking; often uses a saw, nail board, or metal plate to bring the adjoining surfaces to a flat seam

Groove detail line–decorative impression, drawn along the surface, to form a single-angled V-notch shape with the V-notch chisel or a concave line with the gouge chisel

Guide bar–the extension of a chain saw; it guides the chain during motion and acts as the cutting surface

Half-block splitting–procedure of dividing a full block into two equal pieces

Hand broom–cleaning tool made of straw or nylon to sweep away unwanted ice fragments

Hand truck dolly–two-wheeled cart used for moving heavy objects by hand

Heat gun–commercially built power tool used to throw a concentrated flow of heated air onto the ice

Ice fusion–act of joining two segments of ice

Ice sphere–ball carved from a cube of ice

L-cut half block–20 × 35 × 5-inch upright block with a 20 × 5 × 10-inch base left attached for support

Metal plate fusion–act of joining two segments of ice by creating perfectly flat surfaces with a metal plate

Modeling sculpture–method of creating an image by assembling pieces over one another

Multiple-block designs–sculptures that incorporate more than one block of ice to create the display

Ohm's law–mathematical equation used to calculate the number of amps, volts, or watts

Paper template–paper overlay that serves as a pattern to use when tracing design on to the ice.

Peg and notch fusion–method of fusion in which one segment has a peg, or a male section, and the other segment has a void, or female section, to match the shape of the peg

Power tools–electric tools used for speed and specialty application in the carving of ice

Preparatory line drawing–scale sketch of a sculpture design on paper

Protective liner–cardboard, high-density styrofoam (polystyrene insulation works well), plywood, or rubber mats used to cover the carving platform

Prism effect–light refracting through ice into multiple angles and sometimes changing from white light to rainbow colors

Relief cut–saw cut made between a segment to be removed and the intended design, thus allowing rapid removal of the unwanted ice without cracking or damaging the body of the sculpture

Relief sculpture–creation of an image by removing portions from a solid medium

Scale–exact proportion of two images

Sand-fill technique–achieved by pouring a layer of colored sand, through a narrow spout, into a back-filled scrollwork channel

Scrollwork–design technique that involves filling an engraved channel with cloudy snow to create a contrast image within the ice

Sculpture–three-dimensional image that conveys a thought or message

Sculpture charge formula–used to determine how much to charge for each carving; it is based on the expenses involved with producing the sculpture coupled with the value of your time and the quality of your work

Sculpture cleaning–process of removing unwanted ice fragments from the finished sculpture with water, air, heat, or broom sweeping

Shaping die grinder bits–die grinder bits that are straight or slightly conical; used for shaping or rounding

Sharding–condition in which the internal crystals of the ice break down and separate from the structure of the carving block

Sharpening stones–also known as whetstones; used to sharpen the edges of cutting tools

Silhouette image–two-dimensional side view of a sculpture design

Solid template–usually made of wood or cardboard and can be used for multiple applications as a pattern to use when tracing a design onto the ice

Square half block–20 × 20 × 10-inch segment formed by splitting the block down the center of the 40-inch face

Squaring the block–process in which the bottom face is cut flat and perpendicular to the upright position of the carving to create an even surface

Surface scratch–connects the dots during the template transfer process

Template–a design pattern, which can be used as a guide to transfer the initial image to the ice

Template adhesion–process used to secure the template to the ice

Template expansion method–process used to create a full-size template from a small preparatory drawing

Tensioning the chain–adjusting the tension of the chain so that it is tight enough to keep the guides on track with the bar

Third-dimension–a specific artistic image

Third-dimension visualization–imagining what the sculpture will look like once the ice is removed

Three-dimension image–a design with height, width, and depth

Three-dimensional logo–design in which the ice is sculpted into a formation of letters or a specific artistic image

Third-dimension preparatory drawing–diagram used to outline the third-dimension segments to be removed

Tracing–method of drawing in which an image is placed either over or under a comparable image of the intended design and copied to a blank sheet of paper

Visualization–basic practice of examining the ice and formulating an idea of what the sculpture will look like after a carving step is completed

V-notch lines–angular grooves made with a V-notch chisel for either finishing detail or defining the template lines

Water washing–final step of cleaning an ice carving to leave a smooth and sparkling finished sculpture

Wind velocity–speed at which air is traveling

Answer Key

Chapter 1

True or False

1. T
2. F
3. F
4. T
5. T

Short Answer

6. A prism effect is the result of light refracting through ice and projecting into multiple angles and sometimes changing from white light to rainbow colors. These ever-changing qualities truly create audience appeal for ice sculptures.

7. Create a barrier to keep the spectators from gathering too close. Stay aware of any ice or water that may lead to slips in the guest area, and keep tools out of the reach of children.

8. The amortized value of your equipment investment is the expense to your business equal to the amount you would need to charge to pay off your investment in tools and supplies. (This value is paid off over time as an internal expense of business costs as they relate to taxation and real property.)

9. Delivery charges depend on who is delivering the block and the distance traveled.

10. The actual time involved in the project depends on a number of factors, so it is common practice to give an approximate price range.

Chapter 2

True or False

1. T
2. T
3. F
4. T
5. T

Multiple Choice

6. b
7. b
8. c
9. b
10. d
11. a
12. a
13. a
14. c
15. c

Chapter 3

Matching

1. d
2. a
3. g
4. f
5. e
6. b
7. c

Short Answer

8. Ice carvings are generally three-dimensional sculptures.

9. To prevent the loss of detail from melting, first remove the large pieces and then go back and do the head with the details before working on the rest of the body, the detail work would be lost from melting before the rest of the sculpture was completed.

10. To move from the second to the third dimension a carver must imagine where the wide and skinny portions lie within the side view of the silhouette carving and remove the unwanted ice.

11. A stationary fish is simpler. A fish on a coral background would require that only a portion of the second dimension is to be removed, which is difficult for a novice carver.

12. A model or scale drawing provides a guideline to follow when forming the basic and finished detail and helps the carver visualize what the finished sculpture will look like.
13. The carver should be able to see the proportions of the finished piece, despite its lack of detail or finished surfaces, by stepping back and looking at the sculpture from at least five feet away. That will allow the carver to see the proportions correctly.

Matching

14. c
15. b
16. a

CHAPTER 4

Short Answer

1. They give the carver full dexterity, and they offer a slight barrier between the ice and sharp edges. Latex gloves are inexpensive and readily available. The main drawback of using this type of glove is that it offers little protection from the cold and not much protection from sharp edges.
2. Long-sleeve cuffs can be a safety concern, especially with the use of power tools. Cuffs should not dangle into your work zone. Keep the cuffs rolled up, strapped to your wrist, or inserted into your gloves.
3. A large flat chisel will leave a flat, clean surface. It will also shear large segments of ice.
4. A wood saw has centered teeth, and they glide through the cut more than remove ice. Use of a wood saw may require additional pressure, which may lead to breakage of the ice. Woodworking hand saws are not recommended for ice carving. The teeth of an ice saw are slightly offset, which enables them to glide through the ice by removing the ice from the channel while cutting.
5. Freezing spray is a can of gas that emits a cold spray upon application. It can be used as a temporary application to chill the surface of the ice and make quick repairs. It can also be used for ice welding and template adhesion.
6. Always remove the chain after each carving session and dry it with a towel. Take the time to dry off the remaining components of the saw so the chain does not rest in water during storage. Once the chain is reassembled, use the chain oil pump to apply oil and rotate the chain along the bar a few times by gripping the chain with the towel and pulling it.
7. Mineral oil or any other clear food-grade machine oils are suitable for the oil pump, chain, and bar sprocket. Never use cooking oil of any kind for lubrication as it will gum up and damage the equipment.
8. Canvas, leather, and cardboard sheaths can be used to protect carving tools.

Multiple Choice

9. b
10. d

11. a
12. b
13. a
14. b

Matching

15. c
16. d
17. a
18. b
19. f
20. e

CHAPTER 5

True or False

1. F
2. F
3. T
4. T
5. T
6. T
7. T
8. T

Short Answer

9. Paper templates are relatively simple to make, and they adhere well to the ice. They allow a carver to tap markings through the paper or cut directly through to the ice as described in the scrollwork section. They are good for only one use and if positioned wrong on the ice may be difficult to reposition or move.
10. A solid template can be used over and over again. They take longer to make than paper versions. They are durable and easily moved if positioned wrong.
11. Carving ice is expensive, and like any resource it should not be wasted.
12. It saves the carver time and is done in a professional manner.

CHAPTER 6

Matching

1. b
2. c
3. e
4. a

5. f
6. d

Short Answer

7. It is hard on the back to carve at floor level. Also, the hard surface can damage the tools.
8. Wear pants, shoes, gloves, and an apron to keep you warm, dry, and comfortable during the exercise of ice carving. Protective eyewear should be worn when using power tools. If the temperatures are cold, a hat is also important.
9. Oftentimes debris leaves the ice's surface and could easily fly into the carver's eyes.
10. Three carving platforms and two 20-amp, 120-volt circuits are needed. Additional needs may call for ice removal and tool storage tables.
11. Use a squeegee to keep the floor free from ice chunks and to remove large puddles.
12. Make sure the carving area is out of direct sunlight. Work in a covered area or shed or indoors.

True or False

13. T
14. T

Multiple Choiee

15. c
16. d
17. a
18. a

CHAPTER 7

True or False

1. F
2. F
3. T
4. T
5. T

Multiple Choice

6. d
7. b
8. d
9. b
10. b
11. d

12. d
13. a
14. d

CHAPTER 8

Short Answer

1. A base supports the carving. If the base isn't large enough, the carving might crack when moved.
2. You will need to wet the ice with water and then apply the template to the wet surface.
3. A solid template is needed when producing a series of identical carvings.
4. The chipper should be held perpendicular to the ice.
5. A deeper line won't disappear as the ice carving melts or fills up with saw shavings.

Multiple Choice

6. c
7. b
8. a
9. d
10. a

CHAPTER 9

Matching

1. c
2. a
3. b
4. c
5. a
6. c

Multiple Choice

7. c
8. b
9. c
10. b
11. a
12. b
13. a
14. a

Chapter 10

Matching

1. b
2. d
3. c
4. a

Multiple Choice

5. d
6. b

True or False

7. F
8. T
9. T
10. T
11. F
12. T

Chapter 11

Matching

1. a
2. d
3. b
4. a
5. d
6. c
7. a

Short Answer

8. A flat-side chisel stroke is an application of the flat chisel for shaving away areas of a flat surface or a convex curve. A beveled-side chisel stroke is an application of the flat chisel, which is used for shaving away areas of a concave curve.
9. 1. Be conscious of loose clothing, which can become tangled.
   2. Always use GFCI power protection in wet areas.
   3. Keep both hands on the tools at all times.
   4. Allow the tool to come to a complete stop before setting it down. Use sharp chains and bits.
10. 1. The disk sander can throw particles of ice in many directions. The operator should use protective eyewear.
    2. Always allow the disk to come to a full stop before setting the tool down.

Chapter 12

Matching

1. f
2. h
3. d
4. g
5. e
6. a
7. b
8. c

Short Answer

9. Visualization is the basic practice of examining the ice and formulating an idea of what the sculpture will look like after a carving step is completed. Visualization can be simpler when one focuses on a one segment during a single carving step. For example, shaping the tail fins is simplified when the second dimension is followed by the third dimension and then completed by shaping and rounding. Visualizing the finished tail from the initial point of the solid block would require more experience. On occasion, through the step-by-step process, the carver will still need to step away from the block to examine how all the segments are flowing together to form the entire sculpture.
10. Most ice sculptures are on display for a number of hours. There must be an allowance for melting, which requires that the carver exaggerate the size of the features so that they will still show as the ice melts.
11. After the carving process is complete, there may still be ice shavings scattered over the carving. The base area is most likely to have these unsightly fragments. The final step before storing or displaying is to perform sculpture cleaning, which is the process of removing unwanted ice fragments with water, air, heat, or broom sweeping.

Chapter 13

True or False

1. T
2. T
3. F
4. T
5. F

Multiple Choice

5. b
6. a
7. a
8. c

Short Answer

9. NICA stands for the National Ice Carving Association.
10. Scan the design into a positive image with a computer. Use an editing program to transform the design into a negative format.
11. A person's face is about the size of a human hand or about one-seventh to one-eighth times the height of a standing human body.
12. A platter or bowl, a punch bowl or giant martini glass, a bar or piece of furniture, a functional design is used to hold or display food or beverages or to serve a purpose.
13. Peg and notch fusion attaches two sections of ice. One of the segments has a peg and the other has an indentation the size of the peg. A little slush can be used to put into the hole with more packed over the union.
14. Ice spheres can be used for a number of sculptures, including as a globe for a worldwide affair or as a crystal ball for a themed event.

CHAPTER 14

Matching

1. d
2. c
3. d
4. b

Multiple Choice

6. d
7. d
8. c
9. b
10. a
11. b
12. b
13. a

Index

The completed basic angelfish serves as the basic design inspiration for this text.

The basic angelfish rises to new level by using a full block and adding sea coral to the design.

The completed horse head stands upon a Roman column base pedestal.

The martini bottle has been turned into a shot luge that can actually be used to serve beverages.

A swordfish "jumps" out of the ice sea.

A spherical ball is placed
on the palm of a hand.

The clamshell can be used in a buffet line filled with seafood.

The flying swan is a popular design in ice carving.

The angelfish model was an inspiration for the finished angelfish ice carving.

Models help the carver to visualize the finished sculpture.

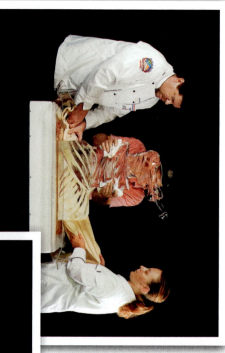

There are a number of methods to use when lifting a finished carving. Here, two lifters move the carving while a third helper is navigating the placement and holding the upper portion of ice steady.

The horse is being placed on a Roman column to elevate the carving.

Men and women alike enjoy the art of ice carving.

The hand saw is being used to shape the fish.

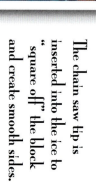

The chain saw tip is inserted into the ice to "square off" the block and create smooth sides.

The six-prong chipper is being used to trace the outline of the template onto the ice.

Specially designed display trays often include a set of colored gels to illuminate the carving in a variety of colors.

The sphere begins to emerge from the square block of ice as the carver rounds the center sections of the ice.